DATE DUE

Jesuit Studies

Contributions to the arts and sciences

by members of the Society of Jesus

Jesuit Studies

JESUIT STUDIES

Diplomatic Protest
in Foreign Policy

ANALYSIS AND CASE STUDIES

Joseph C. McKenna, s.j.

LOYOLA UNIVERSITY PRESS

Chicago, 1962

© 1962
LOYOLA UNIVERSITY PRESS
Printed in the United States of America
Library of Congress Catalog Card Number: 62-15739

FOR MY FATHER
AND MOTHER

PREFACE

Almost anyone who writes a book of this kind must, I suspect, come from his labor with a heartening insight into the cooperative spirit of his fellow men—many of whom he knows and perhaps more whom he does not. Although it is clearly impossible to make public acknowledgment, as I would wish, of all the willing help I have received, I welcome the opportunity to pay my more obvious debts of gratitude. I am grateful to the several people who counseled me as to the structure and presentation of this study: President John A. Logan, Jr., of Hollins College, Professors Samuel F. Bemis and Frederick Watkins of Yale, Gerhart Niemeyer of Notre Dame, and Stefan T. Possony of Georgetown. The book is a drastically revised version of doctoral research presented to the Yale Graduate School; a special word of appreciation is due Director Arnold Wolfers of the Washington Center of Foreign Policy Research for his guidance of this work. I also express my thanks to Mr. G. Bernard Noble, Mr. E. Taylor Parkes, Mrs. Kieran B. Carroll, and Mrs. Mary Ellen Milar for assistance in my consultation of State Department archives, and to Mrs. Zara Jones Powers for aid in the use of the Edward M. House Collection at the Yale University Library. The responsibility for what I have written is, of course, my own.

J. C. McK.

CONTENTS

TABLES

xiii

The Problem
and the Method

On December 11, 1956, the *New York Times* carried a front-page headline: "U.S. Protests Curb on Its Czech Office." In a note to the Prague government, Ambassador Herschel V. Johnson had asserted that police stationed at the entrance to his embassy were inquiring into the identity and the business of all Czech callers, and were thus in effect intimidating all visitors to his establishment. He strongly objected to this procedure and demanded that it cease.

Leafing through the *Times'* files for the past few years, one finds numerous examples of similar diplomatic action. In November 1959 governmental negligence in controlling an anti-American riot was the subject of a protest to Panama. During July 1960 a protest was presented to Cuba against the confiscation of American-owned oil refineries. In July 1954 the loss of three American lives in the destruction of a British airliner and a subsequent armed attack on an American naval search party brought a protest to Communist China. And the United States protested, in November 1953, over the mistreatment of non-Catholic missionaries in Colombia.[1]

The extensive employment of this diplomatic device is not a new development in international relations. A survey of United States experience has uncovered 598 instances of protest in

1

fourteen selected years of the present century; and this survey was restricted to published diplomatic papers.[2] The frequency with which protest is used suggests that those who use it think it achieves something. Yet, oddly, there have been no systematic studies of its effectiveness. Presumably rationality, the correct adaptation of action to maximum goal achievement, is desirable in conducting foreign relations and presumably, therefore, protest should be rationally employed. Yet there have been no inquiries into whether and in what circumstances it is likely to accomplish its purposes.[3] To fill this gap, just such an inquiry is undertaken here. It may be the more worthwhile because an ill-conceived resort to protest can eventuate not merely in failure to produce optimum results but in positive frustration of major foreign-policy objectives. One thinks, for example, of the near approach to unwanted war in the Tampico incident of 1914.[4]

Besides the pragmatic contribution which this inquiry might make to the efficient use of protest, it may also illuminate one theoretical facet of international relations. Some theories tend to emphasize the nations' concern for their coercive capabilities as the central fact of international politics and to regard the acquisition of power as the supreme norm by which national action is and should be governed.[5] There is an unchallengeable and important insight in this conception, especially when it is juxtaposed to the naiveté of the views it was intended to meet. But the validity of the position as a comprehensive theory of international politics depends upon the breadth of its observational base: Has the examination of factual reality been wide enough to justify its fundamental propositions? Will it stand up if attention is shifted from the major tensions between nations—Axis against Allies, Communism against Free World— to the routine day-to-day conduct of foreign affairs? If, more particularly, history records substantial achievement through a noncoercive instrument, the theory would have to take into very careful account a more subtle analysis of power and a more expansive and humane outlook on man's incentives.[6] The present study necessarily undertakes just such a change of observational focus.

As to method, a conceptual framework for the study is provided in Chapter 2, which indicates what is meant by diplomatic protest, how it is supposed to work in implementing foreign policy, what constitutes success or failure, and what circumstances demand attention as likely contributors to either result. The inquiry's examination of the United States' experience with protest then follows two distinct but complementary lines. The first of these, in Chapter 3, is an extended but somewhat superficial historical survey, intended to provide a control for possible inaccuracies in the purely analytic structure. This line has suggested hypothetical conclusions and has furnished a backdrop against which truly representative cases can be singled out for closer study. A second line is by way of five intensive case studies, presented in Chapters 4 to 8. This approach follows the perception, emerging from the theoretical framework, that a fully valid judgment on whether a particular protest has been effective requires an investigation going beyond the mere letter of the diplomatic note and its formal reply. The deeper motivations of the protesting nation, the unavowed countermeasures of the recipient, and numerous apparently extraneous conditions touching both parties must all be taken into account. The case studies try to do this. Chapter 9 summarizes the entire study.

In selecting incidents for special study, ample documentation and some historical distance seemed desirable. With cases too nearly current, the appraisal of results could easily miss delayed reactions and long-term impacts. Even after making allowances for the desired distance and documentation, of course, one must still stress the reservation that, as with all historical inquiry, much data relevant to the cases may very well remain unrecorded or inaccessible.

It was also desirable that the incidents selected should be representative and collectively capable of illustrating the varied circumstances which appear significant for the success or failure of a diplomatic protest. For such a choice, the theoretical framework and the general survey of American experience were helpful. The protests selected were directed to two major powers, Great Britain and the Soviet Union; to two minor powers, Rumania and Canada; and to one power whose peculiar facilities for resistance made it somewhat more than minor, China. In geographical terms, these were European, North American, and Asian nations; in political terms, one of them was engaged in war and one of them was troubled by revolution, while the other three were in more stable circumstances. The United States itself in one case operated under the uneasy apprehension of war; in three cases, felt secure in intense isolationism; in the fifth, experienced some yielding of this mood. On the economic side, the American government rode a wave of prosperity in the two cases from the twenties, wrestled with recession in the two cases from the thirties, and in 1914-1916 dealt with both situations. The protests were concerned with the protection of nationals, consular privileges and immunities, conditions of commerce, and monetary claims.

The pattern for the case studies is more or less the same. Each begins with a brief statement of the historical background, aimed at highlighting the prima facie issue. Detailed examination then centers on the four factors which the conceptual framework has indicated as focal in weighing success or failure. First, what were the policy maker's expectations: Did he hope, for example, to achieve total or partial fulfillment of his formal demand? Did some hidden purpose lie behind the aims expressed in his note? How highly did he value his objective? Secondly, what were his predictions of cost: Did he expect the other nation to yield or to resist, or to press some counterobjectives vis-à-vis the complainant? Did he foresee his own country's use of any instrumentality besides protest? Thirdly, what did he actually achieve: Was the objective of the protest obtained? How completely? How promptly? Fourth, what did this cost him: To what purely diplomatic measures, what sanctions, what concessions did the protesting nation resort? Were any adverse consequences ignored or discounted through the policy maker's miscalculations? A concluding judgment is then made on the effectiveness of the protest, along with a determination of the conditions which had an important bearing on its success or failure.

NOTES

1 See the following items in the *New York Times*: "Panama Rejects U.S. Note on Riots," November 5, 1959; "U.S. Files Protest on Cuban Seizure of Oil Refineries," July 6, 1960; "U.S. Demands Red Chinese End Attacks on Allied Craft," July 28, 1954; "Columbians Stir New Religious Ire," April 3, 1954.

2 This survey is reported below in Chapter 3.

3 See below, Chapter 2, n. 12.

4 United States Department of State, *Papers Relating to the Foreign Relations of the United States with the Address of the President to Congress, December 8, 1914*, pp. 448-76, 480. Washington: Government Printing Office, 1922. (Published annually since 1861, the title of this source has varied through the years. It will be cited in this essay by the short title, *Foreign Relations*, followed by the year.)

5 Hans J. Morgenthau, *Scientific Man vs. Power Politics*, pp. 9-10, 101, 194-95, 200 (Chicago: The University of Chicago Press, 1946); Nicholas J. Spykman, *America's Strategy in World Politics*, pp. 18-19 (New York: Harcourt, Brace and Company, 1942); Robert Strausz-Hupé and Stefan T. Possony, *International Relations*, pp. 2, 5-6, 386 (New York: McGraw-Hill Book Company, 1950). The ideas cited have been attributed to these authors merely as a tendency because they do explicitly qualify their use of the term "power," and they do explicitly recognize other motivations in man (however much these mitigations may be forgotten in their unfolding of their theory); see Spykman, *America's Strategy*, p. 7; Strausz-Hupé and Possony, *International Relations*, p. 382. The latter authors, moreover, omitted the cited passage in their second edition (1954).

6 It is possible that, with the realists as well as with the idealists, generalization has prevailed over observation, while little analysis has been made of existing facts and available means—to the detriment of international relations as a science. See the complaint of Edward H. Carr, *The Twenty Years' Crisis, 1919-1939*, second edition, p. 8 (London: The Macmillan Company, 1949).

CHAPTER II

Protest in Policy Formation: The Theory

Public policy can be defined as "a program of social action." The orderly programing of social action is comprised of four phases, which are not so much successive steps in a chain of reasoning, as aspects of a psychological process that might appear in the form of an instantaneous, intuitive judgment. The four phases of this process can be briefly described in the following fashion. There is a recognition and clarification of the values to which the society aspires; there is an estimate of the situation in which the values are sought; there is a weighing of the probable consequences which alternative courses of action will have; and there is a choice of one of these courses.[1]

All public policies are ultimately aimed at the status of values which are cherished within the community; in this sense, at the national level all policies are domestic policies. But if the program is intended to augment national values primarily by influencing events outside the state's own legal jurisdiction, it may be regarded as foreign policy.[2] Such a program may seek to control situations in other countries, or on the high seas, or in international organizations; it may be directed, for example, at justice for Americans in Andorra, or the repression of piracy, or the development of universal fair standards of labor.

6

Policy making can seldom be as tidy as the four-phased analysis could lead one to believe. A few of its complications may be mentioned to give it realistic perspective.

The clarification of ends is difficult because the participants in any large social enterprise do not all seek the same specific goals for themselves, nor do they all give the same weight to such specific goals as they do seek in common. Secondly, even common goals may show mutually contradictory tendencies when particularized into their component elements. For example, if national security is defined as the preservation of national institutions, specifications of it might include both the development of defensive military power and the adherence to an anticolonial ideology. A proposal, then, to establish air bases on the island territory of some primitive people would present a painful dilemma. Thirdly, many social objectives can never be attained with finality. They cannot be placed in a trophy case, so to speak, with an air of "we have that; now let's get on to something else." They are not things; they are states of things in continuous dependence on numberless operations of nature and of men. This makes them harder to define and to preserve. Nevertheless, it seems a fair assumption that in most nations at most times only a negligible minority stands outside consensus about a dynamic equilibrium of values that gives real guidance for action. Radical and reactionary nonconformists, along with some criminal elements, may actively resist, but most members demonstrate consent at least by acquiescent cooperation in community measures, as opposed to the antisocial pursuit of private ends.[3]

The consideration of values does not stop with the first phase of policy development. The other three phases deal with ends as well as means. For in addition to ultimate goals which are sought as desirable in themselves without conscious reference to any further purpose, there are intermediate goals. These are regarded as both desirable in themselves and as serving some further end. Values like these can inhibit the choice of particular means which might seem, in the abstract, best calculated to achieve ultimate aims. For example, United States adherence to the Monroe Doctrine and Swiss adherence to neutrality have qualified these countries' commitments to international security organizations.[4]

In the very unfolding of the four phases, moreover, there is constant need for re-evaluation and readjustment. New questions of value confront the policy makers at every turn. The unavailability of means may force a modification of ends. The estimate of the situation repeatedly shifts with changes in the facts or the knowledge of the facts. The definitive plans are often extremely general, with wide discretion left to the man on the spot, or perhaps with less desirable alternatives cited to him as acceptable second bests. Often the relevant facts are simply too numerous and too complicated for the policy maker to grasp; an intuitive stab at the salient items may supplant an encyclopedic marshalling of data, and may actually lead to a more intelligent choice. Frequently, problems of substantial magnitude come to the policy maker's attention in fragments rather than in a single piece. Responses made, then, to isolated questions just as they arise, on a short-term or even on a day-to-day basis, establish precedents and even institute series of actions which are irreversible, so that the total situation cannot be met in what would have been the most effective fashion. Finally, not every policy question is or need be examined from its very roots; accepted standing principles may furnish a limiting framework within which the planning process moves toward individual decisions.[5]

Against this background of what foreign policy formation involves, the nature and function of the instruments used to implement policy can be understood. In this context "instrument" primarily means a human action rather than an inert material device. The varieties of human action utilized to realize a nation's objectives are all but infinite. They range from the dropping of a well-timed word to the dropping of a well-placed bomb. In analyzing them, however, one can distinguish two basic tendencies. Action may be "originative" or "responsive." Originative activity attempts to influence the conduct of some other nation by inducing it to contribute in some way, by the grant of a new concession or the maintenance of an old one, to the values of the nation which originates the action. Thus the United States may offer tariff reductions on imported French perfume in return for reductions on exported American motion pictures. Responsive activity is the reaction to action originated in some other country; it is the answer to the proffered inducement, the granting or withholding of the value sought.

Effective initiation calls for different qualities in a nation than does effective response; this is the importance of the distinction. Yet the capacity of the country to act in either direction requires that it have within its borders certain material and spiritual resources—natural wealth, balanced manpower, developed industrial plant, appropriate human skills and temperaments, and appealing politico-economic traditions. It is also required that the country should have discretion to use these resources as it wishes.

The physical possession of nature's bounty is not enough; lack of what might be called moral constraint is necessary, too. Fundamentally, the factors which limit a nation's freedom of action are its own values. A pressing demand for lower taxes will negate moves to provide technical assistance for other countries as a means of winning their favor. In the interest of national good faith, commitments to third parties will preclude other types of measure; the United States could not, in fidelity to its allies, dissolve its bonds with the North Atlantic Treaty Organization in order to placate Soviet Russia. National ideals like peaceableness and nonintervention will work the same way in restricting a country's freedom to act.

The common underlying characteristic of virtually all the originative instruments which spring from this national capacity is that they operate on the motivations of other countries. The action is an effort to persuade that is brought to bear on someone else's psychological field.[6] This may be contrasted with compulsion which, at least in its strictest sense, implies that superior physical force guides the motions of the one controlled; the parent places the recalcitrant child's hands in the water, presses them around the soap, and rubs them together. A threatened trip to the woodshed might achieve the same result, but it would not compel; it would motivate the child to wash his own hands. In this light, even outright warfare is a measure of persuasion. The warring nation does not intend primarily the death of the opposing soldiers, but the fear of death, impelling them to surrender; nor does it intend the destruction of the other nation's property, but the fear of destruction, impelling its policy makers to grant concessions. Other measures to implement policy work less drastically, but they similarly work as inducements.

The persuasive force of a diplomatic action may be aimed at the psychological idiosyncracies of the other country's authoritative policy maker. Spain's Primo de Rivera apparently inclined toward yielding to foreign pressure on the expropriation of oil companies in 1927 simply out of personal irritation with repeated representations over a question which he did not fully understand in the first place.[7] More usually the action is directed at the policy maker as he stands in a relationship to nationally desired objectives. Some favor which has a place in the country's equilibrium of values is offered for some return benefit. For example, the State Department might encourage private American investment in another nation's public works, but only on condition that a government reorganization designed to establish democracy and stability be instituted. The promised recompense might of course be intangible: support, perhaps, of a state's ambition to sit on the Security Council of the United

Nations. On the other hand, intimidation may be used instead of blandishment. A country might be threatened with the deprivation of a value which is part of its national equilibrium; the most drastic threat is war. Obviously, there must be some proportion between the reward or punishment and the sacrifice which a favorable reply would entail for the responding state. Technical assistance appeals strongly to underdeveloped countries, presumably even to Communist China. Yet the Peiping government is unlikely to accept a program of this sort under American auspices, since it would facilitate espionage and cultural penetration. Much less would Peiping accept help at the cost of, say, renouncing its claims to Taiwan.

One should remember too that international relations in their sum total are multilateral rather than bilateral. A third party's pressure on values may neutralize an effort at persuasion. Czechoslovakia responded gladly to the Marshall Plan proposals; but Soviet threats and promises apparently had greater weight and drew the country away from participation. Moreover, international action does not work exclusively in one direction. The nation toward which a measure is directed has objectives of its own vis-à-vis the initiating country, it has resources of its own, and it can take initiatives of its own. The result may be a meeting of minds midway between the starting positions of the two nations.

Because policy instruments are essentially persuaders, their diversity is as wide as the diversity of men's motives. Improvisation is feasible, then, and an alert diplomat may exploit the most fortuitous conjunction of circumstances. The merest hint by the United States minister to Rumania that he would personally visit Oradea Mare, where an American national had been injured in a riot, brought a satisfactory reply from the previously evasive Foreign Office; the Rumanian government apparently feared that the proposed visit would spark an outbreak of public demonstrations.[8]

There are, however, institutionalized methods of eliciting favorable responses from other countries. Brief consideration of a few will illustrate the operation of all and will set off some distinctive features of diplomatic protest. These measures could be set roughly along a continuum running from coercive to non-coercive.[9] After the ultimate coercive instrument, which is full-scale war, come more limited types of military action: punitive expeditions, military occupation, naval bombardment of coastal towns, and pacific blockade. Somewhat less direct are economic sanctions such as the embargo and the boycott. The formation of a military alliance with hostile overtones may also be persuasive. Various diplomatic steps are possible, pitched at different levels of severity, from harsh gestures like nonrecognition and breach of relations through purely verbal formulas, sharp or mild. Diplomatic protest is one such formula. Toward the strictly noncoercive is, first, the treaty of friendship and commerce. More helpful is technical assistance, which was at one time an adjunct of private capital investment but has now become a formalized official instrument of foreign policy. More generous still is economic preferment in the form, for example, of favorable tariff rates or large loans on easy terms. The most extensive inducement one nation can offer another is its cooperation as a military ally.

Costs or potential costs are attached to virtually all these measures. The human and economic sacrifices of a war come high, even for the initiator. Open resort to lesser measures against weaker countries is regarded as dishonorable. An embargo by a single nation plays into the hands of rival suppliers and in any case damages the domestic producers of the embargoed item; the difficulty of universalizing an embargo was demonstrated by the economic sanctions against Italy in 1935-1936. A boycott may also upset the boycotting nation's economy by creating shortages and inflating the prices of crucial commodities. A hostile military alliance is, in the first place, a mere deterrent rather than a spur to positive concession; in the second place, it tends to generate a counteralliance with a consequent increase in international tension. Nonrecognition deprives its victim of prestige, competence for litigation in foreign law courts, and facilities for protecting national interests in the non-recognizing country; but the more annoying of these privations are mutual. While technical assistance programs may be financially inexpensive, they can stimulate autarchic aspirations in their beneficiaries and thus result in unpleasantly large losses to the benefactor.[10] Tariff concessions limit the granting nation's freedom with third parties, and loans carry danger of default. The price of a military alliance is the sacrifice of discretion, in the interest of conciliating allies, and the enormous risk of involvement in "somebody else's war."[11]

Diplomatic protest stands almost in the middle of the scale. So focal a concept in the present study clearly requires close analysis. Yet, despite the frequent use of protest, no sacrosanct definition of the term is discoverable. An intensive search in the likely literature has uncovered only three relatively full studies of the technique and less than a dozen other significant mentions of it. And all these items are in the realm of international law or diplomacy, not politics.[12] One must therefore manufacture, so to speak, a conception of protest, working from the various legal sources and from American usage in an extensive sampling of diplomatic correspondence.

To begin with, a diplomatic protest is a communication; in itself, it is purely verbal. The communications which implement foreign policy vary widely in both form and content. They are oral and written; they are notes, *notes verbales, aides-mémoire*, and manifestos; they are inquiries, representations, reservations of rights, protests, and ultimatums. External style makes no difference; a protest may be written or oral, and may take any accepted form of diplomatic correspondence.[13] As for its distinctive content, this will be indicated presently.

A diplomatic protest must usually be directed by a government to a government. Strictly speaking, other bodies which have a status in international public law, such as the United Nations and the Red Cross, are competent to send and receive protests; completely private organizations and individuals cannot protest in any recognized diplomatic sense. The communication must be transmitted through regular foreign-affairs channels. Ordinarily this implies a message going directly from one head of state to another, or a message proceeding by way of the respective Foreign Offices. Therefore, a presidential message to Congress, a Congressional resolution, a decision of the Supreme Court, or a complaint by the Department of Commerce cannot be regarded as a diplomatic protest. At the receiving end, protests addressed to governmental agencies other than the Foreign Office have no standing until they are referred by the recipient agency (as they should be) to that Office. Regular foreign-affairs channels include not only the foreign minister but also his agents abroad: ambassadors, ministers, special emissaries, and in some cases consuls. Accredited diplomats may accept protests for reference to the home government and may initiate protests which have full validity unless repudiated by superiors. A diplomat may address protests only to the government to which he is accredited; on this principle, the British were expected to ignore a protest from the American minister to the Netherlands, concerning their treatment of mail shipped from that country during World War I.[14] Consuls, military commanders in the field, and local political authorities are sometimes authorized channels. In war and revolution, military leaders or local officials may be the sole foreign representatives in a position to initiate or accept communications.[15]

Protests, like most other intergovernmental communications, may be distinguished as "formal" or "informal." The distinction is related to the subtle symbolism of diplomatic gestures. A formal communication is felt to engage the full faith of the government which originates it; a position taken therein is consequently less flexible than in an informal communication. A formal protest, therefore, implicitly puts greater pressure upon the recipient. But because the language of diplomats does not always make clear their intentions in particular situations, the distinction can be given little attention in this study. In either case protest carries some weight behind it; differences in degree are no greater than those intimated, for example, by the stronger or milder language of the note itself. Diplomatic protests need not be severe in tone. They may be mild and friendly or sharp and hostile. There is no need to detail the differences; the mildness or severity of a diplomatic note is usually so obvious from its language that it can be recognized without effort, although a knowledge of diplomatic convention would make it even easier to recognize. "Demand," "insist," "earnestly protest," all indicate some strength, and a recital of the relevant facts can add great vigor to such terms. Incidentally, the word "protest" need not appear in the communication; the idea may be conveyed in varying phraseology, because the substance, not the language, is what counts.[16]

As regards substance, diplomatic protest is in the nature of a complaint. It expresses dissatisfaction with an official action or policy of the government to which it is addressed. Such policy or action includes public programs or measures, like legislation or executive decrees touching on tariffs, immigration, and commercial regulations. It also includes administrative acts by, for example, tax collectors, the police, and the military. Indirectly, it may even include the activities of private citizens, as will happen when some types of delinquent conduct are permitted or condoned through the collusion or negligence of the government. The policy or action to which objection is made may belong to the past, the present, or the future. There is a place for "prescription" in international affairs, so that some protests may reasonably be rejected on the grounds that they have come too late. But allowance of a reasonable time for an event to reach attention and to be investigated by the protesting state would apparently validate a protest on a situation of some years' standing. There is also a place for a government's refusing to anticipate an injustice; but when the enactment of an inequitable law, or the perpetration of an injurious act is imminent, protest is a legitimate measure of protection—especially if the expected damage is likely to be irreparable.[17]

Of utmost importance as a distinguishing mark of protest is the basis on which it is made. It should rest on the grounds that the act or policy in question violates either positive international law or what is asserted to be universally accepted morality. The complaint must be that a strict right rather than a mere courtesy has been violated. A communication which seeks a favor or an indulgence motivated by generosity, reciprocity, or comity, may be a "request," or "inquiry," or "good offices," but it is not a diplomatic protest. Positive law includes the principles which are thought to possess legal binding force through custom, the case law which has developed through the practices of the parties and the decisions of international tribunals, and the contractual obligations which have arisen from treaties or other agreements between the two nations.[18]

Appeals to international morality are less frequent. They are indicated by such phrases as "humanity demands," "justice requires," "it is unreasonable to expect." The common complaint of "denial of justice" fuses morality with positive law, since customary law legitimates this ground for protest, but "reason," rather than established arbitrary standards, specifies the requirements of justice. Protests are occasionally made on the basis of the recipient state's domestic law; the charge is then that the law has been neglected or misapplied in a particular case affecting the interests of the protesting country. Equivalently this is an appeal to the moral principle of equality before the law.[19]

Almost always it is the rights of the protesting nation that are alleged to be violated. Protests in favor of third parties are doubtfully valid apart from a specific agreement; a treaty of mutual guarantee, for example, might entitle every signatory to protest any breach by any other signatory, not just a breach directed against the protesting nation. Custodianship of a third nation's interests, as after a severance of diplomatic relations, also carries a right to protest any injury.[20]

After expressing dissatisfaction, a protest asks redress of the grievance. The specific redress varies with the specific objectionable conduct. A return to the *status quo ante* may be requested: for example, the evacuation of occupied territory or the repeal of discriminatory legislation. Monetary compensation for assessable material damage may be demanded: reparations for an aerial bombardment, for example. Intangible injury may require a formal apology and a punitive indemnity. If the damage has been merely potential, the plea may be for nonrepetition, as with unauthorized flights over national territory. In fact, measures to prevent future offenses may be sought in almost any case: the issuance of new executive orders, the removal of delinquent officials, the passage of remedial legislation, or the negotiation of a covering agreement between the parties. While a diplomatic protest in itself is purely verbal and noncoercive, sanctions other than the mere presentation of the note may be explicitly or implicitly threatened. These obviously add weight to a complaint's persuasive power.[21]

The whole notion, then, is adequately summarized in the following definition: Diplomatic protest is an intergovernmental communication expressing dissatisfaction with the officially approved policy or action of the recipient state on the grounds that the policy or action violates that state's legal or moral obligations to the sender, and asking redress of the grievance.

The concern here is less with the legal than with the political role of diplomatic protest.[22] As a legal instrument, protest may have one of two purposes. It may be a justificatory piece which recites the recipient state's offenses and the protesting state's efforts to obtain satisfaction through negotiation. In the failure of these efforts, the complainant in effect puts its case before the world to legitimize such measures of self-help as it may undertake. Or protest may be a kind of demurrer. It forestalls appeal to the dictum that silence means consent, or to the argument that an act or policy to which no objection is made acquires legal standing by this very fact. As an explicit refusal to accept some reprehensible act or policy, diplomatic protest may deprive this of legality. If, then, the factual position should change in favor of the complainant, no international litigation will be needed to validate the new situation.[23]

Taken strictly as a legal device, the first of these uses is obsolescent, because legal measures of self-help are now viewed with disfavor. As a political device, it is perhaps growing in significance; the indictment in this fashion of a diplomatic adversary is one weapon of the competitive propaganda which seeks to undermine the adversary's support among third parties. More important for legal purposes is the second use of protest, which precludes the creation of some new and undesirable legal status. In fact, this helps to explain the multitude of perfunctory, almost automatic, diplomatic protests which are filed in many a Foreign Office. Nations often have little choice but to record their objections even when they are unwilling or unable to support them with effective action, for otherwise they may appear to ratify an unwanted legal status through their silence.

While the legal purposes of protest are not central here, one must be aware of them as part of the background. The political conception of protest is more comprehensive. The statesman intends to use the legal instrument, of course, but not merely to block the operation of prescription. He uses it as an instrument of persuasion, directed, at least sometimes, at achieving substantive results.

Results, then, are at the heart of any normative judgment on the political effectiveness of protest. As with every other policy instrument, one must look at national values gained. But one must also look at national values foregone. Borrowing a term from economics, one can call a policy rational if it achieves the maximum goal at minimum expense.[24] If the test of the states-man's skill is the degree to which events conform to his predic-tions, the emphasis will be on subjective rather than objective rationality: the policy maker's personal appraisal of ends, means, and probabilities. The focal questions will be: Has the protest achieved as much or nearly as much as the policy maker intended? Has it done so with as little or nearly as little expense as he expected? The anticipated accomplishment must be weighed against the actual accomplishment, the expected sacrifice against the real. In mathematical terms, the expected unit cost of hopes would be compared with the actual unit cost of realizations, thus:

$$\frac{\text{Anticipated Cost}}{\text{Anticipated Achievement}} - \frac{\text{Actual Cost}}{\text{Actual Achievement}} = \text{Index of Success}$$

Assuming that, as in most things human, the outcome will dis-appoint the expectation, a small negative (as well as a positive) index of success will signify an effective use of protest; a sub-stantial negative figure will show ineffectiveness. The problem, of course, cannot be mathematicized, because unit quantification of qualitatively disparate social values is unrealistic. But the formula clarifies the critical validity of the approach.

To answer the focal questions meaningfully, some refine-ment of their central terms is necessary. In the first place, the patent and the latent aspects of a protest's objectives must be distinguished. Every diplomatic protest has a prima facie pur-pose. This is the redress of the grievance stated in the note: an apology for censoring diplomatic mail, or perhaps the discontin-uance of a restrictive quota on imported American automobiles.

But the policy maker may be reaching beyond the proximate situation to some objective not mentioned in his communication.

Some ulterior purposes have no relation to the instrument's function of influencing other states' conduct. A note may be intended merely to assure domestic interests that the government is active on their problems, even though the policy maker has no hope that his representations will effect any results abroad. A protest of this kind is less a diplomatic action than a substitute for action. Or the note may be aimed at keeping the legal record clear against some future time when the protesting nation can alter an unjust factual situation tolerated now.[25] Or the note may be planned as propaganda for home consumption, intended to bestir in an apathetic public enthusiastic support of the government's policy toward the recipient nation.[26] Objectives of this kind are of no concern here.

Other ulterior purposes do involve the use of protest to effect a new international situation in one or another indirect fashion. A favorable answer to the prima facie demand, for example, may be only an intermediate step to an improved military or economic position. Thus, when a Chilean newspaper asserted that the United States' airmail development program in South America was a military plot, Washington protested the allegation as an insult. However, this action was not primarily motivated by the offensiveness of the newspaper's charge; the principal concern was with the potentially adverse impact of the charge upon the airmail program itself.[27] Notes may also be intended to create a bargaining position for the protesting nation. In the expectation that Spanish resources for compensating expropriated oil companies would be limited, the United States protested Spain's activities in order to keep American claims on a par with those of other nations. Regarding Poland, continued pressure against quotas on imported automobile tires was viewed as a way to win concessions on the whole quota system.[28] The purpose of a diplomatic protest may also be to justify a preordained sanction. The Austro-Hungarian ultimatum to Serbia in 1914 perhaps had this goal.[29] Paradoxically, in this case prima facie success would be long-term failure, whereas short-term failure would be ultimate success, because concession of the protesting nation's explicit demands would deprive it of the excuse for further action.

With costs as with purpose, two aspects must be distinguished. With every diplomatic protest are associated intrinsic costs, which spring from the very concept of the instrument; and with some protests are linked extrinsic costs, which center on other nations' arbitrary reactions. On its face, diplomatic protest is an appeal to reason and principle. It is, either expressly or by implication, argumentative. It is an attempt to convert the mind of the recipient nation or policy maker. Underlying the intellectual approach, there is also an implicit appeal to the nation's will, based upon its sense of honor and its desire to be regarded as fair and just.[30] Two obvious costs are necessarily and intrinsically connected with this technique of persuasion. First, the protesting nation has drawn upon the perspicacity, the literary skill, and the time of its Foreign Office. Secondly, it has committed itself to the principle on which it rests its case, thus diminishing its future discretion; if the roles of the two nations should be reversed, the principle may return to plague the country which first used it. The resources affected by these costs are intangible; differences here between national capabilities are comparatively insignificant, and small countries may be the peers of large ones. But it is also intrinsic to protest that it threatens one subtle sanction. Through the very fact of presenting its note, the protesting nation implies that the other nation's failure to redress or correct its reprehensible behavior cannot help but chill, in however slight a degree, the complaining country's friendship. Just how much weight this sanction carries is hard to determine. Yet governments apparently do not wish to alienate or to face the dissatisfaction of friendly nations.[31] The sanction must be computed as cost because the protesting nation commits itself to continued friendship if the protest succeeds and is prepared for a reciprocal chill if it fails. The entire resource structure of both parties, their entire potential for help or hindrance on the world scene, quietly insinuates itself, since friendship or coolness touches so sweepingly the quest after values and the exertion of international pressures.

The extrinsic costs may be visualized as of three sorts: those concerned with sanctions, those concerned with bargains, and those concerned with the responsive conduct of other nations. A note of protest may indicate that resort to certain sanctions, besides the quickening or cooling of friendship, is contingent upon the reply. Whether the sanctions be coercive or noncoercive, their actual use will almost always mean some sacrifice for the nation which employs them. Instead of forthright acquiescence or rejection, the recipient may grant redress only for some compensating concession by the complainant, and such a concession is clearly cost. Again, the recipient may respond not with mere refusal or with a proposal to bargain, but with some countermeasure—the filing of counterclaims, the raising of tariffs, the cementing of an alliance, or the waging of war—designed to offset the action or to prevent similar future action by the protesting nation. A kindred response may be made by a third state if it sees in the protest an unfavorable policy trend. The mere occurrence of such phenomena does not make the protest a failure. That depends on the policy maker's anticipations. While he presumably envisioned and accepted all the intrinsic costs, he presumably did not—unless there is evidence to the contrary—wish to employ sanctions, or to strike bargains, or to stimulate counteraction abroad.

When one turns from the notion of cost to that of achievement, one notes first that the actual accomplishments of a diplomatic protest may be of different degrees, with relation to the policy maker's hopes. The optimal reply to a well-founded protest is prompt and complete redress of the prima facie grievance. Theoretically, a government imbued with good will recognizes the justice of the complaint and hastens to repair the damage; or the protest clarifies the recipient statesman's understanding of a previously obscure situation and impels him to change his course of action.

The reply may be less than optimal, however, and then the reverse side of some responses mentioned as possible costs appears. The recipient may attempt a compromise, usually hinging on the issue's legal aspects. It may, for example, give substantive satisfaction while denying the juridical ground of the complaint. As an act of grace, Canada granted compensation for the shooting of two American hunters by Canadian militiamen; but it would not admit an obligation in justice, since the Canadian courts found the officers not guilty of crime.[32] Instead of compromising, the recipient may bargain, may seek from the protesting nation a *quid pro quo* which has no intrinsic relationship with the protest. When the British protested against the Panama Canal toll system as violating the Hay-Pauncefote Treaty, the United States bowed; but there is evidence that Great Britain had informally promised to support American policy in a troubled Mexico.[33] The response to a diplomatic protest may also be an express refusal to consider it,[34] or its quiet interment in the archives after a period of negotiation. The note must then be written down as a failure. If, instead, the recipient denies the alleged law, or its applicability to the case, or—after investigation—the alleged facts, then the protest's effectiveness must be estimated in the light of the protesting nation's reaction. It should accept a well-founded denial and withdraw its complaint.[35] If it refuses, its protest remains operative and must be judged on the basis of its final outcome.

Judgment upon effectiveness in any given case faces obvious difficulties. It is not always easy to find out what a statesman hoped to achieve through a diplomatic protest, or what sacrifices he anticipated making to achieve it. This is even true of his prima facie purpose; because the redress he asks is capable of partial concession, he may ask for more in the hope of getting less. As for ulterior purposes, he is still less likely to show his hand.[36] His attitude toward costs will be the same. On its face the note indicates that only the intrinsic costs are anticipated. The statesman often knows in his heart, however, that further sacrifices will be needed. The recipient, for his part, knows that a protesting diplomat makes his threats with the hope of not having to fulfill them; but he should not know how far this hope amounts to downright unwillingness. Search for intentions is more practicable in case studies than in a general survey. Public and private papers, biographies and autobiographies can be examined more carefully, and circumstances, more closely scrutinized, may themselves suggest motivations. The over-all pattern of a nation's policy, like the old German *Drang nach Osten* or the American Monroe Doctrine, could be a helpful indicator. For example, United States pressure for economic stabilization in the Carribean countries often aimed at forestalling intervention by European creditors.[37] The mood of the public can likewise be helpful; an aroused opinion will suggest an official willingness to take serious steps, whereas a reserved popular attitude will raise doubts that strong measures were contemplated. To some extent, even the ultimate settlement may be a gauge of intent; if there is evidence that the diplomat was genuinely satisfied, the outcome presumably came close to his predictions of achievement.

Comparative measurement of the four terms in the equation also faces obvious difficulties. All four must be stated as highly complex social values which are almost always qualitatively diverse. The policy maker, for example, weighs in his mind the safety of nationals abroad as against the loss of prestige if a protest in support of such safety should be rebuffed, the health of the economy's export factor as against the damage of war which some activities promotive of this factor might provoke. Moreover, the establishment of quantitative units of measurement would be unrealistic in most cases. It seems doubtful, for instance, that sociological indices of a war's magnitude can really represent the human valuation of the policy maker and his principals. Helpful here, however, is the apparent existence of broad common-sense standards of value on which there is a consensus in the American community.[38] It is also possible to speak of maximal, extensive, moderate, minor, and minimal actualization of the social values involved, with reasonable hope of being understood.

As indicated in the introductory chapter, the theoretical formulation of how protest works and of how its efficacy should be judged suggests not only the outline for the case studies, but also the variables which should be important and should therefore be illustrated by the situations chosen for examination. Because the concession granted in response to a protest will almost always diminish the values controlled by the grantor, the "size of the request" must be considered. Large concessions would seldom be made simply because of the protest's implicit appeal to the recipient's national honor and intellectual objectivity; some legal subterfuge is a more probable initial answer, since it saves honor and sacrifices nothing else. Small concessions are likely to be made readily in the interests of international good will. Special circumstances may modify the meaning of "large" and "small." For while appraisals of some items may be broadly uniform, account must be taken of the peculiar position held by particular factors, either permanently or temporarily, in the specific country's scheme of values. Oriental and Occidental, Protestant and Catholic, Caucasian and Negro, developed and underdeveloped, established and neo-nationalistic countries may assess differently the integral concept of the common welfare. Less enduring but not less important could be the counterpressure of third parties, who may try to prevent concession by threatening other values which are highly prized.

The character of the response to diplomatic protest, favorable or unfavorable, will likely depend in part on the recipient's capacity for action. A nation strong in resources may be less pliable. A lack of real control over resources nominally possessed may impede a country's ability to reply favorably even if it wishes to. A nation which has no resources can scarcely refuse point-blank the demands of stronger states. It should be remembered, however, that the resources required for resistance are not the same as those needed for an originative role. Switzerland, for example, can better withstand a threat of violence than make one, because the country's rugged terrain contributes notably to defensive strength but does not offset the offensive weakness of so small a population.

The character of the response will depend on the protesting nation's capacities. These will affect both the cogency of the reasoning and the motivational appeal of the promises or threats. The diplomatic skill which enters into the selection of the subject, the timing, and the argumentation of a note is therefore a first resource.[39] But perhaps more to the point are the more general ingredients of strength, their abundance, their coercive potentiality, or their peculiar relevance to the recipient's values. For these should add up to persuasive ability in the protesting nation to help or hinder the other country's national objectives.

A brief summary of what has been said may be helpful. The task of foreign policy is so to influence events abroad as to maintain and amplify community values at home. The shrewd statesman uses the measures at his command to maximize achievements while holding to a minimum the sacrifices which each instrument involves, and the test of his skill is the accuracy of his predictions. The instruments of foreign policy operate primarily on the motivations of other countries. Among these instruments is diplomatic protest. In itself this is a purely verbal, noncoercive, effort at persuasion through intellectual conversion, but it carries with it the possibility of positive and negative sanctions. Because protest may well seek hidden as well as stated objectives and may involve extrinsic as well as intrinsic costs, empirical study of its operation must look deeply into the history of each case. The focal points of study must be the anticipated and real accomplishment, the expected and actual costs. Circumstantial factors most likely to affect a protest's outcome, and therefore most deserving of attention in examining experience, include the size of the request, the peculiar valuations of the recipient, the recipient's capacity to respond as it wishes, and the complainant's capacity to support its demands.

NOTES

[1] See C. Easton Rothwell, in the Foreword to Daniel Lerner and Harold D. Lasswell, editors, *The Policy Sciences*, p. ix (Stanford: Stanford University Press, 1951); Roger Hilsman, Jr., "Intelligence and Policy-Making in Foreign Affairs," *World Politics* 5:26-32, October 1952.

[2] Charles B. Marshall, "The Nature of Foreign Policy," *United States Department of State Bulletin* 26:415, March 17, 1952.

[3] Robert A. Dahl and Charles E. Lindblom, *Politics, Economics and Welfare*, p. 27 (New York: Harper and Brothers, 1953); Hans J. Morgenthau, *Politics Among Nations*, third edition, p. 562 (New York: Alfred A. Knopf, 1960); Marshall, "The Nature of Foreign Policy," p. 416. Gabriel A. Almond, *The American People and Foreign Policy*, pp. 158-59 (New York: Harcourt, Brace and Company, 1950), sets forth the elements of foreign policy on which there is almost universal consensus in the United States.

[4] Marshall, "The Nature of Foreign Policy," p. 416; Robert A. Dahl, *Congress and Foreign Policy*, pp. 78-80 (New York: Harcourt, Brace and Company, 1950). The State Department's booklet, *Our Foreign Policy, 1952*, State Department Publication 4466, p. 12 (Washington: Government Printing Office, 1952), speaks of freedom, economic well-being, justice, and peace as being pursued "for their own sakes."

[5] James L. McCamy, *The Administration of American Foreign Affairs*, pp. 16, 39 (New York: Alfred A. Knopf, 1950); Dahl and Lindblom, *Politics, Economics and Welfare*, p. 62; Morgenthau, *Politics Among Nations*, pp. 540-41.

[6] Dahl and Lindblom, *Politics, Economics and Welfare*, pp. 97-98.

[7] *Foreign Relations, 1927*, Vol. 3, p. 701.

[8] *Ibid.*, p. 644. For some other little considered inducements, see pp. 401, 436.

[9] Coercion is taken to imply a threat of severe deprivation; a favorable response,

if granted at all, will therefore be granted only with great reluctance. This concept of coercion partly conforms with the definition of Harold D. Lasswell and Abraham Kaplan, in *Power and Society*, pp. 97-99 (New Haven: Yale University Press, 1950). The authors include in the term the promise of high indulgence, but this application seems too alien from ordinary usage to make for ready intelligibility. Their requirement that coercion spring from personal activity and not from blind circumstance does appear to be reasonable usage.

[10] Carl McGuire, "Point Four and the National Power of the United States," *American Journal of Economics and Sociology* 11:354-55, April 1952.

[11] *Foreign Relations, 1929*, Vol. 3, p. 494; *Foreign Relations, 1930*, Vol. 3, pp. 749, 754; Albert C. Hindmarsh, *Force in Peace*, pp. 69-70, 73-74 (Cambridge: Harvard University Press, 1933); Antonin Basch, *The Danube Basin and the German Economic Sphere*, pp. 192-93 (New York: Columbia University Press, 1943); John Foster Dulles, "Practicable Sanctions," in Evans Clark, editor, *Boycotts and Peace*, pp. 19-22 (New York: Harper and Brothers, 1932); Francis P. Walters, *A History of the League of Nations*, Vol. 2, pp. 654-88 (New York: Oxford University Press, 1952); Robert Langer, *Seizure of Territory*, pp. 70-72, 102, 116, 145-46, 266-68, 287-88 (Princeton: Princeton University Press, 1947).

[12] The full treatments appear in Josef L. Kunz, "Protest im Völkerrecht," in Karl Strupp, editor, *Wörterbuch des Völkerrechts und der Diplomatie*, Vol. 2, pp. 329-30 (Berlin: Walter de Gruyter, 1925); Franz Pfluger, *Die einseitigen Rechtsgeschäfte im Völkerrechts*, pp. 194-220 (Zurich: Schulthess, 1936); Erik Bruel, "La protestation au droit international," *Revue de droit international* 10:364-70, 1932; this last is a digest of an article appearing in *Nordisk tidsskrift for international ret*, 1932. The other mentions appear in Carlos Calvo, *Dictionnaire de droit international public et privé*, Vol. 2, pp. 129-30 (Berlin: Puttkammer and Mühlbrecht, 1885); Ferdinand de Cussy, *Dictionnaire ou manuel lexique du diplomate et du consul*, pp. 601-02 (Leipzig: F. A. Brockhaus, 1846); Roland R. Foulke, *Treatise on International Law*, Vol. 1, p. 445 (Philadelphia: John C. Winston Company, 1920); Paul Heilborn, *System des Völkerrechts*, pp. 375-76 (Berlin: Julius Springer, 1896); Franz von Liszt, *Völkerrecht*, twelfth edition revised by Max Fleischmann, pp. 151, 242-44 (Berlin: Julius Springer, 1925); Charles de Martens, *Le Guide diplomatique*, fourth edition, Vol. 2, p. 177 (Paris: Gavelot Jeune, 1851); H. Meisel, *Cours de style diplomatique*, Vol. 1, pp. 593-94 (Dresden: Chr. Arnold, 1823); L. J. A. Moreuil, *Dictionnaire des chancelleries*, Vol. 2, p. 257 (Paris: Jules Renouard, 1855); Lassa Oppenheim, *International Law*, seventh edition revised by Hersch Lauterpacht, Vol. 1, pp. 787-90 (New York: Longmans, Green and Company, 1952); Alphonse Rivier, *Principes du droit des gens*, Vol. 2, p. 440 (Paris: Arthur Rousseau, 1896); Ellery C. Stowell, *International Law*, pp. 426-27, 436-37 (New York: Henry Holt and Company, 1931). Several of these loci, incidentally, show an obvious dependence on others cited here. The American State Department's style manual makes no mention of diplomatic protest; see Margaret M. Hanna and Alice M. Ball, *Style Manual of the Department of State* (Washington: Government Printing Office, 1937).

[13] Bruel, "La protestation au droit international," p. 367; Calvo, *Dictionnaire*, Vol. 2, p. 130. The term "protest" need not appear in the communication. Thus, although the word does not occur in a mild American note to Austria-Hungary, no less an international jurist than John Bassett Moore, acting for the secretary of state, calls this communication a protest. See *Foreign Relations, 1913*, pp. 21-23.

[14] *Foreign Relations, 1916*, Supplement, p. 595.

[15] Kunz, "Protest im Völkerrecht," p. 329; Pfluger, *Einseitigen Rechtsgeschäfte*, pp. 202-07.

[16] Harold Nicolson, *Diplomacy*, second edition, pp. 220-21 (London: Oxford University Press, 1950); *Foreign Relations, 1916*, pp. 294-95; *Foreign Relations, 1917*, pp. 1007-08. Recipient governments sometimes express appreciation for an informal rather than a formal approach; see *Foreign Relations, 1901*, p. 28; *Foreign Relations, 1914*, Supplement, p. 235.

[17] Pfluger, *Einseitigen Rechtsgeschäfte*, pp. 208-09, 214; *Foreign Relations, 1918*, p. 787.

[18] Pfluger, *Einseitigen Rechtsgeschäfte*, pp. 207-09; Quincy Wright, *The Control of American Foreign Relations*, pp. 212-13 (New York: The Macmillan Company, 1922). A rather extended interpretation of "contractual obligation" appears with respect to Nicaragua in *Foreign Relations, 1928*, Vol. 3, p. 419. In 1927-1928 the State Department insisted that a flurry of new taxes in China should be met with protest only if they were contrary to treaty or were discriminatory; see *Foreign Relations, 1927*, Vol. 2, pp. 385, 393, 398-99, 427; *Foreign Relations, 1928*, Vol. 2, p. 503.

[19] See the case of Louis Economopoulos, compelled by Greece to perform military service, *Foreign Relations, 1900*, pp. 634-47. See also *Foreign Relations, 1914*, p. 1097; and the protest to Cuba over the seizure of American oil refineries, "Text of U.S. Protest on Refinery Action," *New York Times*, July 6, 1960.

[20] See Pfluger, *Einseitigen Rechtsgeschäfte*, pp. 206-07, 213-14; Quincy Wright, "The Denunciation of Treaty Violators," *American Journal of International Law* 32:530-32, July 1938. The United States acted, for example, for France in Mexico in 1914; see *Foreign Relations, 1914*, pp. 867-84.

[21] Bruel, "La protestation au droit international," pp. 366-67; Pfluger, *Einseitigen Rechtsgeschäfte*, p. 210. The Soviet Union's reaction to the reconnaissance flight of the U-2 over Russian territory exemplifies the demand for nonrepetition of offensive conduct and, in effect, for apology. See "Russian and U.S. Notes on Downing of American Pilot in the Soviet Union," *New York Times*, May 11, 1960; and Premier Khrushchev's vigorous reiteration of the point at the abortive summit conference a week later, "Text of Khrushchev and Eisenhower Statements on Summit and the Plane Case," *ibid.*, May 17, 1960.

[22] Pfluger suggests the distinction, *Einseitigen Rechtsgeschäfte*, p. 196, n. 7.

[23] Meisel, *Cours de style diplomatique*, Vol. 1, pp. 201-03, 593; Liszt, *Völkerrecht*, pp. 151, 243-44; Pfluger, *Rechtsgeschäfte Völkerrechts*, pp. 194-200, 209-11, 216-18; *Foreign Relations, 1927*, Vol. 2, pp. 406, 558.

[24] While it is here assumed that rationality is a desideratum in the formulation of foreign policy, increments of this particular value may themselves cost more than they are worth. An administrative reorganization of the State Department,

for example, might increase rationality by one-hundredth of one per cent, but diminish speed, drain manpower, and reduce the Department's responsiveness to public sentiment. See Dahl and Lindblom, *Politics, Economics and Welfare*, pp. 38-39, 64.

[25] See the recommendations of Ambassador Fletcher in Mexico to the secretary of state, *Foreign Relations, 1918*, p. 789; see also pp. 751, 784.

[26] Wright suggests this possibility in "The Denunciation of Treaty Violators," p. 532; see also Meisel, *Cours de style diplomatique*, Vol. 1, p. 201.

[27] *Foreign Relations, 1929*, Vol. 1, p. 575.

[28] *Foreign Relations, 1927*, Vol. 3, pp. 615, 682-83.

[29] Bernadotte E. Schmitt, *The Coming of the War, 1914*, Vol. 1, pp. 348-49, 357, 376-77, 380, 384-85. New York: Charles Scribner's Sons, 1930.

[30] Pfluger, *Einseitigen Rechtsgeschäfte*, pp. 215-16, asserts that investigation in good faith is the obligation of the recipient.

[31] *Foreign Relations, 1928*, Vol. 3, p. 771; *Foreign Relations, 1929*, Vol. 3, pp. 777, 780, 782-83.

[32] *Foreign Relations, 1915*, pp. 418-23.

[33] Charles Seymour, editor, *The Intimate Papers of Colonel House*, Vol. 1, pp. 192-206. Boston: Houghton Mifflin Company, 1926.

[34] Russia is reported to have returned, "without consideration because of its unworthy character," a United States note complaining of a *Krokodil* cartoon offensive to the memory of the late James Forrestal. See "Forrestal Cartoon Is Protested by U.S." and "Soviet Bars U.S. Protest," *New York Times*, June 18 and June 27, 1954.

[35] See Pfluger, *Einseitigen Rechtsgeschäfte*, p. 210; and, for example, *Foreign Relations, 1914*, Supplement, pp. 771-74, 780.

[36] Morton A. Kaplan, "An Introduction to the Strategy of Statecraft," *World Politics* 4:574-75, July 1952.

[37] Samuel F. Bemis, *A Diplomatic History of the United States*, fourth edition, pp. 519-20, 526-30, 536-37. New York: Henry Holt and Company, 1955.

[38] Almond, *American People*, pp. 158-61.

[39] In the crisis over Congolese independence, the notes transmitted by a fledgling and untutored government to the secretary general of the United Nations manifested a remarkable subtlety, which observers attributed to the assistance of Soviet diplomatic officers. See "Text of Letters Exchanged between Hammarskjold and Officials of the Congo," *New York Times*, August 16, 1960; and "Soviet Hand Seen in Congo Protest," *ibid.*, August 17, 1960.

CHAPTER III

The United States Protests:
1900-1930

Only the more dramatic instances of diplomatic protest are likely to be chronicled in the histories and the current news accounts, and purely abstract analysis of a political concept may easily overlook significant elements of the reality. A theory on either base could be wholly unreliable. A comprehensive look at American experience with protest will safeguard against these pitfalls and will assure the representativeness of the case studies that follow later.

There is no feasible way, it is true, of obtaining a comprehensive look actually covering every diplomatic protest in United States history, but there is no real need of trying to achieve this completeness. An extensive sampling will serve the same purpose. For this the annual *Foreign Relations of the United States*[1] is an excellent source, because it records a large volume of routine, as opposed to spectacular, diplomatic activity, and on a large portion of this activity carries information sufficiently detailed for evaluation. However, to meet the problem posed by the sheer mass of data in *Foreign Relations* itself, three series of years have been singled out for study. The series have been chosen with an eye to circumstantial variation. Because all of them are from the twentieth century, the United States stands throughout as a world power. The first period, 1900-1903, reflects the initial reaction of the country to its new position; the general international environment is neither notably tense nor notably relaxed. The second period, 1913-1918, sees the Democratic party assume control in Washington and watches the nation conducting its affairs first in peace, then as a neutral in a major war, and finally as a belligerent power. The third period, 1927-1930, finds the Republicans in office again; an isolationist mood dominates the country; generally good international feeling prevails; both at home and abroad high prosperity gives way to deep economic depression.

The material published in *Foreign Relations* is a miscellany of State Department documentation. It includes instructions to United States diplomatic and consular personnel abroad and their reports to Washington, correspondence of American missions with foreign governments and of foreign missions with the American government, communications to and from other executive agencies, departmental memoranda recording oral discussions or presenting special studies of specific questions, texts of international agreements, and citations of foreign governmental documents. Correspondence is frequently telegraphic and published in paraphrase. The content rather than the actual text of diplomatic protests is often cited in instructions and reports.

Documentation of this kind does not provide data with the precision of the pollster's questionnaire. The information pertinent to the survey had to be quarried from it, and in this process consistency of classification was a special concern. The standards for this classification are described in subsequent paragraphs. Using these standards, the survey has attempted to extract the fact of protest and a categorization of each instance of protest in terms of subject matter, time, addressee, and prima facie success or failure.

In determining the fact of diplomatic protest, the definition elaborated earlier[2] was used: an oral or written communication from one government to another, expressing dissatisfaction with the latter's conduct on legal or moral grounds and asking redress of the grievance. Nevertheless, if a governmental agent expressed the judgment that he was protesting, his action was considered a protest even though some element of the definition was indiscernible. Local American representatives were regarded as speaking for their government even when the initiative was their own, as long as Washington did not repudiate their act. No distinction was made between formal and informal protest, because the documents rarely permit a safe judgment on which was intended. While reiterated complaints on the same precise question were not counted as separate instances, in any communication which embodied several complaints each item was listed as an individual protest. This was necessary because partial concessions could otherwise be tabulated neither as successes nor as failures. Numerous cases in which *Foreign Relations* mentions the fact of protest and nothing more have been omitted; but cases in which the outcome, despite ample documentation, remained uncertain have been included.

The subject matters of the protests were grouped under eight major headings. The first, protection of nationals, embraces diplomatic action to defend the personal rights of United States nationals, usually abroad, sometimes at home. Typical of this classification are cases arising from denials of justice, laxity in the punishment of crimes against Americans, impediments to their freedom of movement, and infringements of their civil rights and capitulatory privileges. Diplomatic and consular privileges and immunities constitute the second category, although a few incidents involving American overseas officials without this formal standing were placed under this category. The third category, national honor, comprises instances of insult to the flag or the government of the United States. National security as a classification covers threats to territorial integrity, extended for limited purposes to vessels flying the American flag, and threats to the safety of the armed forces. But cases in the survey, it may be noted, scarcely ever affected the sensitive area which the term has connoted since the late thirties.

The fifth category, conditions of commerce, signifies complaints concerned with maintaining market conditions in conformity with the reasonable expectations of United States businessmen. The chief target of these protests was discrimination based on nationality: the award of contracts without open bidding, and tariffs and taxes violating the "most favored nation" clause of commercial agreements. Nondiscriminatory measures, however, can also strike at business, and these too were protested; recurrent examples include exorbitant taxation and harassing or impractical regulations of specific industries. The line between protection of nationals and conditions of commerce was sometimes hard to draw. When a new tax or monetary measure seemed essentially confiscatory, or appeared as an isolated act against a single firm, it was viewed as violating personal rights; but when it seemed to have implications for the business community in general, it was viewed as contravening reasonable commercial expectations.

Monetary claims, the sixth heading, were considered as protests rather than as mere negotiations only when foreign governments appeared negligent in settling or paying the amounts in question. The bulk of these claims centered upon indemnities for personal injury or property damage and upon unpaid debts and breach of contract. Human rights have also been the subject of protest, although the delicate doctrine of "domestic jurisdiction" has made the State Department chary of terming its action on religious persecution, for example, "representations."[3] Washington's scruples have been respected in the tabulation, but appeals for other than United States nationals, when made on such ethical grounds as "justice" or "humanitarian principle," were considered as protests and placed in this category.[4] The eighth category, miscellaneous, is best understood by mention of a few instances subsumed under it: the forcible seizure of con-

cessions at Tientsin, China, by several European powers; aid
and comfort given to Latin American revolutionists by the governments of neighboring states; some admittedly internal problems of Caribbean countries—in which, however, the American
government had a standing based on agreement; and the im-
proprieties of foreign diplomatic and consular personnel resid-
ing in the United States.

Each case was assigned to the year in which it first appeared
as protest, thus ignoring any prior diplomatic discussions. However, if a complaint was first filed in a year outside the survey
and merely reiterated inside the survey, it was placed in the year
of reiterated protest.[5] All the issues were traced to their respective conclusions, even when final disposition fell outside the periods of study. The determination of to whom a protest was made
sometimes presented difficulties. *De facto* revolutionary authorities—military or civil; central, provincial, or municipal—were
regarded as representing the entire country within which they
maintained power. Thus, both northern and southern parties in
the Chinese disturbances of the twenties were listed as "China."
The groups did, after all, claim and exercise power within a
political entity that stood in a basically constant relationship to
the United States. In situations of legal dependency, protests were
placed under the country actually responsible for action. While
Canada, Egypt, and Iraq, in the occasions on record, seem to
have been operating independently of Great Britain, Britain was
the effective agent in Palestine, as was France in Morocco.

Insufficiency of data necessitated the adaptation of norms,
suggested in Chapter 2, for deciding the outcome of protests. For
present purposes these turn out in four different ways: They
clearly succeed; they clearly fail; they evoke a response of du-
bious acceptability; or, due to the limitations of the documented
information, their achievements are "uncertain." Protests were
tabulated as successful if they were followed by unquestionable
concession to the American viewpoint, or if concession was sub-

stantial and at the same time accepted by the American government as satisfactory. Protests were regarded as failures if they met with the unquestionable rejection or nonfulfillment of the American demand, even though the United States acquiesced. Protests were considered as of doubtful result when concessions did not clearly meet demands or when, apparently meeting demands, they drew expressions of dissatisfaction from the American government. Protests were viewed as of uncertain outcome when the documentation trailed off inconclusively. Doubtful and uncertain outcomes were counted under a single heading. To omit them would distort the record, yet their relation to the problem of effectiveness is the same, as neither can be evaluated.

Such were the definitions which guided the extraction of pertinent information from *Foreign Relations*. The results can now be reported and scrutinized. It should be noted, however, that no statistical refinement or subtlety is intended in the discussion of the data which the general survey turned up.[6] Numbers and percentages do state facts and may epitomize even highly complex situations, but the emphasis is on historical and conceptual analysis.

An examination of the diplomatic papers contained in *Foreign Relations* has uncovered a total of 598 protests by the United States in the three series of years under study. Distributed by subject matter over the series in which they occurred, these would be tabulated as in Table 1. In 1900-1903 there were 110 protests, an average of 28 per year. In 1913-1918 there were 338, an average of 56. In 1927-1930 there were 150, an average of 38. The total of all these—comprising, as it does, merely a random sample of diplomatic protests over a time span of only fourteen years—is startlingly higher than was anticipated. Divergences in the volume of printed documentation for the three periods make comparative analysis of the figures impossible.[7] But the figures clearly indicate that the United States has used protest with regularity: as emergent and as established major power, in peace and in war, as neutral and as belligerent, in prosperity and depression, and under Republican and Democratic administrations. The figures also show the importance of protest in the routine relations of the United States with other countries.

Protests over the protection of nationals[8] and conditions of commerce are, as the survey reveals, relatively the most numerous; for no period did the proportion for any other category rise

TABLE I

Diplomatic Protests According to Subject Matter and Period

	1900-1903		1913-1918		1927-1930		All Periods	
Protection of nationals	81	73.6	122	36.0	61	40.7	264	44.2
Diplomatic and consular immunity	5	4.5	10	3.0	9	6.0	24	4.0
National honor	1	0.9	5	1.5	4	2.7	10	1.7
National security	0	0.0	32	9.5	3	2.0	35	5.9
Conditions of commerce	9	8.2	118	34.9	40	26.7	167	27.9
Monetary claims	8	7.3	18	5.3	13	8.7	39	6.5
Human rights	2	1.8	16	4.7	5	3.3	23	3.8
Miscellaneous	4	3.6	17	5.0	15	10.0	36	6.0
Total	110		338		150		598	

In every table in this chapter, percentages are printed in bold type. Failure to carry out decimals results in minor discrepancies in total percentages.

above 10 per cent of the total. The perennially high incidence of protests directed toward protection of nationals is understandable. In terms of sheer numbers, individual Americans in their private capacities are more likely to brush with foreign governments than are American officials who enjoy some type of legal immunity. Incidents touching national security arise in rather special circumstances, and the legal standing of remonstrance on human rights has been tenuous. Conditions of commerce and monetary claims, moreover, are in fact merely more readily identifiable issues over which Americans do come into conflict with other governments. As for the high incidence of protests on conditions of commerce, World War I appears to be a landmark in this development. During the war, belligerent interference with neutral shipping and communication gave prominence to these complaints, while the shift in the balance of trade and investment—expanding United States economic interests abroad—gave them some permanence.

The countries to which protests have been most frequently made are listed in Table 2. Mexico, Great Britain, China, Germany, Turkey, and France head the roster, France showing the lowest figure, 26. For none of the other thirty-seven countries does the number run higher than 17; the average number for each of them is 4.8, as against a general average for all countries in the survey of 13.9.

TABLE II

Countries to Which the Most Protests Have Been Made

	Number of Protests	Percentage of Total
Mexico	115	19
Great Britain	99	17
China	91	15
Germany	57	10
Turkey	31	5
France	26	4
All others (37)	179	30
Total	598	100

There is no uniform reason why the countries named dominate the list. All but five of the instances involving Great Britain were exclusively attributable to the war, and are therefore explicable in terms of British naval supremacy and leadership in the economic warfare against the Central Powers.[9] The German cases dealt mostly with military service early in the century and arose from the conjuncture of considerable migration from Germany to the United States and a treaty between the two countries resolving the problems of double nationality. There were, therefore, frequent occasions for appeal and a written agreement to which appeal could be made. The count for France reveals no distinctive causality. A significant number of Americans, with extensive interests, resided in both Mexico and China; revolution was chronic, widespread, and violent; and the impulse toward economic self-determination was strong. The Turkish scene was a variation of this. A nominally centralized government was in fact quite ineffective during the first two periods; nationalistic sentiment, intensified by religious feeling, ran high; and American interests, especially as represented by Protestant missionary endeavors, were substantial.

The pattern of dominance suggests a conclusion verging on tautology: that the frequency of United States protest may be expected to correspond with the frequency of offensive behavior in other countries. The statement, however, gives point to two observations derived from the regional distribution of protests. For one thing, the Far East of 1913-1918 appears as an illuminating exception. A sharp decline in protests directed to this area at this particular time probably had its rationale in the American desire to support the political integrity of China and the consequent unwillingness to disturb the then delicate environment, whatever the provocation might be.[10] Wartime preoccupation with Europe was probably not responsible for this conduct, because there was no decline in the Western Hemisphere parallel to that in the Far East. By contrast, the entire European tabulation appears as an illuminating confirmation of the suggested conclusion. For if the military service cases and the complaints arising from the war were excluded, the total figure for protection of nationals here would fall to the extraordinarily low sum of 31. The political stability of European countries and the close approach of their standard of justice to that of the United States would account for this fact.

The question might be raised as to whether the power status of the recipient country has qualified the supposed correspondence between remonstrance and offense; in other words, as to whether the greater strength of some recipients has inhibited complaint against their reprehensible conduct. Because the incidence in fact of activity against which protest would have been justified cannot be determined, the answer can only be conjectural. To nations which were ranked as Great Powers when action was taken (the roster has varied from period to period), the United States has made 210 recorded protests. The count for each of the three periods is presented in Table 3. In 1900-1903 there is recorded an average of 6.3 protests to each of the Great Powers; for 1913-1918 and 1927-1930 the averages are 22.3 and 3.2 respectively. The corresponding figures for all other countries listed[11] are 4.7, 9.1, and 4.8. Obviously the United States has not been less articulate in dealing with the Great Powers than with the small. At best one could scale down the 1900-1903 record by subtracting the German military service cases—2.2 would be the new average—and hypothesize that, in peaceful periods, protest to major powers is less likely than to minor ones. But this would not necessarily imply American diffidence in the face of strength; it would more probably mean that the stable internal control of the Great Powers has minimized the number of offensive incidents.

TABLE III

Protests to the Great Powers

	1900-1903	1913-1918	1927-1930	Total
Austria-Hungary	8	9	*	17
France	1	16	9	26
Germany	25	32	*	57
Great Britain	1	94	4	99
Italy	0	4	0	4
Japan	*	1	2	3
Russia	3	0	1	4
Total	38	156	16	210

*Not regarded as a Great Power at this time.

Beyond the mere occurrence of protest and in many ways more important is the question of results. How did the cases turn out? Percentage-wise there is a curious hovering in the same general area for almost all distributions according to outcome. By subject matter, by time span, by recipient's power status, successes run in the vicinity of 55 per cent, failures at 25 per cent, and doubtful-uncertain results at 20 per cent. Success, then, is a somewhat more characteristic outcome of United States diplomatic protest than failure or uncertainty.[12]

TABLE IV

Outcome of Protests According to Subject-Matter Categories

	Success	Failure	Doubtful-Uncertain	Total
Protection of nationals	167 63	55 21	42 16	264
Diplomatic and consular immunity	14 58	4 17	6 25	24
National honor	7 70	3 30	0 0	10
National security	21 60	9 26	5 14	35
Conditions of commerce	76 46	54 32	37 22	167
Monetary claims	19 49	7 18	13 33	39
Human rights	8 35	9 39	6 26	23
Miscellaneous	15 42	15 42	6 17	36
Total	327 55	156 26	115 19	598

This, however, is a general statement of results, and there were particular differences of outcome which merit closer scrutiny. In them, clues as to the influences underlying effective and ineffective protest may appear. Table 4 lists the outcomes of protests in each subject-matter category.

Three categories show relatively poor ratios of success: conditions of commerce, human rights, and miscellaneous. A look at the record for these three may uncover factors which characteristically render protests ineffective.[13] Concessions in these areas have perhaps been made grudgingly because concessions have meant tangible loss to the government which made them.

With respect to conditions of commerce, Mexico and China have resisted markedly. Nationalistic stirrings constituted an important facet of this obstinacy: Mexican pride called for an end to the foreign exploitation of national resources; Chinese pride chafed at economic controls under the "unequal treaties." In both countries one revolutionary faction after another sought funds desperately, through tariffs, taxes, expropriations, and currency schemes. The appeal to nationalistic emotion is a two-edged sword: Once the feeling has been aroused, governments have yielded to foreign pressures or importunities only at their peril; inflamed public opinion is likely to label every concession as an "appeasement." Furthermore, the desperate need for money arises whenever any revolutionary action is prolonged; for unless the movement's military forces are paid, they will begin to evanesce.

Moved by the same factor of tangible high cost, businessmen in peacetime and strategists in wartime are also likely to generate governmental resistance to foreign pressures regarding some commercial matters. The businessmen seek economic advantages through government support; the strategists use economics as a military weapon. Although this kind of resistance was perceptible, its impact was less clear than that of nationalistic fervor and revolutionary indigence. One reason for the difference has been the pluralism of domestic commercial interests in stable societies. Their lack of unanimity on protectionism and associated policies can give outside governments leverage to undermine such programs. The United States, for example, once enlisted the aid of Czechoslovakian automobile dealers in order to win a modification of Czech import restrictions on American vehicles.[14] Another difference is that, even in wartime, the possibly higher reward for concession may be regarded as balancing its higher cost. A nation at war may labor anxiously to keep a neutral from becoming an enemy or even to transform it into an ally.

On human rights seven of the nine failures recorded refer to cases growing out of World War I. Imperious military necessity, real or fancied, blocked compliance with American demands, presumably because sacrifice of strategic advantage is a decidedly tangible cost.

Because the label "miscellaneous" connotes heterogeneity, individual instances here must be more closely scrutinized. At least four failures regarding Latin American nations and two regarding China are attributable to nationalistic feeling. These failures were responses to an effort to end Costa Rican aid to Nicaraguan revolutionaries, an attempt to limit Dominican financial indebtedness, two component measures of the extended American intervention in Nicaragua, a demand that Japan be given a voice in revising China's "capitulatory" judicial system, and a complaint concerning the nationality of high personnel with the Canton-Hankow railroad.[15]

In other miscellaneous cases, the recalcitrance of the recipients was more rational. In Mexico, General Calles felt that an American-sponsored truce between warring factions needlessly neutralized the advantages of his military position. Cuba disregarded some ill-advised pressure for a political amnesty. Four nations rejected United States protests against their territorial acquisitions at Tientsin in 1901. Russia brushed aside American invocation of the Kellogg-Briand Pact in the Sino-Soviet crisis of 1929.[16] The rationally calculated stakes were relatively and perceptibly high, suggesting again that the common factor behind resistance was tangible high cost. Moreover, when the miscellaneous successes were significant, as in several cases with Liberia and Latin America, they were achieved under substantial American pressure.[17] The actual loss was offset by a loss which, though merely prospective, would have been equally tangible and notably larger.

In the categories marked by more favorable results, an important factor behind effectiveness appears to be the reverse of the tangible high cost hypothesis: Concession has usually been less expensive. Demands recorded under protection of nationals have been individualized and unpublicized. Domestic pressure groups have rarely been operative. More often than not, any monetary outlay has been trivial. Frequently a nascent government's desire to prove its responsibility has spurred it to corrective action. On the other hand, resistance has appeared when the precise issue was antiforeignism, as in the China of the Boxers or the Turkey of 1914-1916, or when the government's physical weakness prevented the maintenance of order, as in the Mexico of 1915-1918. The vindication of diplomatic and consular immunity has been analogous to the protection of nationals, and concession assured the premium of reciprocal treatment for the diplomats and consuls of the nation which made it. Favorable responses to monetary claims were made for similar reasons; recalcitrance was manifested only when the sums in question reached large proportions, as they did in China during 1929 and 1930.

Despite the frightfully explosive ingredients in questions of national honor, their proximate danger has depended on the initial dramatization. The Tampico incident, which brought the United States and Mexico to the brink of war over an affront to the American flag in 1914, early became a *cause célèbre*, on which open retreat would have been a bitter pill for either party.[18] The protests on national security have seldom demanded great concessions. On one issue which has been placed in this category, Great Britain strongly resisted United States objections in 1916-1917. This was the British practice of forcibly removing from American ships civilians who were nationals of Germany and Austria-Hungary, claiming that these men were reservists in the Central Powers' military forces. While the release of a handful of individuals might have been a minor matter, surrender of the principle assuredly was not, and it was to this that United States demands tended.

With respect to some categories in which protest was more effective, however, it should be remembered that intangible or low cost was not the sole operative factor. On diplomatic immunity, national honor, and national security, usage has established rather firm principles of international conduct. And protest will perhaps bring a readier response when concession is the logical requirement of principles accepted jointly by the appropriate parties.

Clues to the success or failure of protest may be found not only in their subject matter but also in their temporal relationships. Table 5 presents the outcomes of protest for each of the three periods investigated, both over-all and for the two most numerous categories.

TABLE V

Outcome of Protests Over-all and for Special Categories,
According to Periods

	Success	Failure	Doubtful-Uncertain	Total
1900-1903				
Protection of nationals	57 **70**	13 **16**	11 **14**	81
Conditions of commerce	4 **44**	4 **44**	1 **11**	9
Others	12 **60**	4 **20**	4 **20**	20
Total	73 **66**	21 **19**	16 **15**	110
1913-1918				
Protection of nationals	70 **57**	32 **26**	20 **16**	122
Conditions of commerce	52 **44**	41 **35**	25 **21**	118
Others	45 **46**	30 **31**	23 **24**	98
Total	167 **49**	103 **31**	68 **20**	338
1927-1930				
Protection of nationals	40 **66**	10 **16**	11 **18**	61
Conditions of commerce	20 **50**	9 **23**	11 **28**	40
Others	27 **55**	13 **27**	9 **18**	49
Total	87 **58**	32 **21**	31 **21**	150

The general record of success for the middle period was poor, 49 per cent, as compared with 66 per cent for the earlier and 58 per cent for the later period. Conditions in revolutionary Mexico and in the warring European powers were influential in depressing this record. According to Table 6, which assembles the figures for Mexico, for the European belligerents, and for the rest of the world,[19] the ratio of success in the troubled areas was 48 per cent, as compared with 53 per cent elsewhere in the world. Moreover, virtually all the protests to the belligerents were directly concerned with situations arising from the war, and absolutely all the protests to Mexico were linked with that country's revolution. Since concessions in these circumstances entail greater sacrifices, one would expect wars and revolutions to increase resistance to outside diplomatic pressure.

TABLE VI

Outcome of Protests to World War Belligerents and to Mexico, 1913-1918

	Success	Failure	Doubtful-Uncertain	Total
France	7 44	4 25	5 31	16
Great Britain	44 47	38 40	12 13	94
Italy	3 75	1 25	0 0	4
Austria-Hungary	5 56	3 33	1 11	9
Germany	15 47	6 19	11 34	32
Total belligerents	74 48	52 34	29 19	155
Mexico	49 49	26 26	25 25	100
Total Mexico and belligerents	123 48	78 31	54 21	255
All others	44 53	25 30	14 17	83

On the other hand, the influence of these circumstances could not have been decisive. The differential in the success ratio for countries inside and outside the war-and-revolution framework was not large. It is arguable, however, that the war transformed the attitude even of its nonparticipants. Possibly the other countries were capitalizing on the preoccupation of the United States,

even during the neutral years, with the central conflict—a preoccupation which partly immobilized the nation's diplomatic potential. The peculiar assets of some countries, it should also be
recalled, gave their favor toward one side or the other an inflated value at the very same time that the threat of heavy sanctions from both sides impelled them to yield ground very warily.
One remembers that Turkey chose this period to denounce the
capitulations; and that Spain, the Netherlands, and the Scandinavian neutrals were picking their way carefully through the
agonizing dilemmas imposed by the belligerent powers' rival
economic strategies.[20]

More clearly than in the general figures, the tendency of war
and revolution to stiffen the participants' diplomatic resistance
appears in the specific figures for particular subject-matter categories during the three periods. Table 5 includes the record for
two of these categories.

Successful protests on protection of nationals declined
sharply in the middle period, standing at 57 per cent, as contrasted with 70 per cent in 1900-1903 and 66 per cent in 1927-
1930. Although this dip was rather universal geographically,
it was most notable in Mexico. The influence of revolutionary
conditions, then, is again indicated. As a case-by-case canvass
reveals, favorable responses which would have made difficulties
for military strategy or would have run counter to revolutionary
economics were rare; almost half the failures, in fact, were in
cases arising from monetary reforms or new legislation on the
control of natural resources. The complaints which were successful mostly dealt with the protection of persons from violence,
although even here the governments' promises of help often went
unfulfilled from sheer want of military resources to furnish
such help. A fair number of representations over forced loans to
government and localized double taxation also succeeded; and
these favorable responses are atypical in terms of revolution's
presumed effects.

Outside Mexico the case-by-case canvass uncovered no pattern. The World War I belligerents made few important concessions. The issues on which they did surrender had been drained of magnitude by being individualized. These included specific instances of inequitable blacklisting, violation of safe-conduct pledges, and, after the United States had joined the Allies, improper treatment of American prisoners of war. Even nonbelligerents responded favorably to protests only under heavy American pressure. Satisfaction was given on such items as racial discrimination (against Syro-Americans), unjust and abusive treatment of civilian prisoners, and disputes over joint use of borderland water resources. On the other hand, few refusals in this period can be traced to factors which the more general analysis had suggested as significant: countervailing pressures upon the responding nation, or its dire necessities, or its premium bargaining assets, or the diverted attention of the United States as complainant.

With conditions of commerce, as with protection of nationals, effectiveness was low in 1913-1918. The absolute figure for the earlier period was too small for meaningful comparison, but in 1913-1918 the success ratio was 44 per cent, as compared with 50 per cent for 1927-1930. In the middle period, all but 12 of the 118 protests in this category were filed with the World War I belligerent powers or with Mexico. From Mexico less than a third of the United States complaints won redress, mostly on minor matters. Oil wells and metal mines were at the heart of the revolutionary economic program, and objections to the Mexican governments' actions on these regularly met with unsatisfactory replies. Among the countries at war, Great Britain played the most prominent role. Although the British bowed to American demands more than half the time, they made concessions only in particular cases, seeking to mollify influential segments of the American public; but they gave no ground on principles.

For subject-matter categories other than protection of nationals and conditions of commerce, the protests were too few to warrant separate tabulation or detailed discussion. Outside the 1913-1918 period, only three protests on national security were registered; inside that period, the success ratio was good, 56 per cent. But strictly strategic conceptions were almost never at issue. The eleven complaints to Mexico had to do mostly with border violations by outlaw bands. As one approached true strategy, in fact, the reluctance of a protest's recipient to concede anything became much stronger; one notes here Great Britain's firm stand on the surveillance of neutral commerce by warships of the British navy which "hovered" outside American ports.

Resistance on monetary claims appeared most strikingly in the last rather than in the middle period and was associated with the revolutionary upheavals in China. Exceptionally unstable economic conditions accompanied the political chaos. The sums demanded were huge; other countries had similar large claims, so that settlement with any would set troublesome precedents; and Chinese authorities wanted no more liens on current governmental revenue, which had been a common device for assuring the payment of international creditors.

The reverse side of the quest for the backgrounds of ineffectiveness in the middle period is the quest for the backgrounds of effectiveness in the other two. In 1900-1903 circumstances simply did not make for weighty or highly emotional controversies between the United States and Europe. However bitterly they maneuvered for position, hostility among the European powers themselves was not active, and American competitive economic interest within their territories was small. United States attention was accordingly narrowed to the protection of nationals on their travels. The problem arose almost exclusively from the visit of some naturalized American citizen (or his child) to his ancestral village and the local authorities' effort to hold the visitor for his compulsory military service under the laws of his erstwhile fatherland. Given a naturalization treaty which unravelled the complications of double citizenship between the United States and the country concerned, American complaints routinely received favorable replies; and where no treaty existed, the complaints were not included in the present record. In the Western hemisphere relative serenity prevailed; curiously, no American protest appears in the crisis over the Venezuela blockade and the Panamanian revolution. In the Far East the Chinese recalcitrance which preceded the Boxer uprising gave way to an almost obsequious responsiveness, a normal sequel to severe military defeat.

In the Europe of 1927-1930 one finds neither the imperious necessities nor intense emotional attitudes which might have inspired resistance to the occasional United States pressures. In the Western hemisphere a period of ill-feeling between the United States and Mexico ended in 1927; during subsequent sporadic revolutionary outbreaks "south of the border," the Mexican government never lost its fundamental control. The United States' role in the several bitter inter-American boundary disputes of the period was confined to the exercise of good offices. The Far East was an exception to the relative calm. China was troubled by revolution and the struggle to throw off the unequal treaties. Local and national violations of treaty provisions touching taxation were frequent, and corrective measures requested by the United States were repeatedly refused. Monetary claims made little headway with authorities who simply did not have the money.

An examination of protest's effectiveness specifically in terms of recipient countries adds little to what has been uncovered with relation to subject matter and time span. The oddest indication here is that power status was apparently unrelated to efficacy. The figures for recipients assembled according to power status, following the Great Power-small power grouping used earlier, are presented in Table 7. The ratios of success for all protests to Great Powers and small powers are virtually identical, 54 and 55 per cent, although the ratios differ for the three periods. In interpreting the data, however, some allowances must be made. The omission of the German military-service cases, which were handled almost mechanically, would cut the proportion of successes with the Great Powers in 1900-1903 to about 50 per cent and in the entire survey to 49 per cent; and because the small total for the Great Powers in 1927-1930 may be an inadequate sample, the success ratio for that period may have an unrepresentative basis. More important, the situations in China, Mexico, and Turkey, to which reference has several times been made, gave an unfavorable bias to the small-power record. If the figures for these three countries are deducted from this record, the success ratio for small powers in all three periods would be about 60 per cent. Unfortunately, however, the protests to these other powers would then be distributed so thinly over so many countries that no characteristic background of effectiveness or ineffectiveness could be expected to emerge.

TABLE VII

Outcome of Protests According to Power Status of Recipient Countries

		Success	Failure	Doubtful-Uncertain	Total
1900-1903	Great Powers	30 **79**	5 **13**	3 **8**	38
	Small Powers	43 **60**	16 **22**	13 **18**	72
1913-1918	Great Powers	74 **47**	52 **33**	30 **19**	156
	Small Powers	93 **51**	51 **28**	38 **21**	182
1927-1930	Great Powers	10 **63**	5 **31**	1 **6**	16
	Small Powers	77 **58**	27 **20**	30 **22**	134
Total	Great Powers	114 **54**	62 **30**	34 **16**	210
	Small Powers	213 **55**	94 **24**	81 **21**	388

General American experience with diplomatic protest, therefore, indicates the lines within which cases for intensive study
may be regarded as representative or at least not unrepresentative. Protests in all subject-matter categories have been employed reasonably often in modern American diplomacy. Most
common, apparently in the nature of things, have been complaints dealing with protection of nationals and conditions of
commerce; least common have been complaints in defense
of national honor. Protest has been used constantly, although
available data permits no judgment as to its relative frequency
in changing situations. Diplomatic protests to forty-three countries appear in the documentation of the fourteen years studied.
It is likely, then, that they have been filed with every nation
which has existed in the twentieth century. Only two major
circumstances have been isolated as prompting a great volume
of protests: instability within a country and open warfare
between Great Powers.

In most subject-matter categories, at most times, and with
most countries, about 55 per cent of diplomatic protests have
succeeded, 25 per cent have failed, and 20 per cent have come
(as far as the documents reveal) to a doubtful or uncertain
conclusion. The record of success was somewhat less favorable
for protests concerned with conditions of commerce, human
rights, and miscellaneous than for those concerned with other
kinds of issues; for protests made in time of war and revolution; and for protests directed to nations pressed by these two
circumstances. But the power status of the recipients, in itself,
seemed not related to the effectiveness of protest. The pervasive
factor inspiring resistance appeared to be the greater and more
tangible cost of the demanded concessions, whether calculated
rationally in terms of political and economic advantage or
emotionally in terms of nationalistic sentiment.

The cases chosen for more intense study in the following
chapters fall within these guiding lines of "representativeness."

Close examination of them, it is hoped, will yield a deeper insight into the workings of diplomatic protest.

NOTES

[1] United States Department of State, *Papers Relating to the Foreign Relations of the United States.* Washington: Government Printing Office. (See p. 5, n. 4.)

[2] See above, Chapter 2.

[3] See Secretary of State Kellogg's attitude toward the alleged mistreatment of the Jews in Rumania; he undertook to explain to the Rumanian government the state of American public opinion regarding the issue (*Foreign Relations, 1927,* Vol. 3, pp. 637-40).

[4] Not included, however, were actions taken on official behalf of other countries in favor of their nationals, as during the period when the United States had custody of French interests in Mexico.

[5] *Foreign Relations* for any given year frequently contains material dating from prior years and on rare occasions material from the subsequent year. Footnotes occasionally indicate the ultimate disposition, several years later, of particular cases.

[6] This demurrer is the more necessary because the crossing of categories upon each other seldom yields figures large enough to bear reliable statistical treatment.

[7] The relevant volumes of *Foreign Relations* for the 1900-1903 period contain 3,469 pages of text; for 1913-1918, 12,987 pages; for 1927-1930, 10,715 pages. There is simply no telling whether the divergences represent corresponding divergences in the amounts of diplomatic documentation from which the printed papers were selected. It seems a fair assumption that diplomatic business expanded during the war and that it was more extensive in the last period than in the first.

[8] The extraordinarily high percentage in 1900-1903 is not necessarily significant. A large number of routine military service cases, especially with Germany, has inflated this figure; with them subtracted, the percentage of cases in this category would drop from 73 to 46.

[9] Footnotes in *Foreign Relations* often indicate that parallel notes were sent to the leading Allied or Central powers, as the case may be. All such instances were noted and the protests tallied separately for all the countries concerned.

[10] The United States followed with intense interest the progress of Sino-Japanese negotiations over the Twenty-One Demands, *Foreign Relations, 1915,* pp. 105-59. Prior to these negotiations, the State Department raised objections to specific counts and reserved its rights with respect to any agreement reached, but the actions in question were not clearly protests.

[11] Properly, one should include all countries, even those for which no protests have been recorded. Since only the list of small powers would be expanded in this way, the average number of protests to each of them would drop, while the average number to each of the Great Powers would remain the same.

[12] Analysis has been made of the doubtful-uncertain outcome only when the circumstances have indicated a clear relevance to the question of effectiveness.

[13] The poor record for monetary claims is more apparent than real. During the First World War, six claims against Germany were in the process of satisfactory adjustment when diplomatic relations were broken for other reasons. If these cases are simply dropped from the count, successes run to 54 per cent.

[14] *Foreign Relations, 1928*, Vol. 2, p. 709.

[15] *Foreign Relations, 1914*, pp. 180-85; *Foreign Relations, 1915*, pp. 321-39, and *Foreign Relations, 1916*, pp. 249-56; *Foreign Relations, 1928*, Vol. 3, pp. 418-76, and *Foreign Relations, 1929*, Vol. 3, pp. 606-41; *ibid.*, Vol. 2, pp. 713-22; *Foreign Relations, 1930*, Vol. 2, pp. 609-10.

[16] *Foreign Relations, 1915*, pp. 800-01; *Foreign Relations, 1917*, pp. 371-78; *Foreign Relations, 1901*, pp. 39-59; *Foreign Relations, 1929*, Vol. 2, pp. 367-68, 404-06. A protest parallel with this last was filed with China and met with evasion rather than outright rejection; see *ibid.*, p. 387.

[17] See, for example, *Foreign Relations, 1913*, pp. 369-81 (Cuba); *Foreign Relations, 1915*, pp. 1221-40, and *Foreign Relations, 1916*, pp. 938-43 (Panama); *Foreign Relations, 1917*, pp. 431-56 (Cuba), and pp. 877-87 (Liberia); and *Foreign Relations, 1930*, Vol. 3, pp. 198-251 (Haiti).

[18] *Foreign Relations, 1914*, pp. 448-88.

[19] No protests to Russia have been recorded for these years. Turkey has been omitted from the count as a belligerent because almost none of the complaints made to the Porte concerned the conduct of the war; Turkey's inclusion would impair the record of effectiveness in a minute degree.

[20] On Turkey, see *Foreign Relations, 1914*, pp. 1090-94 and Supplement, pp. 767-68, 777; *Foreign Relations, 1915*, pp. 1301-06; *Foreign Relations, 1916*, pp. 963-75. For examples on the others, see *Foreign Relations, 1918*, Supplement 1, Vol. 2, pp. 1081-1107, 1772-89.

CHAPTER IV

Neutral Rights
on the High Seas, 1914-1916

A traditionally focal issue in American foreign policy has been the freedom of the seas. During the first two-and-a-half years of World War I, a classic controversy with a classic adversary, Great Britain, concerned this issue. In this encounter the United States used diplomatic protest extensively to realize its objectives.

Although the range of problems was broad and their documentation is extensive, the question of what may be labeled neutral trading rights presents a manageable unit of study. This question arises from the use, assertedly under international law, of belligerent sea power vis-á-vis the neutral countries. It centers upon the definition of contraband, the right of visit and search, and the establishment of blockade. Excluded from its purview are matters—such as censorship of mail and cables—less directly concerned with property rights, and matters—such as blacklisting and control over supplies of coal—less clearly within the scope of international law.

For Great Britain the factor of overwhelming importance in the background of its diplomatic struggle with the United States was its military struggle with Germany. The war had brought into conflict armies and navies of unprecedented destructive power. Rightly or wrongly, the English thought that

German ambition was primarily responsible for the war. They accordingly felt that defeat would mean the end of Great Britain as a nation determining its own destiny and that a negotiated peace would only postpone, not end, the battle. Germany was the sole antagonist on the Western Front and was envisioned as the real source of the Central Powers' military and industrial strength. The decisive defeat of Germany was the controlling objective of British diplomacy. One fundamental means of attaining this objective was the economic strangulation of the Central Powers. An army without munitions, food, and shelter must surrender. England advantageously employed its own peculiar strength, therefore, to choke off the enemy's supply of these vital commodities.

Great Britain's geographical position and its possession of the world's most powerful navy dictated this strategy. The British Isles commanded the major approaches to Germany by sea: the North Sea and the English Channel. Island bases and French assistance secured control of the Mediterranean. Widely scattered colonial outposts facilitated the policing of the sea lanes elsewhere in the world. England was physically able to impede all intercontinental shipments to the enemy, but its effective control was limited by two circumstances. First, Germany's naval command of the Baltic Sea made Norway and Sweden virtually contiguous with its own territory, while Denmark and the Netherlands were actually so; goods which reached these countries could pass without hindrance into Germany. Secondly, the prescriptions of international law restricted the measures which the British could take in interrupting the overseas commerce of these neutrals who were potential suppliers of German economic and military needs. The controversy with the United States originated in practices which allegedly violated these legal prescriptions.

The English strategy of strangulation was executed through two devices relevant here. Complaining that Germany had mined the North Sea indiscriminately, the government announced that Great Britain in reprisal and self-defense had prepared mine fields in the neighboring area. The government then indicated to neutral ships the secure routes to the British Isles and suggested that they call at British ports for further safe sailing instructions. It thus became easy to halt merchant vessels for visit and search, even for a leisurely visit and search in port. The United States never protested the mine laying which made the British advice to ships so persuasive. In addition the English government promulgated a series of orders in council which directly regulated the treatment of merchant vessels by naval officers and prize-court officials. The pertinent orders will be discussed later. These did evoke American protests.[1]

Several considerations tended to moderate or intensify the stringency of British action. The principal moderating factor was England's need of military supplies, much more urgent than Germany's need because the English had entered the war with less preparation. The United States was an indispensable source of vital materials and, later, of loans to finance their purchase. Interference with neutral commerce could not, therefore, be carried to the point where it would provoke the American government to curtail the flow of munitions or of money. War with the United States was even less desirable. Prime Minister Asquith, Foreign Secretary Grey, Minister of Munitions Lloyd George, and Ambassador Spring-Rice all recognized the delicacy of the situation.[2]

The British government's impulse to intensify its economic warfare sprang from external military circumstances and from internal politics. The war on the crucial Western Front early reached a stalemate not to be broken by the most reckless bloodletting on either side. This situation gave the German submarine a chance to threaten England's own exceptionally vulnerable line of supply. The frustration on land and the threat at sea tempted Great Britain toward unhampered use of its naval power for quick and cheap victory. This subject readily aroused the British public. It was taken up in Parliament in early 1915 and was seriously agitated again in the winter of 1915-1916, when an American observer was convinced that a relaxation of economic warfare would have precipitated a cabinet crisis.[3]

The American reaction to British restraints on maritime commerce was conditioned by deep-seated public attitudes, legal conceptions, economic circumstances, and the personal prepossessions of governmental authorities.

Almost unanimously, the public at large wished to stay out of the war. This desire reflected the national tradition since George Washington's time: Europe's politics did not concern the United States and war was horrible anyhow. Although long-standing friendship for France, compassion for Belgium, and a decade's dislike for the Kaiser had stimulated emotional identification with the Allies in most quarters, neutrality as an official policy received widespread support. German-Americans, however, tended to sympathize with the Central Powers, and Irish-Americans tended to "sympathize against" Great Britain.[4]

But if detachment from European affairs was an operative tradition among Americans, so was devotion to neutral rights. The very spirit of detachment magnified this devotion. The United States' conception of neutrality had reference to the conduct both of belligerents and of neutrals. The corpus of international law on which the United States had to rely was neither comprehensive nor indisputable. Nevertheless, its relevant principles as of 1914 may fairly be summarized in the following fashion.[5]

There were three classes of merchandise, each subject to different treatment if stopped by a belligerent at sea. Absolute contraband consisted of goods used exclusively for war and destined for enemy territory. These remained contraband, subject to confiscation, even if they were to pass through a neutral state on the way to their "ultimate destination"; the rule of "continuous voyage" was therefore applicable. Conditional contraband consisted of goods susceptible both of peaceful and of warlike use. These were contraband only if they were destined for the armed forces or a government department of a belligerent nation. To them the rule of continuous voyage could not be applied; proximate destination to neutral territory made them immune to seizure. Goods included in neither of the above categories were noncontraband. They were not subject to seizure unless they were destined for a port which was formally blockaded. Even enemy property of this class was exempt from seizure when carried on neutral ships, as was neutral property on enemy ships.

For purposes of discovering contraband, belligerent naval vessels had the right to search neutral ships on the high seas. If the examination developed a well-grounded suspicion of contraband cargo, the suspected merchantman could be sent to port and detained for adjudication in the belligerent's prize courts. Shipments found to be contraband could be confiscated. Unfounded detention, however, rendered the belligerent government liable for damages. As mentioned above, even noncontraband goods could be seized if they were proceeding to a port which a belligerent had declared to be under blockade. But for a blockade to be juridically binding, it had to be formally notified to neutrals; it had to be effectively maintained by an "adequate" naval patrol; it had to bear with equal force, rather than selectively, on all neutrals; and it had to be operative only against enemy ports, not against neutral ones.

As to the legal standing of neutrals, the American positions most important for present purposes concerned commerce in contraband of war, and war finance. In public circulars of August 15 and October 15, 1914, the Department of State indicated that the government was not obliged to prevent its citizens from trading in contraband at their own risk vis-à-vis the belligerents. The second of the announcements emphasized that executive interference with the munitions traffic was not authorized by federal law. Inconsistently, the Department at first discouraged war loans by an extralegal declaration that they were not in accord with "the spirit of neutrality." However, the administration later reversed this stand, privately informing the bankers that the government would not object to their granting credits (not loans) to finance purchases in the United States. Both of these positions touched very closely Great Britain's capacity to wage the war.[6]

The outbreak of the war aggravated already depressed business conditions in the United States. Naval action and military transportation problems limited the availability of belligerent merchant vessels to carry American merchandise, and fear kept other ships in port. Direct trade with Germany, the second largest importer of goods from the United States, was quickly cut to 2 per cent of its 1913 level. Curtailment of agricultural exports threatened the ability of Americans to meet international business obligations, which were customarily paid in London late in the year through the shipment of crops. The rate of exchange fell sharply. The New York Stock Exchange closed (and remained closed until almost the end of the year) in order to prevent the dumping of European-held securities. Bank clearances were drastically reduced. The dismal financial situation joined with shortages of vital imported materials to diminish industrial output. The outlook for the American economy was bleak.

Three months later, however, the picture completely changed. Government-sponsored insurance and higher transport charges revived mercantile shipping. As foreign production fell off, the export of grain reached record levels. A lucrative trade with the neutrals in northern Europe almost compensated for the loss of commerce with Germany. Above all, Allied orders for munitions and other supplies put the United States industrial plant to work. The increase of exports soon reversed the outflow of capital. Prosperity percolated outward and downward. All the standard indices of business activity—bank clearances, stock prices, railroad earnings, and steel output—pointed to boom times for America.[7]

The men chiefly responsible for formulating and executing United States policy did not always agree among themselves, and the views of the same person were not always consistent. But the dominant patterns in their personal attitudes toward the war are clear enough. President Woodrow Wilson played a responsible and frequently active role in shaping policy. He had a sympathy for English political ideas and institutions, and a distaste for the Prussian militaristic tendency in Germany. Although his awareness of economic and power-political factors in international affairs precluded a one-sided view of "war guilt," he did see less peril for his country in an Allied than in a German victory. Even though he did not regard a subsequent German attack on the United States as an immediate danger, as early as September 1914 he feared that the triumph of the Central Powers would compel the nation to sacrifice its progressive ideals in exchange for military security. At the beginning of 1915 he went so far as to assert that "England is fighting our fight," and was unwilling to take any steps which would occasion England's fall. Wilson was also pacifistic; he therefore desired to preserve his own maximum availability as a mediator between the warring nations.[8]

Closely associated with Wilson were his unofficial adviser and personal agent, Colonel Edward M. House; the ambassador to London, Walter Hines Page; and the counselor of the Department of State, Robert Lansing, who later became secretary of state. House felt that Britain's cause was America's, but it could be won by Wilson's mediation. Page too was an Anglophile. He was convinced, moreover, that British necessity rendered substantial concessions to American demands unlikely; that sharp protests would only arouse bitter resentment; and that the United States should, without rancor, place its objections on record, acquiesce in violations of its rights, and await confidently the later payment of its claims.

Counselor Lansing, even before he succeeded Secretary of State Bryan in June 1915, happened to be the acting secretary at several critical periods in Anglo-American relations. As the State Department's expert on international law, he had also been in steady consultation with the president from the very first. Lansing's attitude is puzzling. His papers and his work show the impress of legalistic thinking, of genuine irritation with English encroachments, and of determination to correct them. Yet he reminisces that American cobelligerency against Germany was, in his view, inevitable; that, while awaiting public unity on the issue, he could not allow the controversies with the British to come to a head; and that he therefore designed his communications to provoke peripheral and inconclusive discussions. He was also insistent, however, that the legal grounds of later claims should be firmly laid.[9]

The following chronicle of the controversy between the United States and Great Britain over neutral rights will ignore the American complaints about particular ships and specific commodities. The administration's effort to deal with the general problem consisted of three major diplomatic notes, dated December 28, 1914, March 30, 1915, and November 5, 1915. An important prelude was a protest which was formulated but suppressed before the war was two months old.

In 1909 an international conference had drafted the Declaration of London, a code of maritime warfare. It included rules on the relations between belligerents and neutrals. Although the Declaration had never been ratified, it represented an up-to-date consensus of the jurists on what the law was or ought to be. When hostilities broke out, the United States, seeking a set of definite regulations on which the neutrals could rely, suggested that the belligerents adopt the Declaration for the duration of the war. Great Britain would agree only with modifications which were stated in an Order in Council of August 20. The changes included the extension of the Declaration's contraband lists and the application of continuous voyage to conditional contraband.[10]

Complaints over the subsequent annoyances to American commerce began to deluge Washington. President Wilson himself ordered the State Department to prepare a protest "with teeth." On September 26 an instruction to Page detailed the administration's objections to the Order in Council and indicated that he was to call them to Foreign Secretary Grey's attention. The text of a formal protest was ready for dispatch two days later. However, when the draft reached Wilson for approval, Colonel House was visiting him. Alarmed at the note's sharpness, House persuaded the president to hold it, pending a conference between the British ambassador and himself.

Upon seeing the draft, Ambassador Spring-Rice told House it might have been read as a threat of war. He was sure that his government would be accommodating if the complaint were presented informally. Spring-Rice assisted House in outlining a new cable. How influential this outline was in the revised directions which Wilson and Lansing now drafted for the embassy in London is uncertain. But Page was ordered to tell Grey informally that the Order disturbed the public, that the president wished to avoid a formal protest, but that the terms of the Declaration of London were the maximum to which he could consent. Later, the instruction of September 26 was withdrawn, except as guidance for the American ambassador on the position Washington held.[11]

Wilson also asked Lansing to confer with Spring-Rice. In the course of ensuing conversations, the counselor either made or approved, unofficially and informally, several suggestions through which the British could have accepted the Declaration and yet achieved their strategic purpose with one or another legalistic subterfuge. There was room, he thought, for reasonable interpretation of a rule which could not cover unusual circumstances. Some of Lansing's suggestions actually originated with Wilson, and the British ambassador knew this. The counselor's efforts failed, nevertheless, and on October 22 he instructed Page to withdraw the original American suggestion that the belligerents adhere to the Declaration of London. Instead, the United States would rely on existing international law and would reserve the right to protest every violation. On October 29 England replaced the Order of August 20 with a new one. The new order continued to follow the Declaration, but with more drastic alterations. The American government took no immediate stand. Thus ended the first skirmish over neutral rights.[12]

After the British Order in Council of October 29, the complaints of American shippers, at least shippers of some commodities, continued to accumulate. Ambassador Page attempted to remove at least some problems by negotiating a "working arrangement" with the Foreign Office. This was completed in February of the following year, but the State Department meanwhile thought it necessary to present its first general protest on shipping. Page transmitted this note on December 28, 1914.[13]

This communication explained that the present state of American trade impelled the government to state candidly its attitude on British policy. Five months had passed without correction of irregular practices which the United States had attributed to the initial confusion of the war. Neutral commerce ought not to be molested except under the manifest and imperative necessity of the belligerent's national security. British measures had violated this principle, particularly in the treatment of contraband.

Absolute contraband had been stopped merely because the neutral country of destination had not forbidden re-exportation to Germany; and even when there was such a prohibition, England had sometimes refused to pass the particular commodity. Numerous seizures and long delays had made exporters, ship lines, and insurance firms unwilling to handle such material. The United States therefore wished to know British intentions. Foodstuffs, conditional contraband, had been stopped without any evidence to rebut the normal presumption that neutral destination means innocent use. Some cargoes had been seized on the mere fear that they would reach an enemy destination, regardless of the shippers' intentions.

If evidence of contraband appeared during search at sea, detention was justified, but the English had sent neutral vessels into port for general examination—and under presumptions of Britain's municipal law, which was at variance with international law. Reimbursement did not repair the injury done by detention, since commerce as a whole suffered through increased hazards and diversion from regular markets. The United States had hoped that the British government would instruct its officials to refrain from unnecessary interference and to treat ships and cargoes according to international law. Unless this were done, American public opinion might become deeply incensed at Great Britain.[14]

Sir Edward Grey sent a preliminary reply to this note on January 7 and a definitive answer on February 10. The two documents are complementary. The foreign secretary questioned whether British practices rather than general war conditions should be blamed for any depressed business situation. American trade had not been very badly damaged anyhow. Although exports fell in 1914 as compared with 1913, commerce with European neutrals had substantially increased, especially in meat products and copper. This very fact suggested a sinister ultimate destination for these cargoes. Moreover, the only significant American loss had been in cotton, which England did not treat as contraband anyhow. The enemy government's control of foodstuffs rendered reasonable the presumptions, specified in the Order of October 29, which brought the doctrine of continuous voyage into operation.

The actual annoyance to American commerce had not been serious; only 45 cargoes and 8 ships had been sent to prize court in five months, a period in which 773 vessels sailed from the United States to the neutrals. The American note of December 28 conceded that manifest necessity justified latitude with the law; belligerents were entitled to stop other than bona fide trade; technical developments might alter the methods of exercising their right. Under modern conditions—the size of vessels, the danger of submarines, the impossibility of boarding vessels at sea in rough weather—a ship had to be taken to port for examination; this was more convenient even for the detained merchantman. Modern modes of overland transport gave an urgency, hitherto nonexistent, to belligerent supervision of maritime commerce with neutral ports and justified a wider application of continuous voyage. American precedents confirmed the reasoning on both points. Moreover, the United States' newly established prohibition against publication of ships' manifests, though clearly within the government's rights, contributed to the delay in handling vessels and cargoes.

Aggrieved parties should exhaust British legal remedies before seeking their government's diplomatic intervention. Greater publicity for the many English measures designed to help complainants would reduce American popular objection. For the future, Great Britain was ready to explain any detentions and to make arrangements for the avoidance of errors and the correction of injuries.[15]

Lansing found the British reply lacking in logic, but the president was impressed by its conciliatory quality. He felt that the two countries were in agreement on principles and that the need now was merely to find practical methods of minimizing friction and annoyance.[16] The "working arrangement" which Page had begun to negotiate earlier contributed to this end. On January 5 the Treasury Department announced that upon application it would provide an officer to supervise loadings and certify manifests. By February 16 the order on the publication of manifests, which had been issued at the request of the New York Merchants' Association in October 1914, was revoked. In return, British authorities accepted the certified manifests as evidence on the cargo and relaxed their embargo on rubber, jute, manganese, and other vital needs of American industry. The State Department's trade advisers, who negotiated these relaxations, insisted that they did not act for the United States government.[17]

The United States did not, then, immediately resume the general discussion of neutral rights which had brought Sir Edward Grey's note of February 10. Further provocation was to intervene. On March 1, as a measure of retaliation against the first of Germany's several submarine orders, the Allies declared that they would stop all goods of enemy destination, origin, or ownership. Four days later the American government indicated to the Foreign Office its "perplexities" about the implications of this declaration, especially about whether a formal blockade was or was not intended. The British declaration was implemented by the Order in Council of March 11, the Reprisals Order. Sir Edward Grey hoped that the Order, together with a covering memorandum dated March 15, would resolve the American perplexities.

The salient points of the two documents were as follows. Vessels going to or from German ports had to be stopped and their cargo had to be discharged. It was permissible but not mandatory to treat in the same way vessels traveling to or from other ports but carrying goods of presumed enemy destination, ownership, or origin. The rules of contraband continued to apply. In addition, however, noncontraband goods of German ownership or origin could be detained, requisitioned, or sold, the proceeds to be held for the owners until the war was over. Noncontraband of other ownership or origin could be requisitioned or released to the owner under conditions deemed just by the prize court. Consideration for neutrals, it was said, dictated the decision not to order outright confiscation of all offending cargoes. The Order left to the British courts and executive authorities a wide discretion for moderating or intensifying the severity of its application.[18]

It should be emphasized that Great Britain never instituted a blockade in the juridical sense of that term. Presumably, the "consideration for neutrals" cited in Grey's note dictated this decision. The word was assiduously avoided in the order in council, although it did somehow manage to find its way into the covering memorandum.[19]

Bryan and Lansing wished to challenge sharply the new British policy, essentially on legal grounds. Wilson, however, felt that nothing would be gained by such a challenge, because it would not change the Admiralty's mind. He preferred to rely for practical relief on the judicial and administrative discretion to which Grey's memorandum had called attention. But he did want a declaration that the American government would hold England strictly accountable for all violations of international law. Consequently, a rather mild protest, which Wilson himself had a hand in drafting and which somehow omitted even the call to strict accountability, was transmitted to the Foreign Office on March 30.[20]

The United States government, this note said, wished to preclude any misunderstanding of its position. The British memorandum seemed to give notice of a blockade of neutral coasts. Technical progress might alter the methods of blockade, but not the underlying principles. The blockading squadron might be compelled to stand off neutral shores instead of, as formerly, off enemy ports. But on shipments which were innocent in character and which reached the enemy by way of neutral territory, belligerents had no right to impose the penalties either of contraband or breach of blockade; subject only to their right of visit and search, they had to permit vessels en route to or from neutral ports to pass through their cordon. The United States did not believe that Great Britain would resort to illegal action on the plea that its enemy did so. It anticipated that, in the discretion granted them, British officials would not keep from neutral ports American vessels traveling on otherwise legitimate errands, and would not impose restrictions on trade greater than would attach to an actual blockade of enemy territory. Rigid enforcement of the Reprisals Order would place a heavy responsibility on England. The American government therefore expected that country to avoid violations of the law and to make reparation if any infraction should occur.[21]

The issues raised in this diplomatic exchange were not pursued—at least not very energetically pursued—for several months, partly because the United States had turned its attention to Germany and to the incidents arising from the initiation of the U-boat war against commerce. The British reply to the United States' protest of March 30 was delivered only on July 23. Its principal contention was that the measures in question were merely reasonable and necessary adaptations of an old principle to new circumstances, just as the American Civil War doctrine of continuous voyage had been. The enemy's odd geographical position, which afforded accessibility through neutral territory as easy as through its own, ought not to negate the practical purpose for which international law conceded the right of blockade. A belligerent was entitled to stop enemy goods before they reached or after they left such an intermediate neutral, as long as the trade could be established as not bona fide. There was no blockade of neutral ports; commerce with such ports was impeded only insofar as they were points of access to the enemy. International law did not determine the details of practice as definitely as the United States alleged; the one clear principle was the belligerent's right to stop the sea-borne commerce of its enemy. The challenged measures were no more harassing than if the intercepted trade went through Germany's own ports. It was hoped that the United States would judge the

British action as justified in equity and law. The government would continue, as far as possible, to avoid inconveniencing neutral trade.[22]

The British reply again brought no immediate rejoinder from the United States, but there were several brief diplomatic exchanges on related topics. On July 14 Secretary Lansing had stated that his government could not accept as valid the proceedings of English prize courts operating under municipal legislation. In answer, on July 31 Grey defended his own country's practice but asserted that the United States could, in the last resort, call for judgment by an international tribunal. Rumors became current that Great Britain was profiting commercially from the blockade, as its own exports to the European neutrals expanded. When these rumors were brought to the attention of the Foreign Office, Grey took occasion to reply with comparative statistics, showing a proportionately greater American increase.[23]

Still, there was growing resentment in administration circles over the operation of Britain's Reprisals Order. Whereas about thirty-three vessels with an American interest had been diverted in the seven months before March 11, over three hundred had been detained at Kirkwall alone from March through September. Preparation of a new note to Britain was begun during the summer.[24] Then on November 5 Ambassador Page presented to Sir Edward Grey the United States' most comprehensive protest against Great Britain's maritime policy. It was concerned principally with search at sea, sufficiency of evidence, "blockade" of neutrals, and exhaustion of legal remedies.

The note referred to the earlier general correspondence on neutral rights. The United States had delayed taking up some British contentions because it had hoped that the declared intention of minimizing inconvenience would be implemented. However, the government now feared that objectionable measures would become worse unless they were resisted.

Search had to be made at sea; American naval authorities agreed that this was feasible. The allegation that modern tele-communications facilitated the falsification of ships' papers was untrue; belligerent censorship of mails and cables precluded such fraud. According to established practice, courts should, in the first instance, cognize only evidence taken from the ship or its crew; but the British had been detaining ships on tenuous suspicion while they went looking for extrinsic evidence. The increased imports of a neutral nation could not create a pre-sumption of enemy destination on all goods proceeding thereto; otherwise this presumption would apply equally to England's own vastly expanded shipments to these countries. Great Britain should stop seizing cargoes on conjectural suspicion.

The United States had reserved its rights with respect to the blockade. But the promises of minimal annoyance had not been fulfilled, and now the whole concept of this measure had to be challenged. The blockade was not effective because the Scan-dinavian countries could trade freely with German ports across the Baltic. The blockade did not bear, as it should, with equal severity on all nations; witness again the Scandinavian position and even the British trade with supposedly blockaded neutral ports. Above all, international law prohibited the blockade of neutral nations.

As for redress, the present cases did not fall under the prin-ciple of first exhausting legal remedies. They did not arise wholly within a foreign jurisdiction but in the jurisdiction of interna-tional law on the high seas. The reply that English courts were actually applying international law was inaccurate; those courts were admittedly bound by British municipal law and were un-able simply to declare themselves emancipated from this in favor exclusively of the law of nations. Prize courts, moreover, could not remedy the general damage to American trade which resulted from the anxious withdrawal of vessels from some routes, through refusals of insurance and inability to get shipping space. The British method of acquiring jurisdiction was also objectionable. One nation's municipal law could not authorize its officers to bring other nations' vessels from the high seas into its own territorial jurisdiction, so that they could then be treated according to that jurisdiction. The United States, therefore, could not advise its citizens to submit to English prize courts and could not refrain from using diplomatic channels to seek redress.

Furthermore, it was understood that detained vessels were being charged for the expenses of search in port, harbor dues, freight handling, and so forth; and that masters were being required to waive their right of making claims for these charges. These charges were illegal and the waivers were invalid. The United States hoped that Anglo-American relations would be conducted in accordance not with expediency but with the international law which Great Britain had championed in the past and which the United States now championed on behalf of all neutral nations.[25]

Despite the apparent vigor of this note, Sir Edward Grey took his time in replying. Intervening events strengthened his hand. Colonel House's second mediation attempt, for example, demonstrated his and Wilson's close identification with the Allied cause; and a new crisis in German-American relations was precipitated on March 24, when several Americans were severely injured in the German torpedoing of the French cross-channel steamer, *Sussex*.[26]

The British reply to the American note of November 5 was finally transmitted on April 24, 1916. It was largely devoted to attacking the logic of the American protest. The United States contended that the method of intercepting cargoes had not been used in the past, but new methods of dispatching goods justified new methods of stopping them. British and French naval experts agreed that search at sea was not practical; and while international law prescribed a fair hearing, it left to municipal law the details of prize-court procedure. The techniques for falsifying papers had become so proficient that evidence taken merely from the ship and its crew was no longer of much value. Admittedly, increased neutral imports were not conclusive proof of a cargo's hostile destination, but neither was ostensible consignment to the neutral's general stocks a proof of innocence. The question was one of fact, and the facts on some allegedly neutral consignees (examples were cited) amply justified the use of extrinsic evidence.

Even according to American statistics, trade with European neutrals had not in fact been seriously damaged. To mitigate hardships, however, the British were now elaborating an equitable system of rationing based on normal national needs and normal sources of supply. Shippers could then be given the definite advance information they wanted on the treatment of their merchandise.

The rules of blockade, which the United States said were violated, applied only to a blockade in the technical sense; and German geography would render fatuous such a direct operation against enemy ports. England had observed the spirit of the rules: It had given notice and its patrols effectively stopped all but a few vessels. Scandinavian access to Germany over a few miles of water should have been no more relevant than Dutch access over a few miles of land. To hold that retaliation ought not to injure neutrals seemed to furnish a shield for the unprincipled lawbreaker—who, unfortunately, could not be punished without some repercussions on other nations—and this situation humanity could scarcely approve. Great Britain reiterated that its prize courts were able to do justice under international law in alleged conflicts of municipal law and the law of nations; hence foreigners could safely resort to those courts.

Investigation showed that no dues had been demanded of ships detained without discharging their cargoes and that the American allegation about waivers was inaccurate. However,

where cargo had been discharged, the government could not in-
terfere with the prize-court determination of the conditions for
release. In principle, Great Britain agreed that ships seized on
insufficient grounds were not liable for dues and that no waivers
should be demanded or enforced.

The mitigation of hardships seemed a more practical aim
than abrupt changes in a legally justified policy. For to confine
the examination of suspected vessels to search at sea and to
allow mere neutral consignment or carriage in neutral ships
to protect goods of notoriously hostile destination would nullify
the belligerent right to keep supplies from the enemy. Great
Britain had nothing to fear from the impartial scrutiny, based
on law or humanity, of any neutral concert for the defense of
neutral rights.[27]

This note of April 24, 1916 proved to be the last word in
the general Anglo-American controversy over neutral rights of
trade, at least for the remainder of the war. Several later Allied
measures provoked more limited protests or reservations of
rights. Thus, in April the British virtually abolished the distinction between absolute and conditional contraband. In July
they withdrew even their limited adherence to the Declaration
of London. In the same month American firms were publicly
blacklisted. The State Department sharply protested this step;
Wilson asked, and Congress gave, certain discretionary powers
of retaliation. But the president never used them, partly because
Secretary of Commerce Redfield advised that this would do more
harm than good.[28]

In April 1917, provoked by the now relentless German submarine attacks on its shipping, the United States associated
itself with the Allies in the war against the Central Powers. With
American help, the economic warfare achieved unprecedented
efficiency. The new belligerent employed some, but not all, of
the methods to which it had objected as a neutral. It used the
blacklist, control of coal bunkers, and perhaps an extended con-

ception of censorship of the mails. It expanded the list of contraband. To some degree it appears to have applied continuous voyage to conditional contraband and to have used new presumptions with respect to absolute contraband. It participated in the control of merchant vessels through "safe routing" instructions. It was represented on an inter-Allied committee which rationed the imports of the European neutrals. But the principal American weapon seems to have been the licensing of its own exports, a device which was not within the purview of international law. On paper, the government clung to its principles on search at sea and on the technical notion of blockade; but American naval vessels, operating with the British forces, may possibly have violated the principles.[29]

Action toward the settlement of claims arising from Great Britain's alleged violations of American neutral rights was initiated in 1925 and completed in 1927. The settlement was largely the work of Spencer Phenix, attached to the office of Assistant Secretary of State Robert Olds.

In a careful examination of the State Department's claim files, Phenix discovered that many cases were not formal claims, or had presumably been abandoned by the complainants, or had already been settled, or were for insignificant amounts, or were lacking a legal foundation. In his judgment, only 11 of the 2,658 cases on file called for settlement; these involved about $3,000,000. Ten of these cases, losses of ships or cargoes, were within the scope of the present study; these involved about $2,500,000. He also noted that Great Britain had claims, some clear and some doubtful, of about $5,000,000 against the United States; these arose mostly from the provision of goods and services during the war.[30]

In 1926 the British government and people were highly sensitive about the American claims. They regarded their wartime measures against American commerce with Germany as fully justified in law and equity. They feared claims from other neutrals. They were already irritated over the ungenerous terms on which their war debts to the United States had been settled. They argued that the United States had nullified its neutral complaints by its own belligerent practices. They pointed out that the British blockade had saved American lives and contributed to American victory. Phenix reported that a government which sought a claims appropriation from Parliament would fall. He also suggested that the United States' belligerent conduct would weaken its case in any international adjudication and that even a legal victory might subject the United States to claims from other neutrals.[31]

An executive agreement was therefore effected by an exchange of letters between Secretary of State Kellogg and British Ambassador Howard in May 1927. The agreement was characterized as "not a financial settlement, but as a friendly composition of conflicting points of view." Both countries reserved their rights on the legal questions and therefore remained free to act on their respective interpretations in the future. Neither country would press its claims (of specified categories) against the other, nor espouse diplomatically any citizens' claims which had been fully disposed of by municipal courts. Since the net gain in cancelled claims accrued to the United States, the State Department would seek Congressional action to reimburse the American holders of claims which seemed meritorious but were rejected by the British courts.[32]

With this settlement, the history of American protests over English violations of neutral rights comes to an end. The three major notes can now be examined together in the analysis of United States hopes and realizations. Prima facie, the three notes placed the American position on record, so that silence might not be construed as consent; this was almost their only clearly stated purpose. The November note also aimed at forestalling further encroachments. Implicitly the particular complaints were also pleas for correction. The United States was demanding that the British follow some definite norms, in permitting or refusing passage of absolute contraband, on which commercial interests could consistently count; that they stop seizing contraband on tenuous presumptions; that they stop diverting ships into port for search, particularly for search under standards and procedures of municipal law; that they stop intercepting vessels proceeding to neutral ports on legitimate business; that they deal diplomatically with complaints presented diplomatically; and that they cease imposing port charges and waivers on ships unjustly detained.[33]

Lansing, Bryan, and Wilson felt sure of their ground on most points. Only about the correct interpretation of contraband and continuous voyage were they hesitant, as is clear from an arranged exchange of correspondence between Bryan and Chairman William Stone of the Senate Foreign Relations Committee in December 1914. The administration was earnest in recording its convictions for future reckoning. A total of 2,658 complaints, some of them involving six-digit sums, reached its claim files; and every day's delay of a merchant vessel was known to mean considerable financial loss. Ambassador Page, however, had informed Washington that the British would settle as they had settled the *Alabama* claims, if the matter were properly handled. Moreover, the current, confident justification in administrative circles for differential treatment of German and English offenses was that destruction of property could be compensated at leisure, while destruction of lives could not. The establishment of an effective legal basis for future reimbursement was a highly valued objective.[34]

The expectations as to immediate actual relief of grievances are less clear. In December 1914 England's successful arrangements with some countries against re-export of critical materials must have inspired hope that these arrangements could be universalized, and could thus effect consistent treatment of American cargoes. Bryan's letter to Stone at about this time suggests that anticipations on continuous voyage were not sanguine. There are no reliable clues on search at sea. Yet House had received from Grey a prior intimation of a somehow favorable reply. At this time, then, the government expected some vaguely defined concessions. Neither the note nor its circumstances indicate that the redress which had been requested was valued more than moderately.

The anticipations are clearer for the March 30 communication on the blockade of the European neutrals. The president was certain that his action would not change the British policy in any way whatsoever.

Lansing seems to have been chiefly responsible for the November note. He must have known that reversals of practice on search at sea, on standards of evidence, on blockade, and on prize-court jurisdiction were now improbable. Page was warning that London's current temper was like Washington's after the battle of Bull Run. On the assessment of harbor dues and the requirement of waivers, optimism was possible because these measures were less fundamental to British strategy, and the American consul general at London, Robert Skinner, had won individual relaxations of the rules during the preceding summer. Again there is no evidence that the objectives in question had more than a moderate value.[35]

The British valuation of the United States' prima facie demands was extremely high. There was no objection to the making of a legal record; Great Britain declared it would welcome an international adjudication later. Immediate discontinuance of the challenged practices was another matter. Technically these were only means, presumably flexible, and not ends. But, rightly or wrongly, the English government and people attached to them the supreme value of the nation's overriding purpose: self-preservation. In fact, even these measures appeared inadequate as neutral imports mounted and German exports remained steady; the tightening rather than the slackening of control seemed necessary. Page had concluded early that the admission of war materials to Germany was the one surrender Britain would not make. In the summer of 1915 Grey insisted that to concede most American demands would be to give up economic warfare. In the winter of 1915-1916 compliance might well have meant the foreign secretary's fall from office; his position within the Cabinet was much weaker than it had been a year earlier. In the eyes of the British, the United States was asking very much.[36]

The American protests to Great Britain had no subtle ulterior objectives. The December note was not intended to soften the English attitude toward the "working arrangement" then under discussion, or toward Colonel House's first attempt to mediate between the belligerents, which was then forthcoming. Nor did the March and November notes have such aims. The December protest, however, seemed in some measure a demonstration of impartiality. It was cited as such in Bryan's almost simultaneous letter to Stone, and this letter itself was designed to end currently circulating allegations of favoritism for the Allies. Besides mollifying pro-German, anti-British, and pacifistic opinion in the United States, then, the protest was intended to help preserve Wilson's acceptability to the Germans as a potential mediator. Similar overtones appear with the notes of March and November.[37]

More relevant ulterior aims of the United States' complaints would add up to generic improvement in the conditions of commerce: indeterminate practical adjustments to ease, as much as possible, the burdens imposed by British measures. The only attempt to detail the relief which could be sought was made by Consul General Skinner in early 1916.[38] Although his proposal was not pursued, it suggests the kind of concession which was vaguely expected. Evidence of the pragmatic outlook appears in Wilson's reaction to Grey's note of January 7, 1915: The two governments agreed in principle; attention should therefore be given to practical methods of reducing inconvenience,

annoyance, and friction. Bryan concluded his March 5 statement of perplexities with the hope that Great Britain would at
least limit the geographical radius of its illegal activities. The
March 30 note relied on the British authorities' discretionary
powers to soften the impact of the Reprisals Order. Spring-
Rice was moved by the November note to urge his government
to quiet the United States with marginal concessions. At all
times Page's chief insistence was on the expeditious handling
of detained ships and cargoes. Early in the controversy, American policy makers had reason to hope for this sort of relief.
Page and House, Spring-Rice and Grey repeatedly promised
it would be granted.[39]

The administration appears to have valued only moderately
the relief it sought for trade. Wilson's manifestation of intense
irritation over British conduct postdated these notes and was
evoked particularly by the blacklist. The business press itself
was not anxious that the defense of rights be more than juridical.
Moreover, while the potential losses from British interference
were great, the American government was fully aware, and
Wilson said so in March 1935, that commercial interests were
in generally excellent condition.[40]

The American anticipations of cost were even more modest
than anticipations of achievement. The president and his advisers were convinced that their legal case was absolutely valid
on most issues and were therefore presumably willing to accept
for the United States any future adverse implications of the
principles they were asserting. Lansing alone had misgivings;
he feared that a precisely defined case would prejudice the
country's own freedom of action against neutrals if the United
States should later enter the war. American authorities were
also willing to pay such costs as might be involved in striking
some bargains with the British, although there was little advance
consideration of their details. The willingness appeared in
Lansing's early proposal for compromise on the Declaration

of London and in Wilson's later receptivity to pragmatic adjustments of difficulties.[41]

Beyond this the American view of costs was almost wholly
negative. Wilson was unwilling even to risk British resentment
by a vigorous presentation of his demands. Page and House
warned that sharpness would affect unfavorably both the president's acceptability as a mediator and the nation's political and
economic positions in England's postwar policies and programs.
Much less did Wilson wish to invoke sanctions of any kind. As
a historian who was also a near-pacifist, he feared a recurrence
of 1812. He must have been particularly sensitive to Spring-
Rice's hint that the abortive protest of September 1914 might
have meant war, and to Page's judgment that fighting was the
only alternative to acquiescing. It seems certain, then, that
he must have dismissed out of hand the possibility, suggested at
one juncture, that the United States Navy convoy ships through
British patrols.[42]

The president's historical judgment upon Jefferson's policies
also predisposed him against an embargo. Although he placed
his rejection on the legalistic ground that it would be unneutral
to change the early announced toleration of munitions exports,
the economic argument was perhaps more persuasive. Allied
orders contributed to unprecedented prosperity, commerce with
European neutrals was astonishingly active, and England sup-
plied raw materials indispensable for industry. An American
embargo of goods or of funds would imperil all this. In addition, one factor of high strategy entered Wilson's calculations.
By the spring of 1915 he had decided that a German victory
would not be in the American national interest, that it would
be a cost too high to pay for diplomatic successes against
Britain, for in his view it was fighting America's fight.[43]

Such were the American expectations. What of the event?
The monetary settlement of 1927 was a response to the United
States' wartime protests, and according to the preponderant

evidence the compensation awarded at this time was adequate.[44] Spencer Phenix, the man who examined this question most closely, was satisfied that the sum covered the just complaints of Americans. Consul General Skinner, at this time stationed in Paris, thought similarly; it was actually he who first suggested to the Department that the public estimate of the claims outstanding was greatly exaggerated. The fact that so few shippers pursued their complaints with formal claims further supports this conclusion.[45] It should be added that the link between the settlement and the American protests was in some degree causal. While the *Alabama* arbitration was not re-enacted as Page had so confidently predicted, the American notes had laid the ground for a judicial or arbitral appeal; and the British, however persuasive their defense might have been, were unwilling to risk a decision.[46]

Among more immediate achievements, the United States' protests largely brought an end to the capricious and unpredictable treatment of contraband materials destined for neutral countries, as the British government, the continent's import trusts, and American shippers worked out helpful informal arrangements. But Consul General Skinner's itemization of desirable improvements in 1916 shows that not all difficulties were eliminated. The United States' protests also helped diminish the annoying diversions of vessels for search in port, although in this achievement shippers again had to lend their cooperation and the government its informal collaboration. For many ships operating within this framework, visit and search became a mere formality that was often executed at sea. Furthermore, the British established a special committee to expedite the search of the numerous vessels calling voluntarily at Allied ports; on the basis of data gathered beforehand, this committee could often release incoming merchantmen almost immediately. The United States' protests also won an oblique concession on port charges and waivers.[47]

On other issues, the American notes were less successful. The British Foreign Office persisted in its refusal to receive claims through diplomatic channels before judicial remedies were exhausted. It clung to its conception of blockade and of sufficient evidence; in fact it strengthened its blockade regulations through Orders in Council of March 1916 and February 1917. Regarding Germany, Washington's notes seemed to have had no substantial influence on the attitude of that government toward mediation.[48]

As for the actual costs of the American protests, the most obvious was the embarrassment which the country's legal position as a neutral occasioned for its later operations as a belligerent. But even though its practice violated its theory on the scope of contraband and the extension of continuous voyage, the countries which remained neutral made no notable claims against it on these grounds. The United States' stand on other legal points might have seriously hampered its own economic warfare, had not the British naval forces borne the brunt of blockade duty.[49]

Extrinsic costs were not large. The "working arrangement" developed in 1914-1915 called for only one official act by the United States: the revocation of its futile order prohibiting the publication of manifests. The later American acquiescence in the seizure of copper and cotton was compensated by the British purchase of these cargoes at a fair price. Bargains like these certainly fell within the range of the ill-defined concessions which the United States had been prepared to make. Even if pride was hurt, the exporters were satisfied.[50]

Moreover, Wilson was never called upon to pay the potential costs he had feared. In the main, his protests provoked little resentment in England; according to Page, the public reception of at least the first two notes was gracious. Great Britain's failure to accept the president's mediation sprang from more complex causes. There was no war, no decisive impediment to the Allies' victory, no British reprisal or other significant counteraction, no economic recession.[51]

To this record of hopes and realizations, however, there is an appendix. The American protests eschewed vigor and threatened no sanctions. It is arguable that because of such timidity the United States failed to achieve through them as much as it might have. The first two notes and the earlier correspondence on the Declaration of London unnecessarily volunteered the opinion that new conditions of warfare may justify new adaptations of legal principles. True though this may be, England never conceded its relevance to American neutral conduct—on armed merchant vessels, for example—or to German belligerent practices. Yet the citation of this view introduced the very nebulosity about the rules that the United States had originally struggled to avoid. Moreover, Wilson himself softened the tone of the first two notes, and all the notes were prolix, failing to highlight specific demands for relief.[52]

This mildness of presentation was combined with an unconcealed and astonishing ambivalence in the attitudes of key personnel. Inept timing of moves and blindness as to the available instruments compounded these weaknesses. In the initial skirmish over the Declaration, extreme nervousness about the British reaction was manifested, the impact of a strong note was blunted by the hesitations surrounding its composition and delivery, American officials themselves suggested subterfuges to the British, and the United States finally withdrew completely from its original stand. On one unidentifiable occasion, Ambassador Page told Grey that he himself disagreed with the note he was presenting to the foreign secretary. In negotiating with the British, administrative spokesmen more often emphasized the soothing of American public opinion than the merits of their case. Colonel House, in Europe during the spring of 1915, simultaneously discussed with Allied statesmen American annoyance over their restrictive policies and plans for American cobelligerency against Germany, which he felt would surely follow upon the *Lusitania* crisis. In the spring of 1916 his House-Grey agreement committed the country to a virtual guarantee of Allied victory. There was apparently little consideration of using this agreement or the supply of arms and money to strike some bargain with the British.[53] In fact, the administration announced its approval of the munitions trade while the negotiations over the London Declaration were at a critical juncture, and it disavowed Senator Hitchcock's bill for an embargo just a few weeks before dispatching its first protest to England. At the very time when the final note was in preparation, moreover, Lansing and Secretary of the Treasury McAdoo were urging the president to reverse the earlier "moral embargo" on war loans (McAdoo's suggestion that Britain be pressed for some counterconcessions was ignored). Finally, while still awaiting an answer to this final note, Wilson and House proposed in the *Sussex* crisis that Grey should invoke his agreement with House, and the State Department revealingly asked the Foreign Office what the American embassy in Berlin should do about British interests there if a German-American break should occur.[54]

All of this must have contributed to the impression that the United States was not really earnest in its protests to Great Britain. True, injudicious vigor in the notes or in their presentation could perhaps have involved the United States in war earlier and more tragically. Yet greater deliberation in reaching decisions, wiser timing in their announcement, and firmer inscrutability in negotiating issues would probably have led the British to grant more extensive and more rapid relief to American shipping. But in mitigation it must also be said that United States policy makers understood the war-enkindled fervor which inflated British evaluation of the issues. They also recognized the large economic advantage which, despite all interference, Great Britain's trade was bringing to American merchants, manufacturers, farmers, and laborers. Therefore, they could reasonably be less concerned with immediate and possibly costly remedies than with future and possibly valuable legal assurances.

In the final calculation, then, the United States maintained its legal position, won substantive relief on the minor points where it had been most sanguine, and failed on the major points where it had been most pessimistic. In turn, the country suffered some legal embarrassment as a belligerent and made some counterconcessions, mostly unofficial, to Great Britain. In terms of the policy makers' expectations, the American protests were fairly rational and mildly successful.

NOTES

[1] *Foreign Relations, 1914*, Supplement, pp. 454-66; Alice M. Morrissey, *The American Defense of Neutral Rights, 1914-1917*, pp. 15-16 (Cambridge: Harvard University Press, 1939).

[2] Edward Grey, *Twenty-Five Years, 1892-1916*, Vol. 2, p. 107 (New York: Frederick A. Stokes Company, 1925); Burton J. Hendrick, *The Life and Letters of Walter H. Page*, Vol. 2, p. 169 (Garden City: Doubleday, Page and Company, 1926); Charles Seymour, editor, *The Intimate Papers of Colonel House*, Vol. 1, pp. 446, 464 (Boston: Houghton Mifflin Company, 1926); Stephen Gwynn, editor, *The Letters and Friendships of Sir Cecil Spring-Rice*, Vol. 2, pp. 282-83 (Boston: Houghton Mifflin Company, 1929).

[3] Louis Guichard, *The Naval Blockade, 1914-1918*, pp. 66-68 (London: Philip Allan and Company, 1930); Seymour, *Colonel House*, Vol. 2, pp. 132-33; Ernest R. May, *The World War and American Isolation, 1914-1917*, pp. 305-07 (Cambridge: Harvard University Press, 1959). In the autumn of 1914 Russia and France also pressed strongly for action by their British ally against German commerce; see *ibid.*, pp. 21-25.

[4] Charles C. Tansill, *America Goes to War*, pp. 3, 10-16, 23-25. Boston: Little, Brown and Company, 1938.

[5] Philip C. Jessup, in the Preface to Edgar Turlington, *Neutrality, Its History, Economics, and Law: The World War Period*, p. x (New York: Columbia University Press, 1936); Morrissey, *American Defense*, p. 42. The historical development of this law from 1856 to 1914 is conveniently summarized in Marion C. Siney, *The Allied Blockade of Germany, 1914-1916*, Chap. 1 (Ann Arbor: The University of Michigan Press, 1957).

[6] *Foreign Relations, 1914*, Supplement, pp. 275, 573-74, 580; *Foreign Relations, 1915*, Supplement, p. 820; *Papers Relating to the Foreign Relations of the United States. The Lansing Papers* [henceforth cited as *Lansing Papers*], Vol. 1, pp. 136-44 (Washington: Government Printing Office, 1939); May,

American Isolation, pp. 45-46; William J. Bryan and Mary B. Bryan, *The Memoirs of William Jennings Bryan*, p. 376 (Philadelphia: John C. Winston Company, 1925).

[7] Alexander D. Noyes, *Financial Chapters of the War*, pp. 80-83, 88-93, 123-25, 128-31, 135-42. New York: Charles Scribner's Sons, 1916.

[8] Ray S. Baker, *Woodrow Wilson: Life and Letters*, Vol. 5, pp. 59-63, 71, n. 1, 169, 214 (Garden City: Doubleday, Doran and Company, 1935); Ray S. Baker and William E. Dodd, *The Public Papers of Woodrow Wilson: The New Democracy*, Vol. 1, pp. 224-26 (New York: Harper and Brothers, 1926); Seymour, *Colonel House*, Vol. 1, pp. 293, 298; Vol. 2, p. 50; Gwynn, *Spring-Rice*, Vol. 2, p. 223; Joseph P. Tumulty, *Woodrow Wilson as I Know Him*, p. 231 (Garden City: Doubleday, Page and Company, 1921); Harley Notter, *The Origins of the Foreign Policy of Woodrow Wilson*, pp. 380, n. 315, 432 (Baltimore: The Johns Hopkins Press, 1937).

[9] Seymour, *Colonel House*, Vol. 1, pp. 285, 309, 457; Hendrick, *Walter H. Page*, Vol. 1, pp. 327-28, 334, 370-72, 382-84, 411; Vol. 2, pp. 29, 67-69; Vol. 3, pp. 139, 164, 182-83; Robert Lansing, *The War Memoirs of Robert Lansing*, pp. 18-23, 123-29, 166-67 (Indianapolis: Bobbs-Merrill Company, 1935); *Lansing Papers*, Vol. 1, pp. 106, 151-52, 247, 270-82, 287.

[10] The text of the Declaration appears in James Brown Scott, editor, *The Declaration of London, February 26, 1909*, pp. 112-29 (New York: Oxford University Press, 1919). See *Foreign Relations, 1914*, Supplement, pp. 216-20; Tansill, *America Goes to War*, pp. 135-37.

[11] *Foreign Relations, 1914*, Supplement, pp. 225-33, 239; Baker, *Woodrow Wilson*, Vol. 5, pp. 197-98, 205; Seymour, *Colonel House*, Vol. 1, pp. 306-08; Gwynn, *Spring-Rice*, Vol. 2, p. 233. Arthur S. Link, *Wilson: The Struggle for Neutrality, 1914-1915*, pp. 108-14 (Princeton: Princeton University Press, 1960). According to Link, the accepted version of this incident as derived from Colonel House's account is misleading. Link argues convincingly from the manuscript sources that Wilson and Lansing rather than House and Spring-Rice wrote the new instructions to Page, and that in significant ways this new cable was stronger, not weaker, than the original. May questions the accuracy of Cone Johnson's recollection that Wilson had asked for a protest "with teeth"; see *American Isolation*, p. 55, n. 1.

[12] *Foreign Relations, 1914*, Supplement, pp. 235-58, 260-63; May, *American Isolation*, pp. 59-60.

[13] See *Foreign Relations, 1914*, Supplement, pp. 356-58; examples of complaints appear in *ibid.*, pp. 336-56. There appears never to have been any formal acceptance of the working arrangement on the part of the United States; see Siney, *Allied Blockade*, pp. 58-59.

[14] *Foreign Relations, 1914*, Supplement, pp. 372-75.

[15] *Foreign Relations, 1915*, Supplement, pp. 299-302, 324-34.

[16] *Lansing Papers*, Vol. 1, pp. 261, 266.

[17] *Foreign Relations, 1914*, Supplement, pp. 331-33, 356-58, 369-70; *Foreign Relations, 1915*, Supplement, pp. 297, 334; Morrissey, *American Defense*, pp. 38-40.

[18] *Foreign Relations, 1915*, Supplement, pp. 127-28, 132-33, 143-45; *Lansing Papers*, Vol. 1, pp. 270-73.

[19] Guichard, *Naval Blockade*, p. 13; Siney, *Allied Blockade*, p. 67.

20 *Lansing Papers*, Vol. 1, pp. 273-79, 281-82, 285-95. Siney regards this note as a protest (*Allied Blockade*, pp. 69-70). May does not (*American Isolation*, p. 325).

21 *Foreign Relations, 1915*, Supplement, pp. 152-56.

22 *Ibid.*, pp. 168-71

23 *Ibid.*, pp. 472-74, 478-80, 486-87, 496-98, 502-03, 511-16.

24 *Ibid.*, pp. 499, 594-601; Link, *Wilson: 1914-1915*, pp. 594-96.

25 *Foreign Relations, 1915*, Supplement, pp. 578-89; a lengthy statement regarding vessels detained by British authorities was appended, pp. 590-601.

26 See Seymour, *Colonel House*, Vol. 2, Chaps. 5-7, especially pp. 90-91, 163-64, 201-02.

27 *Foreign Relations, 1916*, Supplement, pp. 368-82.

28 *Ibid.*, pp. 385-87, 411-15, 421-22, 466-78; Hendrick, *Walter H. Page*, Vol. 2, p. 186; Morrissey, *American Defense*, p. 149.

29 *Foreign Relations, 1926*, Vol. 2, pp. 258-62; Grey, *Twenty-Five Years*, Vol. 2, p. 117; Guichard, *Naval Blockade*, pp. 102-04, 108-10, 114-19; Turlington, *Neutrality*, p. 24; James W. Garner, "Violations of Maritime Law by the Allied Powers during the World War," *American Journal of International Law* 25:47, January 1931.

30 *Foreign Relations, 1926*, Vol. 2, pp. 265-66, 269-86; *Foreign Relations, 1927*, Vol. 2, p. 749.

31 *Foreign Relations, 1926*, Vol. 2, pp. 214-23, 246-49, 262, 287.

32 *Foreign Relations, 1927*, Vol. 2, pp. 750-55; Edwin M. Borchard, "The Neutrality Claims against Great Britain," *American Journal of International Law* 21:764, 766, October 1927.

33 *Foreign Relations, 1914*, Supplement, pp. 372-75; *Foreign Relations, 1915*, Supplement, pp. 152-56, 578-89.

34 *Lansing Papers*, Vol. 1, pp. 121, 221-22, 230-31, 273-77, 281, 294; Lansing, *War Memoirs*, p. 23; Baker, *Woodrow Wilson*, Vol. 5, pp. 180, 384; *Foreign Relations, 1914*, Supplement, pp. vi-xiv; Baker and Dodd, *Public Papers of Woodrow Wilson*, Vol. 2, p. 282; Hendrick, *Walter H. Page*, Vol. 3, pp. 253-54.

35 *Foreign Relations, 1914*, Supplement, pp. vi-xiv, 235; *Foreign Relations, 1915*, Supplement, pp. 488, 544; *Lansing Papers*, Vol. 1, pp. 257-58, 271-73, 288-90; Baker, *Woodrow Wilson*, Vol. 5, pp. 231, 261-62, 384; Seymour, *Colonel House*, Vol. 1, p. 314; Hendrick, *Walter H. Page*, Vol. 2, p. 65.

36 *Foreign Relations, 1915*, Supplement, p. 498; Gwynn, *Spring-Rice*, Vol. 2, p. 242; Hendrick, *Walter H. Page*, Vol. 1, pp. 370, 381, 420; Vol. 2, pp. 75, 97, 103-04; Vol. 3, pp. 177-79, 253-54, 268; Seymour, *Colonel House*, Vol. 1, p. 461; Vol. 2, pp. 76, 132-33; Guichard, *Naval Blockade*, pp. 66-68; May, *American Isolation*, pp. 314-19, 352.

37 *Lansing Papers*, Vol. 1, pp. 184-88, 257-58, 290; Baker, *Woodrow Wilson*, Vol. 5, pp. 234-37; Gwynn, *Spring-Rice*, Vol. 2, pp. 282, 297; Seymour, *Colonel House*, Vol. 1, pp. 457-58; Vol. 2, p. 63; letters, Lansing to House, July 30, 1915; House to Wilson, September 3, 1915, in Edward M. House Collection at Yale University.

38 *Foreign Relations, 1916*, Supplement, pp. 340-41.

39 *Foreign Relations, 1914*, Supplement, pp. 258-60, 362; *Foreign Relations, 1915*, Supplement, pp. 133, 147; *Lansing Papers*, Vol. 1, pp. 258, 266; Baker, *Woodrow Wilson*, Vol. 5, p. 355; Gwynn, *Spring-Rice*, Vol. 2, pp. 282-83; Hendrick,

Walter H. Page, Vol. 3, pp. 177-78, 182-83; Seymour, *Colonel House*, Vol. 1, p. 462.

40 *Lansing Papers*, Vol. 1, p. 289; David F. Houston, *Eight Years with Wilson's Cabinet*, Vol. 1, pp. 137-38 (Garden City: Doubleday, Page and Company, 1926); Harold C. Syrett, "The Business Press and American Neutrality, 1914-1917," *Mississippi Valley Historical Review* 32:220-21, September 1945.

41 *Foreign Relations, 1914*, Supplement, pp. 233-35, 240-42, 249-50, 252-53, 356-58, 361; *Lansing Papers*, Vol. 1, pp. 258, n. 27, 266, 293; Lansing, *War Memoirs*, pp. 127-29; Seymour, *Colonel House*, Vol. 1, p. 457.

42 Hendrick, *Walter H. Page*, Vol. 1, pp. 371-72; Vol. 3, p. 179; Seymour, *Colonel House*, Vol. 1, pp. 307, 457; *Lansing Papers*, Vol. 1, p. 291; Baker, *Woodrow Wilson*, Vol. 5, p. 215; Grey, *Twenty-Five Years*, Vol. 2, pp. 115-16; House to Lansing, July 29, 1915, House Collection.

43 Baker, *Woodrow Wilson*, Vol. 5, pp. 181, 188-90, 212-13, 215; *Lansing Papers*, Vol. 1, pp. 121-22, 125, 179-82, 289; Seymour, *Colonel House*, Vol. 1, pp. 303-04; Vol. 2, pp. 58, 84; *Foreign Relations, 1916*, Supplement, pp. 466-78; Tansill, *America Goes to War*, pp. 205, 520, n. 15; Notter, *Foreign Policy of Woodrow Wilson*, p. 380, n. 315.

44 A calculation, based on Turlington's "scholarly guess" of total neutral losses through Allied blockade and contraband measures, produces a much higher figure: $82,700,000. But the figure does not substantially affect the conclusion in the text. Ship charter losses, through delay and reduced efficiency, constitute about 78 per cent of this amount; and in the last analysis, these were largely absorbed by the increased price of goods to the European consumer. Losses through condemnation of ships and cargoes constitute an additional 16 per cent; and many of these condemnations must have been justified. Phenix retained claims of about $2,500,000 for improper condemnation on his list of meritorious cases. Considered in this fashion, about $4,500,000 would be left unindemnified—scarcely significant in view of the imprecision with which the figures have necessarily been estimated. My method of calculating the sum of $82,700,000 need not be detailed. In general, I have adjusted aggregate neutral losses to the American tonnage which Turlington says was involved, or—in the case of condemned cargo—to the number of vessels captured while voyaging from the United States to Europe; on this item I therefore make the "safe" but unlikely (see Department of State files, file number 441.11 W892/27, Skinner to Kellogg, March 22, 1926) assumption that the cargoes aboard these ships were owned wholly by Americans. See Turlington, *Neutrality*, pp. 4, 24-33, 65-66, 100, 144-48, 150-51. (Materials from the Department of State files will henceforth be cited by the symbol "DS" plus the file number.)

45 *Foreign Relations, 1926*, Vol. 2, pp. 270-94; DS #441.11 W892/27, Skinner to Kellogg, March 22, 1926 (initialed, significantly, by Phenix). Senators Borah, Swanson, and Warren, Speaker Longworth, and Representative Madden all approved the settlement before it was executed; see ##441.11 W892/113a and 134, respectively a letter from Kellogg to Coolidge, May 19, and a memorandum by Phenix, May 6-19, 1927.

46 *Foreign Relations, 1926*, Vol. 2, pp. 265-68; DS ##441.11 W892/3 and 5, memoranda from the Office of the Solicitor, March 19 and April 10, 1925.

[47] *Foreign Relations, 1914*, Supplement, pp. 356-58; *Foreign Relations, 1915*, Supplement, pp. 190-91, 297, 309-10, 331, 334, 559-60; *Foreign Relations, 1916*, Supplement, pp. 340-41, 379; *Foreign Relations, 1917*, Supplement 1, pp. 496-97; David Lloyd George, *The War Memoirs of David Lloyd George*, Vol. 2, pp. 118-19 (Boston: Little, Brown and Company, 1933); Morrissey, *American Defense*, p. 91; Turlington, *Neutrality*, pp. 30, 61-62. Immediately after the Reprisals Order, the number of detentions increased, but the average delay decreased. At this time the delay in clearing vessels which carried American cargo appears to have been about 3.5 days; this was 2.5 days less than the average figure (for all neutrals) had been under the contraband measures alone. This new average was calculated from the list of detentions—exclusive, however, of vessels actually held as prize—given in *Foreign Relations, 1915*, Supplement, pp. 594-600.

[48] *Ibid.*, p. 330; *Foreign Relations, 1916*, Supplement, pp. 353-54, 361, 385-87, 490-91; *Foreign Relations, 1917*, Supplement 1, p. 493; May, *American Isolation*, pp. 387-89.

[49] *Foreign Relations, 1926*, Vol. 2, pp. 223, 259-62; Garner, "Violations of Maritime Law by the Allied Powers during the World War," p. 47. In the postwar years, the United States persisted in the view of neutral rights which it had held prior to 1917. At the Hague Naval Conference of 1923, the American government, supported by the Dutch and Japanese, challenged the British and Italian contention that diversion of ships to port had now acquired the sanction of international law; see Morrissey, *American Defense*, p. 41, n. 52. And in 1939-1941 the United States again maintained its original legal position with a series of protests directed to Great Britain; see C. H. McLaughlin, "Neutral Rights under International Law in the European War, 1939-1941," *Minnesota Law Review* 26:42-49, 178-80, December 1941 and January 1942.

[50] *Foreign Relations, 1914*, Supplement, pp. 356-58; *Foreign Relations, 1915*, Supplement, pp. 174, 334, 478, 487-88, 502-03, 516; Lloyd George, *War Memoirs*, Vol. 2, pp. 118-19; Morrissey, *American Defense*, pp. 39-40; Lansing to House, July 30, 1915 and House to Wilson, August 6, 1915, House Collection. According to Lansing, dropping the rule on manifests involved some sacrifice; see *Lansing Papers*, Vol. 1, p. 265.

[51] *Foreign Relations, 1914*, Supplement, pp. 377-78; *Foreign Relations, 1915*, Supplement, pp. 158-59; *Lansing Papers*, Vol. 1, p. 701; Hendrick, *Walter H. Page*, Vol. 3, pp. 71-80. Some contrary indications appear, however, in *Lansing Papers*, Vol. 1, pp. 291-92; and Seymour, *Colonel House*, Vol. 1, pp. 347-48.

[52] *Foreign Relations, 1914*, Supplement, pp. 250, 353; *Foreign Relations, 1915*, Supplement, pp. 133, 153-54; Lansing, *War Memoirs*, pp. 112, 120, 122-23, 128-29; *Lansing Papers*, Vol. 1, pp. 273, 293, 295; May, *American Isolation*, pp. 63-64.

[53] House appears to have made a single diffident effort in this direction in January 1916; see Seymour, *Colonel House*, Vol. 2, p. 124.

[54] *Foreign Relations, 1914*, Supplement, pp. 578-79; *Foreign Relations, 1916*, Supplement, p. 241; Baker, *Woodrow Wilson*, Vol. 5, p. 217; Seymour, *Colonel House*, Vol. 1, pp. 434-36, 453-54, 465-66; Vol. 2, pp. 201-02, 231, n. 1; Tansill, *America Goes to War*, pp. 96-113, 517-18.

CHAPTER V

The Rumanian Mining Act
of 1924

A preoccupation of world diplomacy during the twenties was petroleum. In one shape assumed by this protean preoccupation, underdeveloped countries reserved for themselves, in their oil-bearing lands, benefits which they felt had been accruing disproportionately to foreign capitalists, while advanced countries reacted to protect the interests of their injured nationals. A secondary encounter of this kind took place when the United States government responded to Rumania's Mining Law of 1924.

On the Rumanian side, the background of the controversy was dominated by three factors: the severe economic dislocation of World War I and its aftermath, the unshakeable though unpopular ascendancy of the Liberal party, and the nationalism of the party's program.

In 1916 Rumania had entered the war on the side of the Allies. The country's resources were devastated by military expenditure, direct war damage, and destructive enemy occupation. Gold reserves shipped to Czarist Russia for safekeeping were lost through the Bolshevik Revolution. Warfare and reconstruction left a large inter-Allied debt. The postwar redemption of German occupation currency and of Austrian and Russian currencies in the annexed territories all multiplied obligations, the more so because the redemption was badly handled. The agrarian reform of 1918-1921 decreased, just when an increase was most needed, the agricultural output which was the largest source of foreign exchange. In addition, the reform required the government to compensate dispossessed landowners. In the territories annexed as a result of the war, the regime redirected commerce away from their former possessors—Austria, Hungary and Russia—and toward the so-called "Old Kingdom" of Rumania; this policy interfered with established lucrative trading patterns. Unbalanced budgets, plundered resources, unfavorable trade balances, agricultural disorganization, and heavy internal and external indebtedness all drained Rumania's capital and depreciated its basic currency unit, the leu. The nation which faced these difficulties was dominantly agricultural, with a numerous peasant class at the base of its development. But the country possessed considerable long-range industrial potential, great mineral wealth in particular. Its most highly developed enterprise was the extracting and refining of petroleum, a business which had always been largely in the hands of foreigners.[1]

The job of effecting economic recovery after the war fell first to the Liberal party. After three years of ephemeral cabinets, the Liberals assumed power in January 1922 and maintained it either openly or by subterfuge until late 1928. The Liberals were the party of the urban upper class. Before and during the war, when they were opposed by the landowning Conservatives, they had been a progressive force. Whether from principle or from expediency, they had enacted extensive electoral and agrarian reforms, for example. Nevertheless, even in the late nineteenth century they had inclined toward the nationalistic economic conceptions which now ruled their program for recovery.[2]

The Liberal party was led dictatorially by Ion Bratianu, its perennial prime minister, and by his brother, Vintila, who formulated its economic policy. The key to Ion Bratianu's political power lay partly in the factionalism of the opposition and partly in King Ferdinand's extraordinary personal confidence in him. After the destruction of the Conservative party through war and agrarian reform, the Liberal party was opposed only by splinter groups which took fully eight years to achieve a sizable and stable coalition. In Rumania the constitutional strength of the king was real, especially as reinforced by extra-constitutional tradition. His was the prerogative of calling a ministry at will and commissioning it to conduct elections for the legislature; rigged elections had long been the accepted and infallible method of achieving a parliamentary majority and of thus ratifying the king's choice. Enjoying King Ferdinand's favor, Ion Bratianu had no trouble in keeping the premiership for himself or his designate.[3]

The nationalistic tendency of the Liberals' earlier economic policy was intensified by the experience and the outcome of the war. The difficulty of getting supplies from the Allies suggested the desirability of economic, and especially of industrial, self-sufficiency. Prewar financial subordination to Berlin and Vienna had produced unhappy repercussions. The possibilities of irredentism in the newly annexed territories stimulated fear of Hungarian or Russian attack. Accordingly, the Liberals took as axiomatic for policy the purpose proclaimed by Vintila Bratianu, *"prin soi insine,"* "by ourselves." Two specifications of this autarchic ideal were economic recovery, centering on the revalorization at its prewar level of the badly depreciated leu, and forced development of the country's industries under domestic auspices. This is not to say either that these aims were realizable or that the measures taken to implement them were mutually consistent. High tariffs on manufactured goods protected nascent industries but put the prices even of necessities beyond reach of the peasantry. Deflationary price ceilings on farm produce depressed the agricultural market at home, while heavy export duties (intended to increase government revenue) handicapped Rumanian farmers in competition abroad. Discouraging restrictions limited foreign investments and aggravated the country's shortage of capital.[4]

One measure in the Rumanian policy of self-sufficiency under the Bratianus was the Mining Act of 1924. Only as it affected petroleum is it of concern here. Foreign enterprise had been largely responsible for the development of the country's rich oil resources. By 1913 annual crude production had reached 1,886,000 tons, 3.6 per cent of the world's total. At least 83.5 per cent of this tonnage had been turned out by foreign firms. But the business activities of the foreign companies had not been blameless and had evoked some measures of government regulation in the early nineteen-hundreds. Already in 1911 Vintila Bratianu had urged greater state control to make the industry serve the interests of the nation rather than the advantage of foreign financiers. The experience of wartime, when the industry was wholly under government administration, doubtless helped further to shape these ideas. When the Liberals acceded to power in 1922, he had the opportunity of putting his conceptions into practice.[5]

The first important step in the Liberal party's petroleum program was taken in the summer of 1923. Article 19 of the new constitution adopted at that time provided that all subsoil wealth was the property of the state; a subsequent law was to spell out the regulations for exploiting these resources, but in it due account was to be taken of previously acquired rights.[6] In late 1923 and early 1924 the government began to elaborate this law, and here the controversy with the United States arose.

In the background of the United States' attitude toward the dispute three factors seem significant: a lack of any great economic stake besides oil in Rumania, an intense concern with petroleum everywhere, and some irritation over a number of already existing issues with the Danubian kingdom.

In 1924 the only sizable American investment in Rumania was held by Standard Oil of New Jersey. The Rumanian war debt to the United States government was not large as sums owed the United States on this account went. There was no commercial treaty between the two countries, and while the balance of trade at this time favored the United States, the value of exports was only $1,200,000.[7]

Small though American interests were, questions were outstanding on several of them even before the controversy over oil began. Not until 1925 did Rumania take any steps toward refunding its debt to the United States government. On two substantial private accounts against the Rumanian government, payments were badly in arrears: those of the Baldwin Locomotive Works and the Transoceanic Corporation. In addition, several pieces of legislation, especially the Commercial Indebtedness Law and the Term of Grace Law, were apparently aimed at compelling private American creditors to settle with Rumanian debtors on disadvantageous terms.[8]

The United States government's general interest in foreign petroleum was partly strategic and partly economic. It had been greatly stimulated by the war. Oil starvation had contributed importantly to Germany's defeat, and United States oil production had contributed indispensably to Allied victory. Requirements in any future war would be even larger. The crucial role of the automobile, and consequently of petroleum, in the nation's peacetime economy was coming to be recognized ever more clearly. Yet the United States, possessing only 12 per cent of the world's known oil reserves, was consistently turning out 60 to 70 per cent of the world's oil production. Other powers meanwhile had been quietly pre-empting future sources of supply all over the globe. An intensified effort to exploit foreign fields through American firms seemed absolutely essential. Shortly after the war the State Department had evolved a standing policy of quick protest over interference with the rights of Americans and of active support for American concerns seeking concessions abroad. There is no convincing evidence, however, that the personal interests of some cabinet members in the petroleum industry had any influence on the course of events in Rumania.[9]

In Rumania the State Department's support had only to be given to the Romano-Americana Oil Company. This was wholly owned by the Standard Oil Company of New Jersey. Whatever its other holdings, Standard sought no assistance for them, and no American company besides Standard was operating here. The Romano-Americana's postwar troubles antedated the Mining Act. In 1922 the corporation claimed that in abolishing a governmental commission for the registration of leases, Rumania was unsettling its titles to new concessions. A few months later it complained that the Rumanian government was forcing the company to sell fixed quotas of its production at confiscatory prices. It charged, too, that administrative bias favoring Rumanians in the validation of leases prevented foreign firms from obtaining new, badly needed oil lands.[10] After the new constitution was adopted, Romano-Americana watched with increasing anxiety the development of the law which would give form to the prescribed nationalization of the subsoil. So things stood when the United States clashed with Rumania over the Mining Act of 1924.

In November 1923 Peter A. Jay, the United States minister to Rumania, sought and obtained the State Department's authorization to protest against particular features of the mining law as it then appeared, from unofficial information, to be taking shape. In the spring of 1924 a draft copy of the prospective law came into his possession along with the news that its enactment was scheduled for mid-April. As previously authorized, he presented a courteous note to the Rumanian Foreign Office on March 29, referring generally to "manifestly discriminatory and unsatisfactory" provisions, of which he singled out two for special mention: a clause determining the national character of oil firms operating in the country and a regulation calling for validation of previously acquired rights. The note voiced a hope that legislation of this kind or otherwise injurious to the rights of American nationals would not be passed. Foreign Minister Duca replied that the so-called draft of the law was in fact "a simple study of the matter which has not yet left the . . . Ministry of Industry and Commerce." The legation was given to understand that Parliament would not take up the entire question until the autumn.[11]

Late in May, however, Jay learned that the bill—with no substantial modification—was about to be rushed through Parliament, apparently in the hope of forestalling concerted foreign action. Thereupon, in a protest dated June 6, he made a comprehensive statement of United States objections to the contemplated mining act. The note complained again of the articles affecting the national character of corporations, now very slightly altered, and of administrative arrangements for confirming acquired rights. In addition, it expressed dissatisfaction with provisions for the expropriation of equipment without compensation. Duca's reply on June 24 conceded that Jay's concern for acquired rights had been justified but asserted that modifications in the bill met his objections; it denied the validity of the complaint about the national character of corporations, since Rumania was merely seeking for the question of petroleum a reasonable solution which accorded with "our economic interests and our national defense."[12]

The United States minister presented a further note on June 26. This took issue with some of the supporting arguments in Duca's reply. It also raised one further point: It cited a specific declaration made by the Rumanian government to the Romano-Americana Company in 1919, to the effect that the company could make new and important investments "with full confidence in the spirit of equity which the Rumanian

Government has invariably shown in the past." Jay charged that these assurances, which constituted an invitation for American capital to invest in the country, were being overridden by the prospective mining law.[13]

Despite the objections of the United States and of the several other powers which filed protests, the Mining Act was passed by Parliament on June 28, signed by the king on July 3, and promulgated as law on July 4. Only two alterations in the draft, both relatively minor, made any concessions to the American government's complaint.[14]

The Department of State now took drastic action. On July 3 it recalled Jay for consultation on the generally unsatisfactory state of relations with Rumania: the Mining Act, the war debt, the treatment of commercial creditors, the Baldwin claim and others. Jay was to tell the Rumanian government the reason for his summons to Washington and was to threaten publication of this reason. But because the Ministry of Industry and Commerce, apparently disturbed by the increasing weakness of the country's foreign credit, had meanwhile promised foreign oil firms a benevolent application of the new law, the minister was permitted to delay his return. He attempted to promote the conciliatory tendency in the Rumanian government's attitude by exploiting the threat of recall.[15]

The results were impressive on every issue but the Mining Act. Rumania signed an extradition treaty on which it had long delayed action. A partial payment was immediately transmitted to the Baldwin Company, and negotiations for a complete settlement were initiated. Sudden progress was made toward meeting three additional claims. A Foreign Office memorandum to the State Department dated July 21 expressed hurt surprise at the severity of the United States' attitude and sought some indulgence in view of Rumania's difficulties; but it held to the view that the Mining Act met all legitimate objections. Prince Bibescu, Rumanian minister in Washington, likewise manifested surprise. He pleaded that Jay's recall be delayed six weeks and gave assurances that the issues would all be quickly settled.[16]

In spite of Bibescu's plea and Bucharest's concessions, when further progress seemed stalled the United States minister proceeded to Washington. In consideration of the friendly measures already taken, he promised the Rumanian government not to publish the reasons for his journey. At this time he anticipated that the Bratianu cabinet might soon fall because of its financial embarrassments and the attitudes of Great Britain and the United States, an anticipation which proved illusory.[17]

While Jay was in the United States the Romano-Americana faced its first concrete difficulty with the Rumanian authorities over the interpretation of the Mining Act. In September a ruling of the Ministry of Industry and Commerce applied to old as well as to new concessions the law's prohibition of drilling within thirty meters of any concession's boundary. The oil company had acquired many leases on the basis of the old law, which had set fifteen meters as the corresponding limit. Since the configuration of these properties would often make exploitation under the new legislation impossible, the firm was disturbed at being refused permits for drilling on two such concessions.[18]

Washington instructed B. Reath Riggs, the chargé d'affaires, to protest the refusal as an impairment of acquired rights. Before he could act, the Rumanian government promised the firm it would grant the permits, but without prejudice to the government's principle. This satisfied the company, and the legation refrained from representations. In October the promise remained unfulfilled. The chargé d'affaires informed the Foreign Office of his previous orders and asked quick action. Duca promised that he would put pressure on the Ministry of Industry and Commerce.[19]

Shortly thereafter, in anticipation of Jay's return to Bucharest, the chargé d'affaires was instructed to present a note summarizing again the issues between the two countries and the principles on which the United States minister would stand in seeking settlements. The Mining Act, war debts, and the treatment of creditors were, as before, central. During the interview which accompanied presentation of the note, Duca again asserted that he was pressing for action on the drilling permits. Riggs felt that the general note just filed would stimulate fulfillment of the promise.[20]

By November 8, however, the permits had not yet been granted, and the chargé d'affaires again protested. This time the Rumanian reply, dated November 18, set forth the rationale of the regulations as an inducement to the pooled exploitation of adjacent small properties—that is, the sharing of both costs and profits of a single boring through which the entire deposit, regardless of surface boundaries, could be drained. The reply denied that the thirty-meter rule impaired acquired rights, but it nevertheless gave new assurances of benevolent administration. Minister Jay, who had now returned to his post, wished to pursue the matter further. However, the Department of State preferred not to prolong discussion of a single provision in a mining act which included so many other obnoxious features. Under instructions of December 1, the minister merely pointed out that Washington's fear of serious jeopardy to American interests was confirmed by the government's first action under the new law. Rumania now directly assured Standard Oil that pending applications would be approved. But in March 1925 they were still pending.[21]

In the meantime, however, Rumania had become more actively interested in obtaining a foreign loan. Apparently to prepare the ground for such a move in the United States, the government showed itself more responsive to Jay's proddings. In March, when he urged the need of some "good news" for Washington, the Ministry of Industry and Commerce was suddenly moved to grant the permits Romano-Americana had been seeking. Curiously, the letter communicating the grant included a clause which in effect assumed the company's willingness to undertake pooling arrangements, the very issue on which it had so long held out. When Jay told Foreign Minister Duca that this maneuver would create the very opposite of a good impression in Washington, the offending letter was corrected and the Ministry of Industry explained lamely that the guileful clause had been inserted through a clerical error.[22]

From this time on, the United States government seems to have been less active in meeting the problems created by the Mining Act. The Standard Oil interests tried several times to reach a general settlement through direct negotiations with Rumania. Between May and July of 1925, for example, Standard proposed to back a loan to Rumania as a *quid pro quo* for satisfactory arrangements on new exploitation. But Secretary Kellogg, who had succeeded Charles Evans Hughes in March, told the oil people he would oppose a loan in the United States until the war-debt question was settled. By the time this was settled in December, Standard Oil's plan appears to have died. The State Department's attitude should be viewed, however, in the light of the corporation's admission in November 1925 that it had not had any recent trouble with Rumanian authorities; it was only anxious for the future. Moreover, the Liberal party lacked direct control over the government from early 1926 to early 1927 and even while it held power was slow to implement some of the vague clauses which the oilmen had feared.[23]

During the lull in diplomatic activity, from early 1926 until early 1927, there were several noteworthy developments in Rumania's internal political life. The Liberal government's retirement had been induced by popular excitement over the exile of Prince Carol, the establishment of a Regency Council, and the stirrings of dissatisfaction with the Liberal economic policies. Ion Bratianu had providently seen to his replacement by an "opposition" premier whose ideas on nationalization and foreign investments were safe. However, in September 1926 the definitive fusion of the Peasants and the Transylvanian Nationalists into the National Peasant party threatened the Liberals with their first effective rivalry since the wartime destruction of the Conservatives. King Ferdinand died in July 1927 and his power passed to the cumbersome Regency Council. Ion Bratianu died four months later, leaving the leadership of party and nation to his brother Vintila. Several moves toward direct *rapprochement* between Standard Oil and the Liberal government, from April of this year through July of the next, proved to be abortive.[24]

As the year 1928 progressed, the position of Vintila Bratianu's government became increasingly precarious. The Liberal program had not achieved the national self-sufficiency it had intended; failure of the maize crop seriously aggravated its difficulties. Bratianu had to surrender his cherished plan for revaluing the leu and had to look in real earnest for a stabilization loan abroad. In August, however, the Standard Oil Company's representative in Bucharest was suggesting that his firm should recruit the support of American bankers for a financial boycott of Rumania; he anticipated fairer treatment from the Peasant party, which could be granted a loan when it succeeded the Liberals. One must suspect that the suggestion was accepted. In September, British oil interests advised London bankers to extend no financial help to Bratianu until he amended the Mining Act, especially since to save his political position would be to perpetuate his discriminatory policy toward foreigners. Rebuffed in London, Paris, and New York, Bratianu turned to Berlin. His conversations there were progressing satisfactorily until he overplayed his hand at home. He asked a guaranteed extension of his tenure if the negotiations were successful. The Regency refused his request. He submitted his resignation on November 3, perhaps as a bluff. The Regency accepted it, however, and called upon Juliu Maniu to form a National Peasant government.[25]

The National Peasant party had long favored the importation of foreign capital in the interests of national development. Its program therefore aimed at destroying the barriers set up by the Liberals. Among its measures to this end was a new Mining Law, enacted on March 28, 1929. Many of the provisions in the new law satisfied foreign objections to the old; the pertinent clauses will be cited later.[26]

The reflective processes of American diplomacy concerning the Rumanian Mining Act are not explicitly revealed in any available documents. The government's conceptions of aims and methods, and its anticipations of achievements and costs, must be largely the object of inference.

Clearly the fundamental issue in the case was what has been categorized earlier as conditions of commerce. The State Department intended that the Romano-Americana be allowed to conduct its business in accordance with its prior reasonable expectations as to the security of property and opportunity. Insofar as the Mining Act—first as contemplated, then as enacted—threatened these expectations, it specified the State Department's grievances. The most objectionable features of the legislation will bear summarizing.[27]

Under the Mining Act, leases for exploiting the subsoil would be granted only to companies which were Rumanian in their national character. This meant that Rumanian citizens had to hold 60 per cent of the capital shares, and that the president and two-thirds of the board of directors, of the committee of management, and of the auditors had to be Rumanian. As a concession to the United States protests which had preceded passage of the law, existing foreign firms could thus be "nationalized" through the transfer of only 55 per cent of their shares to Rumanian hands; and the transfer was to be made within ten years, an extension of the five-year period contemplated prior to the American representations. The law required, moreover, that 75 per cent of the firm's personnel in each determinate category should be Rumanians.[28] These regulations threatened Standard Oil's control over its entire investment or, alternatively, its access to the new fields so necessary for continued production.

According to the Act, those who had acquired rights of exploitation previous to the promulgation of the new Constitution in 1923 could protect them only by filing them for governmental validation within a year. The burden of proof was placed upon the applicant. Especially because in January 1922 the Rumanian government itself had abolished the registration commission through which these rights could most conveniently have been established, the law's requirement was onerous. It threatened Romano-Americana's access not merely to new fields but to fields it already held in reserve. The law further provided that upon the expiration of any lease, properties and equipment were to revert to the state. No provision was made for compensation. A similar clause as it applied to the immediate expropriation of pipelines, if the government so wished, had been modified before passage of the Act by directing that compensation be granted.[29] This alteration was intended to satisfy United States complaints. The rule calling for reversion appeared directly confiscatory of property rights.

The Standard Oil Company had several other objections to the law. Some of these the State Department altogether ignored; others it espoused only after the actual administration of the law gave them full validity. The principal grievance of this kind was the prohibition against drilling within thirty meters of property boundaries. Finally, the vagueness of the law throughout was unsettling for foreign enterprise generally, since the Rumanian government's administrative interpretation was so unpredictable.[30]

The prima facie aim of American representations on the Mining Act was the correction of the Act's objectionable features. There was no purpose ulterior to this. The United States had no political interests in the Danube Basin or the Balkans. There was no consciousness of the national defense factor in this case. Once and only once, an oilman suggested that Romano-Americana's production would contribute to security. The suggestion was rightly ignored; in almost any war, the Rumanian fields would have been inaccessible to the United States.[31] Nor was the petroleum issue subordinate to the other outstanding questions of war debts and commercial debts. These problems constituted a coordinate triad, with the State Department both reacting to their cumulative annoyance and employing their cumulative weight to exert diplomatic pressure. The United States demand, therefore, was fourfold. This was the elimination from the contemplated law of its requirement of Rumanian ownership and management, its imposition of a regime comprising 75 per cent Rumanian personnel, its obligation of registering and validating previously acquired concessions, and its provision for expropriating pipelines and other equipment without compensation. After the law was passed, the grant of drilling permits on old lands which could not meet the thirty-meter rule was also demanded. The American government gave no indication at the outset that anything less than full satisfaction was expected.

The value which the State Department placed on its demands is best described as simply "high." The actual and potential American stake in Rumania was much smaller than in Mexico, Venezuela, Russia, and the Near East. Standard Oil's principal investment was about $70,000,000 in 1924. In 1923 its Rumanian output of crude oil had been 164,000 tons; this figure was about 0.17 per cent of the production (in part by foreign firms) in the United States. As for the future, an estimate of 1920 had placed the reserves of Rumania together with Poland and Western Europe at only 2.64 per cent of the world's total. The advantage of Standard's Rumanian enterprise lay in its conserving domestic supplies while helping the firm compete in the markets of Italy and the Near East, where transportation costs would have killed the demand for oil originating in the western hemisphere. The American public, moreover, appears to have had virtually no interest in the entire question. From 1924 through 1929 the *New York Times* carried no expression of editorial opinion on Rumanian oil.[32]

On the Rumanian side, the specific concessions demanded by the United States would have undermined arrangements very highly valued by the Liberal party's policy makers. Nationalization of the petroleum industry had been a long-cherished and very tenacious ambition of Vintila Bratianu. It is possible too that the quest for personal gain affected the entire party's evaluation of the Act. The Liberals controlled or shared heavily in all the larger banks; the direction of the foreign enterprises which would undertake to "nationalize" themselves under the new legislation would naturally gravitate toward their institutions. Even if the foreign firms hid behind "dummy" corporations, Liberals could expect to reap the profits of serving as dummies. In an analogous situation, the threat to Transylvanian manufacturing enterprises through government control of methane gas, native Transylvanian industrialists reportedly bought "protection" by placing Liberal politicians gratuitously or for merely nominal fees among their shareholders and board members. After passage of the Mining Act, Minister Jay discounted the government's promise of benevolent administration with the comment: ". . . general impression is that it will only be possible to evade the law successfully by employing the right intermediaries i.e. the Liberal banks and lawyers."[33]

The valuation of the Mining Act by the Rumanian government and by articulate Rumanian public opinion did not correspond. No one could question the country's need, in its utterly prostrate economic condition, to make the most of its rich petroleum resources; and no one could question the need,

in a nation bordered by two hostile neighbors, to oversee production of so strategic a commodity. But there could be, and
was, widespread questioning of the particular measures used to
these ends. When Minister Jay's recall was announced, all but
two Bucharest newspapers sympathized with Washington's
action. The National Peasants' objection to the Mining Act was
only one aspect of their attack on every major point in the
Liberals' program: revalorization of the leu instead of its mere
stabilization, forced industrialization at the expense of agriculture, and the discouragement of foreign investment. Several
peasant demonstrations in the spring of 1925 indicated the depth
and extent of popular feeling on these issues, but were without
political effect.[34]

There is no evidence that the State Department, in the initial
stages of the controversy, reflected much on whether any backing would be needed for its protest and, if so, what kind. It
appears to have relied on the intrinsic persuasiveness of its
legal case and on an assumed unwillingness of Bucharest to face
Washington's displeasure.

In the State Department's view, and it had so informed
Standard even before the new Rumanian Constitution was
adopted, the American government could not object to nationalization in principle but could object if confiscation or discrimination were involved.[35] As the case developed, the substantial
arguments supporting the oil company's complaints were put
thus by Minister Jay: The Act's requirement of Rumanian
majority participation was confiscatory because there was no
assurance of adequate payment for the stock which Romano-
Americana would be forced to place in Rumanian hands,
especially if one recalled the lack of capital in the country's
economy. The regulation that 75 per cent of officials and
employees had to be Rumanian threatened the profitable management of operations and therefore contravened the government's prior promise of equitable treatment for foreign

enterprises. The rule that previously acquired concessions had to be validated violated the principle that rights obtained in good faith according to prior existing laws should be unquestioned *res adjudicatae*; the Mining Act, moreover, established no norms satisfactorily guaranteeing respect for these rights. Finally, the provisions for expropriation of various facilities without compensation were patently confiscatory.[36]

The Department of State was more hesitant on the thirty-meter issue. The purpose of the pertinent articles in the Mining Act was to encourage pooling arrangements. Judicious pooling would cut the costs of exploitation by minimizing the number of borings; it would also facilitate the adjustment of output to market demand by forestalling production rivalries among neighbors who were drawing on the same deposit. Strictly speaking, Romano-Americana had an alternative to leaving its concessions untapped. But its practical objection to pooling arrangements was that its neighbors were often financially irresponsible "wildcatters" who could not meet the prorated costs of unsuccessful borings.[37] In intradepartmental conversations, American officials first inclined to regard the Rumanian government as within its rights, but the position finally taken showed no sign of this hesitation. The inclusion of the thirty-meter clause in the Act was not protested, but only its *ex post facto* application. The ruling was said to render valueless rights acquired before the passage of the new Act. Presumably the State Department saw this as equivalent to confiscation.[38]

The belief that American displeasure would be persuasive was implicit in the recall of Minister Jay but was explicitly stated only in the note which prepared the way for his return to Bucharest. Herein the potentialities of the Mining Act were viewed with "serious concern," and Rumania was reminded that "cordial relations . . . depend upon mutual . . . confidence."[39]

Apparently only after the Act was passed did the United States give any thought to possible bargains or compromises.

In a dispatch of July 6, 1924, Jay asked permission to accept *ad referendum* any reasonable Rumanian proposal for negotiation, but this willingness to negotiate was never specified any further. As events unfolded, the State Department evidenced its readiness to let Standard Oil reach an agreement with Rumanian authorities on any terms satisfactory to the company, provided that the terms were also unprejudicial to third parties.[40]

Similarly with sanctions, consideration only followed passage of the Act. American policy makers apparently expected that Rumanian authorities would recognize the minister's recall as a gesture severe enough to shake the country's already weakened credit abroad and to effect the government's dismissal at home. A like measure was suggested to Jay, but never used, in the instructions for his return to Rumania: If the government did not give his representations due consideration, "the Department might consider that no useful purpose would be served by maintaining a man of your rank and experience in Bucharest." In the same instruction two additional, directly financial sanctions were indicated: The State Department would be inclined to warn potential commercial investors of the obstacles they were likely to encounter in Rumania, and it might object to the floating of a Rumanian loan in the United States. The second could not have been effective unless the attitudes of other financial powers were similar, and on this point a slight nervousness (on one occasion perhaps purposely stimulated by Rumania) sometimes appeared in State Department deliberations.[41]

As long as the Bratianus held political power, actual concessions to American demands on the Mining Act came sparingly, grudgingly, and slowly. The initial series of protests, from March to June 1924, fell on virtually deaf ears. The draft copy of the law as it had first reached Minister Jay and the Act as enacted were different in only two respects which were even remotely significant. The final Act assured compensation for expropriated pipelines and thus satisfied his first complaints fully

—on a single aspect of oil operations. The Act also reduced for existing firms the percentage of stock which had to be transferred to Rumanian citizens and extended the period within which the transfer had to be made. This by no means touched the fundamental issue, which was the whole idea of a forced sale on conditions tantamount to confiscation. At best it can be said that Romano-Americana gained time to meet the Act's challenge; even in 1928 it had taken no steps toward changing its national character, while it used various legal devices to evade the impact of the law.[42] The State Department's sudden resort to sharp measures, precipitated by the passage of the Mining Act, galvanized the Rumanian government into action on other issues: the long-delayed extradition treaty and the satisfaction of private American creditors.[43]

On the major issue which arose from the administration of the Act, permits for drilling as close to the property boundary as fifteen meters, a compromise solution was reached. Without prejudice to its legal stand, Rumania adopted a policy of approving applications freely. The United States won this concession, however, only after six months of wrangling; and a financial boycott as well as the imminence of negotiations on the war debt strengthened the State Department's hand. In Minister Jay's opinion, the Rumanian government was giving full satisfaction where it could in order to mollify the United States on issues where it could give only partial satisfaction; it recognized the need of "some good news" for Washington.[44]

With the fall of the Liberal government and the passage of the revised Mining Law, the specific purposes sought by the United States were substantially achieved. The new law did not modify the fundamental principle of the old, which was the nationalization of the subsoil as provided in the Constitution. In order to encourage foreign investment, however, it explicitly conceded to foreign capital perfect equality with domestic in the exploitation of petroleum. The onerous prescriptions as to the distribution of shares and as to the nationality of the director general, the technical director, the business manager, and the members of the board were repealed; but the requirement that 75 per cent of the subordinate personnel in each category should be Rumanian citizens was retained. The new law thus removed the primary cause of the American complaint by assuring to foreigners the continued full ownership of their own enterprises and by eliminating the really obnoxious element in the 75-per-cent requirement. The new law also retained the basic rule of the old on the validating of acquired rights, but exempted petroleum lands (as distinguished from other mining properties) and simplified the process. Rights acquired before the promulgation of the Constitution in 1923 could be validated if they were in normal exploitation at any time between August 1, 1914, and July 4, 1924, or would be put into exploitation within a stated period. Although the new law incorporated without change the old law's provisions for reversion of equipment to the state, one finds no subsequent complaint by Romano-Americana on this count. For foreign firms the important things were the security they now enjoyed for their older lands and the equal opportunity in new territories. In its annual report to its stockholders, the Standard Oil Company expressed its satisfaction with the new Mining Law.[45]

The cost of achieving American aims was not great. The United States' legal case, which the Rumanian Liberals rejected anyhow as impinging on domestic jurisdiction, did not propound the sort of argument that could be turned against its author. Moreover, such tension as developed in relations with Rumania had no untoward results. Exports to that country, the one value on which the United States was even tenuously vulnerable, actually rose steadily during the years of contention from $1,200,000 in 1924 to $9,400,000 in 1928.[46]

The State Department did accept, at least tacitly, one compromise, by ceasing to press its legal argument on the thirty-meter issue as long as Rumania substantively satisfied Romano-Americana with the grant of drilling permits for its old properties. The State Department also invoked two sanctions of doubtful relevance. The recall of Minister Jay for consultation adversely affected Rumania's international credit but made little effective impression on the stubborn and strongly entrenched Liberal faction. In 1925 the State Department's unfavorable attitude toward the floating of a Rumanian loan in the United States fulfilled a threat of the previous November, but was explicitly directed at the war debt rather than the Mining Act. In 1928 the same sanction was employed again, but by private interests. In the abortive negotiations of this year, Standard Oil proposed to back a loan if Rumania met its terms, or to use its financial influence against a loan if Rumania refused; British oilmen acted similarly. Although the Department of State passively approved this approach, it refused to participate actively.[47] In any event, neither the compromise reached nor the public and private sanctions employed involved any real loss. A private loan to the Liberal government would, in fact, have been a risky investment.

In addition, the State Department successfully rejected several Rumanian efforts to bargain. Rumania's softening on problems touching Standard Oil and other private American interests in the spring of 1925 was apparently intended to induce in the United States a more lenient view of the war debts. Yet the agreement reached between the two countries at the end of that year shows no reduction of the principal; whether the terms of payment were generous or merely realistic is impossible to say.[48] The State Department was similarly unreceptive to Standard Oil's suggestion that approval be given to a Rumanian loan in consideration of an agreement on petroleum.

Although the Liberal government would not heed the American complaints, these did have an influence on the revision of the Mining Act. The position taken by the United States in its protests and in the persistent attitude which surrounded its protests early convinced the Peasant party that the Act was unduly restrictive of foreign capital and detrimental to the Rumanian economy. The sanctions which backed the protest, moreover, blocked Vintila Bratianu's efforts to get a stabilization loan in New York, London, and Paris; and thus contributed to his replacement by the leader of the party which had this clearer view. One notes, therefore, that the effect of the protests was not to persuade but to replace the Liberal government by making obvious the economic consequences of its stubbornness. One notes also that the like-mindedness of other financially powerful countries gave fortuitous aid to the United States. Helpful also was the enormous disparity in the noncoercive resources of the two nations. Rumania's economy was limited, unbalanced, and devastated. The United States enjoyed a large and varied output, diffused international commerce, and solid financial strength. Severe pressure could thus be applied without fear of serious economic repercussions.

There was some negligence among American policy makers in giving advance consideration to these factors, but substantively their protest on the Mining Act of 1924 achieved solid results at very little cost. It was, on the whole, a successful tactic of diplomacy.

NOTES

[1] George C. Logio, *Rumania*, pp. 122-23 (Manchester: Sheratt and Hughes, 1932); Florin E. Manoliou, *La Réconstruction économique et financière de la Roumanie et les partis politiques*, pp. 64-105 (Paris: Librairie Universitaire J. Gambier, 1931); Leo Pasvolsky, *The Economic Nationalism of the Danubian States*, pp. 385-94 (London: George Allen and Unwin, 1928); Joseph S. Roucek, *Contemporary Roumania and Her Problems*, pp. 162-64, 309, 340-41 (Stanford: Stanford University Press, 1932).

[2] Roucek, *Contemporary Roumania*, pp. 68, 73-74, 106; Charles U. Clark, *United Roumania*, p. 318 (New York: Dodd, Mead and Company, 1932).

[3] Roucek, *Contemporary Roumania*, pp. 67, 73-75, 230, 235.

[4] *Ibid.*, pp. 109, 347-48; Clark, *United Roumania*, p. 318; Pasvolsky, *Danubian States*, pp. 394-97; Henry L. Roberts, *Rumania*, pp. 120-21, 124 (New Haven: Yale University Press, 1951).

[5] See Georges Pilpel, *Le Pétrole en Roumanie*, pp. 9, 39, 61-63, 78-79 (Strasbourg: Editions Universitaires de Strasbourg, 1925); the figure of 83.5 per cent was computed from data on pp. 50-51. See also Roucek, *Contemporary Roumania*, p. 265.

[6] *Ibid.*, pp. 225, 265-66.

[7] *Ibid.*, p. 338, n. 13; Manoliou, *La Réconstruction*, pp. 92-93; *Foreign Relations, 1925*, Vol. 1, p. 168.

[8] *Foreign Relations, 1924*, Vol. 2, pp. 613-14, 618-19, 621-27, 634-36.

[9] Herbert Feis, *Petroleum and American Foreign Policy*, pp. 6-11 (Stanford: Food Research Institute, 1944); Henry C. Morris, "Development of the Foreign Oil Policy of the United States," *Annals of the American Academy of Political and Social Science* 116:262-63, November 1924; Ludwell Denny, *We Fight for Oil*, (New York: Alfred A. Knopf, 1928), pp. 17-20, 271, 279 (on which the percentage figures for reserves and production, 1921-1925, are based); Merlo J. Pusey, *Charles Evans Hughes*, Vol. 2, pp. 562, 567, 637-38 (New York: The Macmillan Company, 1951).

[10] DS # #871.6363/111 and 101, conversations between the Department of State and Standard Oil, November 17, 1922 and January 12, 1923.

[11] *Foreign Relations, 1924*, Vol. 2, pp. 597-602.

[12] *Ibid.*, pp. 604-11.

[13] *Ibid.*, pp. 612-13.

[14] *Ibid.*, pp. 606, 609-10, 617.

[15] *Ibid.*, pp. 613-16, 618-19, 626-28.

[16] *Ibid.*, pp. 619-26; DS # #871.6363/192, 193, 202, and 237, conversations of Bibescu with Department, July 21, August 1 and 24, 1924. Vintila Bratianu, then in London, took a similar tack in a note to the American ambassador there; see the latter's dispatch of July 29, DS #871.6363/206.

[17] *Foreign Relations, 1924*, Vol. 2, pp. 628-29.

[18] *Ibid.*, p. 630.

[19] *Ibid.*, pp. 631-33.

[20] *Ibid.*, pp. 634-37.

[21] *Ibid.*, pp. 642-47.

[22] DS # #871.6363/263 and 265, and 800.51 W89 Rumania/57, dispatches of March 7, 11, and 27, 1925.

[23] DS # #871.6363/268, 272a, and 279, respectively conversation of Bibescu with Department, April 9; Kellogg with Standard Oil, May 6; and Department with Standard Oil, November 21, 1925. *Foreign Relations, 1928*, Vol. 3, p. 808.

[24] Roucek, *Contemporary Roumania*, pp. 91-92, 110-16; Logio, *Rumania*, pp. 33-34; Clark, *United Roumania*, p. 319; DS # #871.6363/298 and 299, dispatches of November 23, 1927 and January 9, 1928.

[25] DS # #871.631/6 and 871.63/45, dispatch of August 10 and letter from Standard Oil to Department, October 8, 1928; Denny, *We Fight for Oil*, p. 149; Clark, *United Roumania*, p. 322; Roucek, *Contemporary Roumania*, pp. 116-19.

[26] *Ibid.*, pp. 266, 314-15.

[27] The text of the Law, in French, appears in *L'Economiste roumain* nos. 2-6, pp. 1-51, 1924. The relevant provisions are summarized in Roberts, *Rumania*, pp. 122-23, and Denny, *We Fight for Oil*, pp. 146-47. For the American objec-

tions, see *Foreign Relations, 1924,* Vol. 2, pp. 601, 603, 606, 608; DS # #871.6363/104, 101, 170, and 164, respectively an intradepartmental conversation, January 6, 1923; two conversations with Standard Oil, January 12, 1923 and May 21, 1924; and an instruction to Bucharest, May 31, 1924.

[28] See Articles 1, 32, 33, 80, 135, 180, and 184 of the Act. The government did not attempt to apply the personnel provisions to "nonnationalized" companies until early 1928; categories then established included director general, technical director, and business manager. This specification of the Act was still in controversy when the Liberals fell from power; see *Foreign Relations, 1928,* Vol. 3, pp. 808-13.

[29] See Articles 98, 195, 235-40 of the Act; DS #871.6363/111, conversation of Department with Standard Oil, November 17, 1922; *Foreign Relations, 1924,* Vol. 2, p. 603.

[30] DS #871.6363/247, a memorandum prepared by Standard Oil's attorney in Rumania, July 18, 1924, and transmitted to the Department in September.

[31] DS #871.6363/272a, conversation of Kellogg with Standard Oil, May 6, 1925.

[32] *American Petroleum Institute Bulletin* 5:1, March 7, 1924; Albert D. Brokaw, "Oil," *Foreign Affairs* 6:101-02, October 1927; Denny, *We Fight for Oil,* pp. 147-49; Karl Hoffman, *Oelpolitik,* p. 219 (Berlin: Ring-Verlag, 1927); DS #871.6363/101, conversation of Department with Standard Oil, January 12, 1923. Some figures in my text have been calculated from the places cited, rather than taken directly.

[33] *Foreign Relations, 1924,* Vol. 2, p. 617. See Pilpel, *Le Pétrole en Roumanie,* pp. 78-79; Denny, *We Fight for Oil,* pp. 147-48; Roberts, *Rumania,* p. 118; Roucek, *Contemporary Roumania,* pp. 94, 349; DS #871.6363/197, conversation of Department with Doctor Arthur Zentler, an American citizen of Rumanian origin, July 28, 1924.

[34] DS # #871.6363/203 and 223, dispatches of August 5 and September 26, 1924; *Foreign Relations, 1924,* Vol. 2, pp. 614-15; Logio, *Rumania,* pp. 33-34; Manoliou, *Le Réconstruction,* pp. 179-81; Virgil Madgearu, *Rumania's New Economic Policy,* pp. 19-22, 30 (London: P. S. King and Son, 1930).

[35] DS # #871.6363/101 and 104, conversation of Department with Standard Oil, January 12, and intradepartmental conversation, January 6, 1923.

[36] *Foreign Relations, 1924,* Vol. 2, pp. 600-01, 607-08, 612-13.

[37] See articles 190, 113-18 of the Mining Act; Mihail Pizanty, *Petroleum in Roumania,* p. 24 (Bucharest: Cultura Nationala, 1930); *Foreign Relations, 1924,* Vol. 2, pp. 644-45; DS #871.6363/223, dispatch of September 26, 1924.

[38] For the hesitant view, see DS #871.6363/240, a memorandum from the Office of the Solicitor, October 6, 1924, with attached chit from the solicitor to the head of the Near Eastern Division. For the action taken, see *Foreign Relations, 1924,* Vol. 2, pp. 642-43.

[39] *Ibid.,* p. 636.

[40] *Ibid.,* p. 615; DS #871.6363/272a, conversation of Kellogg with Standard Oil, May 6, 1925.

[41] *Foreign Relations, 1924,* Vol. 2, pp. 614-15, 627, 629, 638; DS # #871.6363/271 and 800.51 W89 Rumania/74, dispatch of June 5 and conversation of Kellogg with Standard Oil, June 19, 1925.

[42] *Foreign Relations, 1924*, Vol. 2, pp. 601, 603, 606-10; DS #871.631/6, dispatch of August 10, 1928.

[43] *Foreign Relations, 1924*, Vol. 2, pp. 619-20.

[44] *Ibid.*, pp. 631-32, 644-47; DS # #871.6363/263, 265, and 800.51 W89 Rumania/57, dispatches of March 7, 11, and 27, 1925.

[45] The text of the new Law is published, in French and English, as *The Mining Law* [of 1929] (Bucharest: Cultura Nationala, 1929); see especially Articles 1, 4, 30, 79, 92, 135, 183, 238, 239, 256, 258, 260; see also Madgearu, *Rumania's New Economic Policy*, pp. 22-27, 30, 32; Pizanty, *Petroleum in Roumania*, pp. 8, 51; *Report of the Standard Oil Company (Incorporated in New Jersey) for the Year Ended December 31, 1928*, p. 9.

[46] *Foreign Relations, 1924*, Vol. 2, pp. 611, 625, 644; Roucek, *Contemporary Roumania*, p. 338, n. 13.

[47] *Foreign Relations, 1924*, Vol. 2, p. 638; *Foreign Relations, 1925*, Vol. 1, p. 169; *Foreign Relations, 1928*, Vol. 3, pp. 814-15, 818; DS # #871.6363/272a and 296, conversation of Kellogg with Standard Oil, May 6, 1925, and dispatch of October 13, 1927; 871.63/45, letter from Standard Oil to Department, October 8, 1928; 871.631/6, pencilled notation on a letter enclosed in dispatch of August 10, 1928. In the early part of the year, Standard Oil had indicated to Rumania its willingness to support a loan and had thus evoked a flurry of beneficence; this, however, was short-lived; see *Foreign Relations, 1928*, Vol. 3, pp. 811-13.

[48] United States World War Foreign Debt Commission, *Combined Annual Reports of the World War Foreign Debt Commission*, pp. 244-48 (text of agreement) and 242-43 (summary of terms). Washington: Government Printing Office, 1927.

CHAPTER VI

The Nanking
Incident, 1927

On March 24, 1927, the revolutionary troops of southern China drove their northern opponents from Nanking. They then turned upon the several hundred foreigners, including Americans, who were still inside the city in a short-lived but systematic orgy of abuse, terror, pillage, and murder. Such, briefly, was the Nanking incident. In itself it was a minor episode, but upon it hung for a short period the fate of both the Chinese nation's inner revolution and its relations with the rest of the world.

In 1923-1924 a new revolutionary force which had been taking shape in southern China under Dr. Sun Yat-sen effected an entente with the agents of Soviet Russia. Under terms of this understanding, Michael Borodin was sent from Moscow to reorganize Sun's Nationalist party, or Kuomintang. This he did on the Russian Communist pattern: tight discipline and an activism which thrived on agitation and propaganda. On his part, Sun agreed to accept Chinese Communists, as individuals, into the Kuomintang. This facilitated an infiltration directed at domination of the Nationalist movement through the capture of strategic posts. The Nationalist party's doctrine was provided by Sun Yat-sen. Among its major tenets were anti-imperialism and antimilitarism. Anti-imperialism aimed at liberating the country from its status as a "hypocolony" of the more progres-

117

sive nations. Antimilitarism aimed at welding China into an effective political entity by destroying the power of the war lords who had ruled their respective spheres of influence and fought for control of the nominally centralized, official, republican government at Peking since the overthrow of the Manchu emperors in 1911.[1]

The revitalized Kuomintang soon seized power in the Canton area and established a government in that city. Following Sun Yat-sen's death in 1925, factional maneuvering for the succession to leadership began between the organization's Right and moderate Left wings. Particularly at issue in this conflict was the degree of influence which the Communists were to have in Kuomintang affairs.[2]

Despite this factionalism, in 1926 the Nationalists initiated their northern expedition, under command of General Chiang Kai-shek; the expedition aimed at the unification of the country and the seizure of Peking. By December the Cantonese army, aided greatly by an extensive propaganda campaign among peasants, laborers, and opposing troops, had swept most of China south of the Yangtze river. The government was transferred from Canton to Hankow, and during the winter the Left recovered some of the strength which it had lost to Chiang in a coup of the previous March. The Nanking incident would bring to a climax this struggle for control of the Nationalist movement.[3]

While China's domestic affairs took this course, its foreign policy was focused on the so-called "unequal treaties." From 1840 on, humiliating servitudes had been imposed on China in its treaties with the European Powers and with the United States. Through extraterritoriality, China had surrendered civil and criminal jurisdiction over foreigners to their respective consuls. Through agreements fixing the country's import and export duties, and interdicting alterations except by mutual consent of the parties, China had lost to the Powers control over its own tariffs. Through the concession of territorial leaseholds to particular nations (the United States was not among them), China had yielded its right to rule certain portions of its own soil. All these arrangements were nonreciprocal. By the early nineteen-twenties nationalist sentiment among the Chinese had been powerfully stimulated in the quest to end these agreements.[4]

The Washington Conference of 1922-1923 discussed the question and decided upon very modest measures. The Powers promised to send a commission which would investigate the administration of justice in China and would draft recommendations on the extraterritorial system. They also granted a small upward revision of duty schedules, while promising a future special conference on this problem; this conference would consider a further specified customs surtax. However, the commission and the conference were delayed in meeting, and neither of them reached the conclusions desired by the Chinese.[5]

Anti-imperialist feeling intensified. In mid-1925 a clash at Shanghai between a disorderly crowd of Chinese and police under British command resulted in the death of several Chinese, and a similar incident (involving the French also) followed at Shameen. The Kuomintang organized a devastating boycott which lasted fifteen months against the British at Hong Kong and Canton.[6] Inspired with the same fiery spirit, the Peking government began threatening unilateral termination of its treaties with various countries as the dates for their decennial review arrived, unless new, equal, reciprocal agreements were reached; in this way, negotiations were initiated with Belgium, Spain, France, and Japan. In early 1927 unilateral action was similarly used by Peking and Hankow in the premature levying of the surtaxes contemplated at the Washington Conference. Designedly or not, unilateral action was employed again by the Hankow government in the mob seizure of the British concessions at Hankow itself and at Kiukiang, confirmed by Great Britain's formal retrocession of these leaseholds in March 1927. Anti-imperialism had become a power to be reckoned with.[7]

American policy toward China at this time rested on four principles which are relevant here: respect for China's integrity; nonintervention in the country's domestic affairs; insistence, nevertheless, that Chinese authorities furnish proper protection for foreign nationals; and cooperation with other nations in developing and implementing a program with respect to China. It was admitted that action in accordance with all the implications of all the principles in all situations was not possible. The Washington Conference established American leadership among the Powers on Chinese policy; and the orientation of the Nine Power Treaty, elaborated there, toward the maintenance of China's sovereignty, integrity, and stability was of American inspiration.[8] This liberal trend was continued in the State Department's instructions for its delegation to the Special Tariff Conference and for its representative on the Extraterritoriality Commission. In early 1927 Secretary of State Kellogg even expressed a qualified willingness to negotiate directly for complete tariff autonomy and the relinquishment of extraterritorial arrangements.[9]

Moreover, Kellogg's policies appeared to have wide public support in the United States. The Shanghai incident of 1925 dramatized the Chinese demand for treaty revision, and Congressional debate on the Porter Resolution again made this demand a public issue eighteen months later. The mission boards of Protestant churches, mission publications, and mission specialists declared for a liberal program toward China. Most responsible newspapers agreed with them. The *New York Times* and the *Chicago Tribune* were rare exceptions. The *Tribune* decried the disregard of American rights abroad and was apprehensive of Soviet influence in the Kuomintang; the *Times* feared the new Russian imperialism but hopelessly saw both conciliation and force as futile. In China most American missionary organizations favored generosity. But the American business community there advocated firmness; in the chaotic conditions of China any change seemed to these people inopportune.[10] The Porter Resolution, introduced in the House of Representatives in January 1927, requested the president to replace extraterritoriality and tariff control with equal and reciprocal treaties negotiated "with duly accredited agents of the Republic of China, authorized to speak for the people of China." At this very time the danger to Americans at Shanghai from the clashing factions was grave. Yet the debate on the Porter Resolution revealed sympathy with China's patriotic aspirations and dissatisfaction with the treaty system. No speaker urged prolonged maintenance of the existing treaties; no one argued that Chinese chaos impeded the ending of foreign special privileges; some did feel that the concern of the moment should be the protection of American nationals. The Porter Resolution was carried by a vote of 262 to 43.[11]

The lines of three social conflicts therefore converged in the Nanking incident, transforming a commonplace of war into a historical crisis. Within China, Right confronted Left in a struggle to control the Nationalist movement and ultimately the national government. In the international community, Chinese leadership, backed by an inflamed public opinion and maneuvering with apparently irresponsible boldness, challenged the Powers on the issue of foreign privileges. Within the United States, conciliation faced firmness in a contest for the direction of American policy toward China, and a parallel contest seems to have taken place within the other Powers.[12]

In the spring of 1927 the Nationalists' northern expedition was resumed. Chiang Kai-shek remained in general command of its eastern column. An early objective of the movement was the capture of Nanking.

Most of the foreign community here had no intention of being caught in the crossfire of Nationalist and Northern troops.[13] Many had left even before the city was immediately endangered. The evacuation of the rest to vessels lying in the Yangtze was begun when the sound of artillery was first heard on March 23. The rapidity of the Nationalist advance prevented its completion. As the Southerners entered the city early on March 24, those who had been stranded simply stood by, counting—though with some misgivings—on the troops' reputation for discipline and their record of respect for the persons of foreigners.[14]

But events took a surprising turn. Word quickly spread that soldiers were looting foreign property, that several foreigners had been attacked, that an American missionary had been killed in cold blood. The American consul, John K. Davis, after fruitless attempts to reach responsible Nationalist officers, decided to abandon the consulate and seek a more secure position in the Standard Oil residence on Socony Hill. His party of twenty-four found itself under constant and direct riflefire during most of its trek, despite its displaying the American flag.

Socony Hill was a bluff about 130 feet high, in an isolated area at the north edge of the town. From the residence a stretch of open field swept down to the top of the city wall; the wall dropped perpendicularly about seventy feet to the flatlands which bordered the river. Clearly visible from the Yangtze, the house could readily communicate by semaphore with naval vessels in the river; American signalmen and a small naval guard had been assigned to the residence for this purpose. Davis, his party, and a few later arrivals brought the group in the house to number fifty-two, including two women and two children. There were Americans, British, White Russians, and Scandinavians. Beginning shortly after noon, small groups of Chinese troops began successively to appear at the door, menacing the consul and the Standard Oil manager with their guns, threatening to search the house, ignoring the consul's credentials, and finally permitting themselves to be bought off with bribes of money and jewelry.

At about 2:00 P.M. one of these bands seemed on the point of forcing an entrance. At Davis' command, the sailors emerged from hiding and attempted to tie them up, but the Chinese escaped to the surrounding fields and opened fire on the building. The naval guard returned the fire, shooting high to scare off the attackers. Only when reinforcements began to join the Chinese did the consul give his order: Shoot to kill. Fearful now of a Chinese attempt to rush the house, Davis signalled the warships for a landing party. This could not but be slow in coming, and the situation became more precarious. The consul called desperately for more immediate relief: a barrage. Two American gunboats and a British cruiser opened fire about 3:30 P.M., accurately laying a protective screen around the house. Thus covered, the foreigners fled down the slope to the top of the city wall and clambered down improvised ropes to safety.

General Cheng Chien, commander of the Nationalist Sixth Army, now communicated with the ranking naval officers: He had just reached the city; he regretted the antiforeign agitation, which he attributed to local hooligans; he requested that there be no more bombardment. Numerous foreigners, including about 120 Americans concentrated at Nanking University, were still trapped in the city. The naval authorities insisted on their evacuation. When Cheng appeared evasive, a threat of further bombardment brought action; the foreigners began coming out at about 2:00 P.M. on March 25.

Elsewhere in Nanking, troops had behaved much like those on Socony Hill. In all, six foreigners, including one American, had been killed; six or more, including two Americans, had been wounded; there had been two attempts at rape; other indignities had been perpetrated; foreign consulates—including the American—mission buildings, business establishments, and homes had been looted and vandalized. Americans, British, Japanese, French, and Italians had borne the brunt of the damage. An early report cited one thousand Chinese casualties, including civilians. The actual figure was about seven killed and fifteen wounded; Consul Davis insisted that the barrage had been accurate, that Socony Hill was isolated, and that consequently only attacking soldiers could have suffered. General Cheng attributed the antiforeign outburst to local rowdies; Eugene Chen, Nationalist minister of foreign affairs at Hankow, blamed it on retreating Northern soldiers. But Consul Davis argued convincingly, from his own observations and the observations of others, that Nationalist troops were responsible, that they were at all times under the control of their officers, and that the attack was organized and deliberate. The United States maintained this view in the subsequent negotiations.[15]

Soldiers running amok: This is an ordinary incident of war and revolution. In this light, the death of a half-dozen innocent bystanders might have been regarded as deplorable but inevitable, and hence as nothing to get excited about. However, the evidence of deliberation perturbed the Powers. Foreigners in China wondered whether a new Boxerism threatened them all. They asked whether the British retreat at Hankow and Kiukiang had encouraged violence as a tactic of treaty revision. The Foreign Offices reappraised their programs, suspecting that conciliation had failed and that "gunboat" policy should be resumed. Inside China, Chiang Kai-shek appeared to view the incident as the handiwork of his Communist enemies in the Kuomintang; he felt they had operated through the Sixth Army's Soviet-style Political Section for the purpose of embroiling him, as commander of the eastern column, with the Powers.[16]

Viewing the situation as he did, Chiang acted swiftly. At Shanghai the workers had seized the town from the Northerners shortly before the arrival of the Nationalist forces. Chiang hurried to the city, ruthlessly purged the labor unions—in this way forestalling any serious incident with respect to the International Settlement—effected a public entente with the Chinese business community, and thus initiated in the Kuomintang the open split which was consummated four months later with the political isolation of its Communist segment.[17]

Immediately after the Nanking incident, the American consul general at Hankow, Frank B. Lockhart, on orders from Minister MacMurray, presented a perfunctory protest to Eugene Chen, the foreign minister. In reply Chen expressed sincere regret "regardless whether acts were committed by Nationalist or Northern troops."[18] Meanwhile, in lengthy discussions, representatives of the United States, Great Britain, France, Japan, and Italy drafted a more specific diplomatic note. There was no question but that a protest should be presented. The essential demands were quickly decided upon. The principal issues in these negotiations, however, concerned the prospective addressee of the note—Chen, Chiang, or both; the desirability of setting a time limit for compliance; and especially the extent to which a vague threat of "appropriate measures" constituted an advance commitment to joint sanctions. The United States admitted no commitment and the Powers struck out the time limit. On April 11 they presented the identic notes to Eugene Chen at Hankow and to General Pei, representing Chiang Kai-shek, at Shanghai.[19]

The note set forth as "terms . . . for the prompt settlement of the situation" created by the Nanking outrage:

1. Adequate punishment of Commanders of the troops responsible for the murders, the personal injuries and indignities and the material damage done as also of all persons found to be implicated.

2. Apology in writing by the Commander-in-Chief of the Nationalist Army including an express written undertaking to refrain from all forms of violence and agitation against foreign lives and property.

3. Complete reparation for the personal injuries and material damage done.

Unless the intention of prompt compliance was satisfactorily demonstrated, the several governments concerned would "find themselves compelled to take such measures as they consider appropriate."[20]

In a press conference on March 31, General Chiang had already deplored the incident and stated it as the settled policy of the Nationalist government that force or mass violence would not be used to change the status of the foreign settlements. But he did not answer the Powers' protest.[21]

On April 14 Eugene Chen replied in separate notes to the complaining nations. He used slightly different terms in each, but similar substance. This maneuver was intended to divide the participating nations. To the United States, Chen promised to make good all damage done to the consulate, whether caused by Northerners or others, because in any case "an American consulate on Chinese territory had been violated." He guaranteed compensation for personal injuries or damages, unless they were demonstrably caused by the Anglo-American bombardment, by Northerners, or by *agents provocateurs*. He insisted that punishment must wait upon the establishment of Nationalist responsibility (which, according to him, the United States had simply assumed) and proposed that a joint Sino-American commission of inquiry should investigate both this question and the circumstances of a seemingly illegal bombardment. Next, Chen argued that the requested apology must likewise await the outcome of the inquiry; but he reiterated his previous expression of regret. He stated that the Nationalist military authorities would give a written undertaking to protect foreign lives and property, and would make it effective—since this was already the government's policy. Finally, Chen blamed the unequal treaties for the general peril to foreigners and proposed negotiations for their revision.[22]

Despite the unexpectedly moderate tone of the foreign minister's reply, the five governments considered his substantive answer evasive and unsatisfactory. They believed that the basic facts needed no further investigation and felt that the questions of the bombardment and of treaty revision were irrelevant. The Powers therefore began a new series of discussions among them-

selves on a projected second note to Chen. In essence, the text
developed by the ministers at Peking would have required a
speedy and unqualified affirmative reply to the principal demands already made or "the Governments concerned will be
obliged to consider such measures as may be necessary to obtain
compliance."[23] Secretary Kellogg, however, saw no harm in
waiting until the then uncertain conditions within the Kuomintang had been resolved; and he thought that the sanctions which
Britain, France, and Italy were contemplating were neither
feasible nor likely to be effective. Whether moved by this reasoning or by the lack of practical help from the United States and
Japan, the other Powers followed the American lead by deciding
in early May to take no further action for the time being.[24]

Meanwhile, Chiang Kai-shek was establishing at Nanking
a Nationalist government to rival Hankow's. By mid-July, tension within the regime at Hankow and pressure from without
forced the leadership there to dismiss Borodin and the Russian
advisers, and for the most part to join the new Nanking government. Eugene Chen was among the few who preferred not to
cooperate with Chiang and who chose, instead, to "go abroad for
a rest." As early as May 1927 the Nanking government took up
the incident with American representatives. The discussions were
inconclusive.[25] Final negotiations and settlement came in the
spring of 1928, as will be related presently.

Prima facie, the United States was asking an apology, monetary compensation, and an assurance of future protection.
Initially, the State Department seemed pessimistic about getting
any of these. An early instruction to MacMurray dryly supposed
"some formal demand for reparation and apology must be made
by us," conjectured that Chinese refusal was possible, and
warned against an ultimatum.[26] Yet Kellogg was in no hurry to
follow up hopeful elements in Chen's reply and the Nanking
government's earliest initiative. His confidence perhaps grew
with the passage of time. As far as available evidence goes, the

United States sought no objectives beyond those that had been stated in its note.[27]

The demand for compensation was unassessable. No estimate of the damage had been possible; the monetary stake for both the Chinese and the Americans was simply unknown when the protest was made. The requested apology and assurance of future protection, it was recognized, touched sensitive values for the Chinese. However rightist Chiang's sympathies might have been, he understood the potency of propaganda and agitation as military weapons. Chen and his leftist associates at Hankow depended heavily on the aroused laborers and peasants. Even if either man were personally willing to accommodate the United States, they could do so only at serious risk to their political positions.[28]

On the American side, the requested amends and promise were differently valued in Peking and in Washington. Minister MacMurray judged that the Hankow government had been boldly probing the dispositions of the Powers to see how far it could go with impunity and that only insistence on the Nanking demands would maintain the prestige of the American government, respect for the treaty system, and security for American nationals in China.[29]

The State Department also wished to protect Americans; armed forces had been sent to China for this purpose, and President Coolidge had taken issue with Senator Borah on the point.[30] But the State Department was not anxious to preserve the treaty system and did not identify prestige with "firmness." Several years previously, in fact, the United States had been urging that the Special Tariff Conference be empowered to recommend complete Chinese tariff autonomy, and had instructed its delegation to press at this meeting for more generous customs dues than those authorized by the Washington Conference, or even to negotiate a treaty wholly ending foreign tariff control.[31] Moreover, Kellogg could not have been seeking infallible security for Americans. To Silas Strawn, American representative on the Extraterritoriality Commission, he had earlier recommended that only absolutely necessary safeguards be made prerequisites for the relinquishment of extraterritoriality: "Ideal conditions are not expected by us, but we must have assurances that American citizens be fairly protected by the government." Neither the State Department nor the president seemed to look for an early end to the turmoil of which the Nanking incident was a virtually inevitable outgrowth. Official policy sought the Chinese apology and guarantee with moderate earnestness.[32]

As for costs, the United States showed no anxiety about its legal position. It regarded its complaint as unassailably just and therefore validated future use of the principle against itself: A government is obliged to give reasonable protection to the persons and property of foreign nationals within its jurisdiction.[33] Although Kellogg did not wish to sacrifice leadership in the policy of sympathetic consideration, and although he feared, on expediential grounds, to inflame Chinese popular feelings against Americans, he was willing to show coolness toward the Nationalists for an indefinite period. The Chinese, after all, needed American friendship more than the United States needed theirs, both for diplomatic support and for the revenues derived from American commerce.[34] Kellogg was also willing to accept disruption of the united diplomatic front. In earlier years the concert of Powers had carried weight in getting action from the Chinese; in later years it kept China from a self-debilitating auction of favors among the nations: It was an instrument of mutual restraint. However, the front appeared now to be leading away from restraint and toward a violence which Kellogg shunned. The United States was ready, in fact, to accept a temporary loss of face, considering it a lesser evil than some drastic sanction.[35]

There were other possible repercussions of its action which the United States discounted as costs. A Chinese counterclaim on the Anglo-American bombardment of Nanking was to be expected, but the American government had no intention of making any amends. The State Department was mildly interested in minimizing Eugene Chen's opportunities for propaganda. Curiously, no anxiety about a boycott appears anywhere, despite Great Britain's bitter experience of a few years before. Chinese efforts to bargain on recognition and treaty revision were also to be expected, and Washington was confident that it could evade them. Since the collapse of the Peking government in 1926, the United States would recognize no government *de jure*. As long as ultimate control remained doubtful, a premature step of this kind might encourage the permanent division of the country. Even gestures which could be interpreted as *de facto* recognition were studiously avoided. Although Secretary Kellogg was disposed to satisfy China's aspirations for full equality and had even proposed bilateral negotiations to this end in January 1927, he apparently would not employ American concessions on this issue as leverage for settling the Nanking incident. He did not wish the two questions linked.[36]

What Washington was clearly unwilling to risk as a possible cost of settlement was the use of coercive sanctions. This attitude appeared early and was consistently maintained. Other governments, except Japan, leaned to Minister MacMurray's opinion that unbacked protest would be "worse than useless, it would be calamitous,"[37] and considered local action like bombardment of military installations on the Yangtze or broader operations like a blockade of the Nationalist coastline. Already on March 31, however, Secretary Kellogg warned against anything like an ultimatum, because the Powers might then "be compelled to seek some kind of reprisal or take drastic action."[38] He developed his position fully during the negotiations on the projected second note.[39] Drastic steps anywhere, he argued, would imperil Americans everywhere in China. There was little sense in striking at Chinese national property when its control by an irresponsible faction might be purely temporary; it was virtually impossible to reach the really guilty parties with punitive measures. Even if they wished, factional leaders could not comply with the Powers' demands, because they could not control each other. Moreover, he concluded, American newspapers almost unanimously insisted that force should not be used; sanctions would have no public support. The State Department did not compute the probable cost of military action in money and in lives; but even Silas Strawn, who had now become the foremost public opponent of treaty revision, admitted that military intervention in China "would be like spanking a featherbed. It would have no effect because there were so many of them. It would cost a great deal more than could be got out of it. . . . The result would be to solidify the Chinese and that would mean interminable guerilla warfare."[40]

Two other factors in the situation confirmed this American inclination to be moderate: distaste for Soviet influence in the Kuomintang[41] and concern for the internal status of Chiang Kai-shek. The Powers quickly learned of the dissension within the Kuomintang and accepted the theory that the Communists had engineered the incident to embarrass Chiang. While the general was an enigmatic figure, the United States felt that he was more likely than the Hankow group to develop a moderate and stable government. Missing the chance to undermine the Russian influence or to stabilize China internally would have been regarded as loss. The American government fully concurred, therefore, in the decision not to irritate or humiliate Chiang through excessive pressure. For this reason the first note was addressed to Chen as well as to Chiang, and the Powers did not bother with the latter's failure to answer.[42]

Measurement of the anticipations against the actuality requires an account of the incident's final settlement. In the inconclusive negotiations of 1927, C. C. Wu, Nanking's minister of foreign affairs, showed some eagerness to settle with the United

States and offered terms somewhat better than those of Eugene Chen. While Minister MacMurray was not altogether dissatisfied with the proposal, he saw no hurry about settling; especially since the Nanking government desired diplomatic recognition, the incident clearly remained a liability to it. Moreover, the new government's durability was uncertain. In any case, the American consular officials who had first been approached suspected that the proposal would lead only to evasion and equivocation by the Chinese.[43]

The offer did, however, prompt the State Department to clarify its views on an acceptable basis of settlement. In a memorandum of November 3,[44] Assistant Secretary of State Nelson T. Johnson laid down these fundamental points. Sincere acceptance of responsibility by the Chinese was absolutely essential. Guilty individuals should be stigmatized, but to press for actual punishment would likely result in the substitution of innocent parties and would therefore be unwise. Regrets rather than apology on Chiang Kai-shek's part would be satisfactory. Rather than a highly specific undertaking for the future, a general commitment not to support agitation would be desirable. There was no objection to a joint Sino-American commission if its terms of reference confined its work to the verification of facts and the assessment of damages, excluding any judgment on responsibility for the incident. The United States could regret the necessity for the bombardment. It was willing, too, to take up treaty revision, but this was to be clearly indicated as independent of the Nanking settlement.

In February 1928 General Huang Fu became foreign minister in the now stabilized Nanking government; part of his declared program was the settlement of the issues outstanding with other countries. At about this time, Minister MacMurray was making a survey tour of southern China, and Huang invited him to travel as a guest of the Nanking government. MacMurray refused, pointing out that the incident was not yet settled and

that American property at Nanking was still being damaged.
But while he continued on his journey, studiously avoiding the
city of Nanking, he authorized the American consul at Shanghai
to negotiate with Huang Fu's representative. Huang's first proposals appear to have been less generous than Wu's terms in the
previous year. The sudden withdrawal of the British from
parallel negotiations, however, shook the Chinese foreign minister's already precarious position in his own government, and
he became most anxious for an agreement with the United States.
As a result, in a single direct conversation, he and MacMurray
came to terms. The formal settlement of the Nanking incident
took place a few days later, March 30, in an exchange of three
carefully prepared notes and their replies between Huang Fu
and the American minister.[45]

In the first note,[46] the foreign minister dealt with the points
raised in the original protest of the Powers. He regretted the
indignity to the flag and the official representatives of the United
States, and the material or personal damage done to the consulate and American nationals. Although investigation had shown
that the Communists had instigated the incident prior to the
establishment of the Nanking government, that government
accepted full responsibility. The new government had issued
orders for the protection of foreigners, felt confident that this
task would now be easier, and specifically guaranteed that
"there will be no similar violence or agitation against American
lives or legitimate interests." The guilty military division had
been disbanded, and effective steps had been taken to punish
guilty individuals. In conformity with international law, the
government would compensate for personal injuries and for
damages done to officials, private residents, and the consulate.
The foreign minister proposed that a joint Sino-American commission verify the damages and assess the payments due. Mac-
Murray's first note accepted the regrets and the proposed terms
of settlement.

Huang's second note requested an American expression of regret over the bombardment of Nanking. MacMurray's reply pointed out that the action was strictly a protective barrage in intention and in fact, and had been indispensable for the protection of Americans. Nevertheless, he regretted that circumstances had made the bombardment necessary.

The third Chinese note suggested that steps be taken toward treaty revision and toward readjustment of other outstanding questions, on the basis of equality and reciprocity. The United States answered that the question was not germane to amends for the Nanking incident. Nevertheless, MacMurray would reiterate what he had already told the Chinese foreign minister: The United States sympathized with the Chinese desire for sovereignty unimpeded, as far as possible, by exceptional international obligations. Hence, the United States hoped that improved conditions would, from time to time, provide opportunities for revision; especially did it hope for the establishment of a truly representative and effective national authority which could assure the fulfillment of the obligations involved in new agreements with foreign powers.

Subsequently, the joint commission on claims operated smoothly. It awarded $498,000 in damages, rejected claims of $77,000, and permitted the withdrawal of claims amounting to $78,000. Although there were some later defaults in installments, all sums had been paid by 1933.[47]

Huang had also suggested Chinese participation in a ceremonial reopening of the Nanking consulate, which would include formal honors to the American flag. Secretary Kellogg accepted the reasoning of American officials in China that such a ceremony was almost indispensable to assure safety for returning American nationals. But the Nanking government first postponed action and finally, due perhaps to a news "leak" which aroused Chinese extremists, cancelled it. Pressed now by American newspapers and possibly by business interests, and personally convinced that official representation at the Nationalist capital was desirable, Kellogg vetoed further delay. The Nanking consulate was opened without fanfare on November 15, 1928.[48]

Although by this time the Nationalists had captured Peking and had nominally unified the country, they maintained their capital at Nanking. In July, MacMurray concluded a new tariff treaty with T. V. Soong, who was minister of finance. The treaty guaranteed full tariff autonomy to China and reserved most-favored-nation treatment for each country. *De jure* recognition of the new government, which was implicit in the very signing of the treaty, was then confirmed in an explicit public declaration. Informal Sino-American discussions on the abolition of extraterritoriality, however, proved inconclusive.[49]

Meanwhile, Chiang Kai-shek's government succeeded in maintaining itself largely in traditional fashion. Its effective authority was limited in its reach. The ousted Communists regained enough power to hold one strong enclave; maneuvers with and against the generals were still necessary; tension between Right and Left persisted; Japanese aggression soon divided the government's energies. Many of the old United States complaints therefore persisted: unauthorized taxation, military brigandage, kidnappings, and occasional murders. These were not the same thing as government-sponsored anti-foreign agitation, and the government frequently did its ineffective best to meet the annoying or perilous situations. But by and large, in this respect China appears to have gone the way it had always gone.[50]

The actual gains and losses of the American protest can now be gauged. Within a year the Nationalist government had accepted responsibility, granted full compensation, and given assurances of future protection from antiforeign agitation and violence. This was the American achievement. The punishment of the guilty was perhaps fictional, but given the internal turbulence of the intervening year, more could not be expected;

according to Johnson's memorandum three months before, the public disavowal implicit in the fiction sufficiently served the Department's purposes. Regrets in lieu of apology, the formula Huang Fu used, were also acceptable to Washington. The plea of Communist instigation as an extenuating circumstance did not affect the substance of Nationalist concessions, and the United States could not have affirmed or denied this interpretation anyhow. Nanking's later refusal to honor formally the American flag was irrelevant; the United States and the other Powers had deliberately excluded from their original note a demand for such amends, considering it beyond hope.[51] Although the chaos in China continued to endanger foreign lives and thus limited the effectiveness of the Chinese promise, this was not the danger implicit in an inflammatory mass movement enjoying governmental favor. Missionaries and business people took their chances, but they did return, increasing by 2,500 up to 1931. American trade with China expanded until the Great Depression of 1929.[52]

The achievements were, in considerable measure, attributable to the operation of the American protest itself. In a manner of speaking, it froze the situation. Almost a year later Minister MacMurray could point out to Huang Fu that the question was still open and that it was an insurmountable obstacle to friendly relations. His point was reinforced by American avoidance of the city of Nanking.[53] The Nanking government's desire for friendship was then leverage enough to effect an agreement.

The support of its protest had required the United States to maintain for a year its aloof attitude toward the Nationalists. American prestige as conceived by MacMurray suffered somewhat more than if the course he urged had been followed. Coercive measures might have precluded China's later tendency to resume unilateral measures. However, such sanctions would have been vastly more expensive; it is arguable, in fact, that the greatly superior coercive resources of the United States were balanced by the peculiar strength of China's sheer numbers. The cost of the face-saving formula which met the expected Chinese complaint about the bombardment was negligible. Eugene Chen was unable to exploit the propagandistic potentialities of the barrage. No boycott developed. The United States escaped entanglement in any bargain. It withheld *de jure* recognition until a time of its own choosing and preserved treaty revision as a separate question. The later grant of tariff autonomy was part of a previously established American program. Extraterritoriality was not relinquished. The weakening of the united front among the Powers was viewed by Washington with mixed feelings of satisfaction and regret.[54]

American forbearance about pressing its case in a second and more stringent note to China left the field clear for the struggle between Right and Left which resulted in the latter's sacrifice of the Communists. The moderation which thus helped eliminate the Russians also helped establish Chiang Kai-shek. In practical terms, this did not mean all that could be hoped, but it meant much of what could be expected. The unhappy aspects of later history are not exclusively attributable to Chiang, much less to American support of him. The problems intrinsic to Chinese social development would be difficult for any government; for Nanking, they were aggravated by Communist subversion and Japanese aggression. Who can say that the reactionary tendency of the Nationalist government would not have been moderated if such pressures were absent?

At a cost little more than anticipated, then, the stated demands of the American protest were met almost to the letter. In addition, the United States' very manner of handling the situation won an achievement of its own: The conciliatory trend of the Powers' policy toward China stood still at Nanking and bade fair to be reversed by the reinstatement of the gunboat; American moderation braked this reaction and revivified the more accommodating and, one suspects, wiser tendency.[55] The United States government's protest on the Nanking incident was eminently successful.

NOTES

[1] Arthur N. Holcombe, *The Chinese Revolution*, pp. 161-66 (Cambridge: Harvard University Press, 1930); Robert T. Pollard, *China's Foreign Relations*, pp. 291-92 (New York: The Macmillan Company, 1933); Harold M. Vinacke, *A History of the Far East in Modern Times*, sixth edition, pp. 437-42 (New York: Appleton-Century-Crofts, 1959).

[2] Holcombe, *Chinese Revolution*, pp. 181-200; Harold R. Isaacs, *The Tragedy of the Chinese Revolution*, revised edition, pp. 74-75 (Stanford: Stanford University Press, 1951).

[3] Vinacke, *Far East in Modern Times*, pp. 444-46; Pollard, *China's Foreign Relations*, p. 330; Isaacs, *Tragedy of Chinese Revolution*, pp. 89-99; H. H. Chang, *Chiang Kai-shek*, pp. 159-65 (Garden City: Doubleday, Doran and Company, 1944). Isaacs is sympathetic with the radicalism of early Chinese Nationalism and therefore severely critical of Chiang; Chang is an apologist for the generalissimo. Louis Fischer, *The Soviets in World Affairs*, second edition, Vol. 2, pp. 632-79 (Princeton: Princeton University Press, 1951), sympathetically outlines Borodin's strategy during these years.

[4] Vinacke, *Far East in Modern Times*, pp. 43-46, 149-50, 284-87; the Sino-American treaty of 1844, Articles II, XXI, XXIV, and XXV, as printed in Paul H. Clyde, editor, *United States Policy toward China: Diplomatic and Public Documents, 1839-1939*, pp. 13-21 (Durham: The Duke University Press, 1940).

[5] Pollard, *China's Foreign Relations*, pp. 210-19, 270-87.

[6] Dorothy Borg, *American Policy and the Chinese Revolution, 1925-1928*, pp. 20-23, 39-46 (New York: American Institute of Pacific Relations, 1947).

[7] Pollard, *China's Foreign Relations*, pp. 298 (and n. 18), 310-27.

[8] Stanley K. Hornbeck, *China Today: Political. World Peace Foundation Pamphlets*, Vol. 10, pp. 483-84, 487 (Boston: World Peace Foundation, 1927); Borg, *American Policy*, pp. 7-13.

[9] David Bryn-Jones, *Frank B. Kellogg*, p. 215 (New York: G. P. Putnam's Sons, 1937); *Foreign Relations, 1925*, Vol. 1, pp. 767, 844-45, 849, 855-56; *Foreign Relations, 1926*, Vol. 1, pp. 933-34; *Foreign Relations, 1927*, Vol. 2, pp. 350-53.

[10] Borg, *American Policy*, pp. 47-48, 68-94, 190-201, 255-66. In Catholic missionary work among the Chinese at this time, Americans played an insignificant role; see *ibid.*, p. 68, n. 1.

[11] The text of this concurrent Resolution, strikingly similar to Kellogg's declaration of January 27, appears in *Congressional Record*, 69th Cong., 2nd Sess., Vol. 68, p. 4386 (Washington: Government Printing Office, 1927). It was permitted to die in the Senate Foreign Relations Committee. Kellogg may have viewed it as a trial balloon; with the trend of Congressional and public opinion clear, he perhaps preferred the Senate to ignore the matter so that the State Department could resume control. See Borg, *American Policy*, pp. 238-39, 242-56.

[12] *Ibid.*, p. 422; H. Owen Chapman, *The Chinese Revolution, 1926-1927*, p. 108 (London: Constable and Company, 1928); *Foreign Relations, 1927*, Vol. 2, p. 168.

[13] The following narrative of the incident is substantially that of Consul Davis as it appears in his full report to State, March 28, 1927, *Foreign Relations, 1927*, Vol. 2, pp. 151-53, complemented by shorter dispatches of American officials, *ibid.*, pp. 146-51, 168-69. Alice T. Hobart, *Within the Walls of Nanking*, pp. 197-229 (London: Jonathan Cape, 1928), also gives a first-hand account; see frontispiece for a photograph of Socony Hill, p. 93 for description, and p. 82 for map of the city. Mrs. Hobart's husband was the Standard Oil manager. See also Borg, *American Policy*, pp. 290-96.

[14] Chapman, *Chinese Revolution*, pp. 104-05.

[15] *Foreign Relations, 1927*, Vol. 2, p. 159; Isaacs, *Tragedy of Chinese Revolution*, pp. 144-45. Note the varying figures on Chinese casualties in *ibid.*, pp. 144-45; Borg, *American Policy*, p. 295, n. 16; Bryn-Jones, *Frank B. Kellogg*, p. 218; Chapman, *Chinese Revolution*, p. 72, n. 2.

[16] *Foreign Relations, 1927*, Vol. 2, pp. 166-67, 172, 200, 222; Chapman, *Chinese Revolution*, pp. 160-61.

[17] Holcombe, *Chinese Revolution*, pp. 233-34; Isaacs, *Tragedy of Chinese Revolution*, pp. 137-41, 175-82.

[18] *Foreign Relations, 1927*, Vol. 2, pp. 148, 150-51.

[19] Documentation on these negotiations appears in *ibid.*, pp. 164-92; Borg gives an adequate and brief account in *American Policy*, pp. 297-305.

[20] *Foreign Relations, 1927*, Vol. 2, pp. 189-90.

[21] *Ibid.*, pp. 213, 220; Isaacs, *Tragedy of Chinese Revolution*, pp. 150-51.

[22] *Foreign Relations, 1927*, Vol. 2, pp. 192-99.

[23] *Ibid.*, p. 198. Curiously, the British version of the agreed text read "obliged to *concert in* such measures" (*ibid.*, p. 202, emphasis added).

[24] Documentation appears in *ibid.*, pp. 196-219. See also Borg, *American Policy*, pp. 305-17. The American community at Shanghai favored forcible measures, *ibid.*, pp. 342-43, 355-56.

[25] Holcombe, *Chinese Revolution*, pp. 222-24, 236-38; *Foreign Relations, 1927*, Vol. 2, pp. 219-36.

[26] March 31, 1927, *Foreign Relations, 1927*, Vol. 2, p. 170.

[27] *Ibid.*, pp. 201 (Undersecretary Joseph C. Grew), 207, 213, 215-16, 220. The unpublished Department of State files give no clue to the Department's intentions; very little reflection on the American position appears in the earlier phases of the written record.

[28] *Foreign Relations, 1927*, Vol. 2, pp. 166-67, 204-05, 207, 213. Chiang's public statements were often thoroughly radical; see Chang, *Chiang Kai-shek*, p. 167; Pollard, *China's Foreign Relations*, pp. 295-96; Leon Wieger, *Chine moderne*, Vol. 7, pp. 117-18 (Siensien: Hien-Hien, 1926-1927).

[29] *Foreign Relations, 1927*, Vol. 2, pp. 166-68, 173-174; on the treaty problem, his attitude had been expressed earlier; see *Foreign Relations, 1926*, Vol. 1, pp. 996-97. Miss Borg regards the personalities of responsible officials (especially Kellogg and Nelson T. Johnson) as "possibly the main factor that determined" American policy on basic Chinese problems. Johnson, who had

recent field experience in China, was chief of the Far Eastern Division and, after August 1927, assistant secretary of state. MacMurray had attended the Washington Conference in his capacity at that time as chief of the Far Eastern Division; see Borg, *American Policy*, pp. 151, 414, n. 81, 419; Bryn-Jones, *Frank B. Kellogg*, p. 219. MacMurray should not be written down as a rigid reactionary; his constructive criticism prevented serious blunders, and his alert and perceptive diplomatic tactics achieved notable advantages in this and other current issues.

30 In early 1927 it appeared that the Shanghai International Settlement might become a no-man's land between the northern armies under Chang Tsung-chang and the southern armies under Chiang Kai-shek. The United States reinforced its marines and its naval vessels in the area, and President Coolidge publicly asserted the legitimacy of defending American nationals in the treaty ports. But the administration proposed to defend only people, not territory, and to defend them principally from mob violence. See Borg, *American Policy*, pp. 270-72; *Foreign Relations, 1926*, Vol. 1, pp. 662-63; *Foreign Relations, 1927*, Vol. 2, pp. 45-47, 49-50, 64-66.

31 Bryn-Jones, *Frank B. Kellogg*, pp. 214-15; *Foreign Relations, 1925*, Vol. 1, 767, 844-45, 855-56.

32 Borg, *American Policy*, pp. 271, 320-21, 423-24; *Foreign Relations, 1926*, Vol. 1, pp. 978-79; *Foreign Relations, 1927*, Vol. 2, pp. 210-11; Hornbeck, *China Today*, p. 487. Neither the legation in Peking nor the Department in Washington appeared to consider quantitatively, even in a general way, the American interests whose protection was at stake. In 1927 the estimated American population in China was 7,000. In that year direct American trade with China totalled $150,000,000. In 1930 (the only figures available) American industrial property holdings in China were $175,000,000; Chinese financial obligations to Americans amounted to $35,000,000; no reliable estimates of investment can be obtained. (All figures are approximate and have been reduced to United States currency.) These figures are all small relative to the total foreign enterprises of American business. Leading American interests were raw cotton, petroleum, electrical equipment, and machinery (exports); and wood oil, bristles, and eggs (imports). See Hornbeck, *China Today*, p. 482; Grover Clark, *Economic Rivalries in China*, pp 44-45, 47, 112-14, 116-17 (New Haven: Yale University Press, 1932); H. G. W. Woodhead, editor, *The China Year Book, 1929-1930*, pp. 4, 163 (Tientsin: Tientsin Press, n.d.).

33 Almost a year later, Stanley K. Hornbeck, the newly appointed chief of the Far Eastern Division, noted that the complications of federalism rendered the American legal position somewhat dangerous; this, however, was after the settlement of the incident; see his memorandum of March 31, 1928, DS #893.00 Nanking/245.

34 *Foreign Relations, 1927*, Vol. 2, p. 226; *Foreign Relations, 1927*, Vol. 2, pp. 324, 328. The general turmoil at Hankow in 1927 had cut foreign trade with that city by two-thirds; Chapman, *Chinese Revolution*, pp. 162-63.

35 Bryn-Jones, *Frank B. Kellogg*, pp. 215-19; Holcombe, *Chinese Revolution*, pp. 343-44; Hornbeck, *China Today*, pp. 483-84, 487-89. The Department insisted, however, that the Powers be kept informed about later Nanking

negotiations, *Foreign Relations, 1927*, Vol. 2, pp. 220, 228. MacMurray, in a final effort to get Washington's consent for a new note, suggested that the failure of the United States to cooperate might lead to a new Anglo-Japanese understanding and an undermining of American commercial interests. The Department simply rejected this prophecy; see *ibid.*, pp. 209-11.

[36] *Foreign Relations, 1926*, Vol. 1, pp. 688, 914, 937; *Foreign Relations, 1927*, Vol. 2, pp. 177, 198-99, 214, 234; Holcombe, *Chinese Revolution*, p. 202.

[37] Dispatch of April 1, *Foreign Relations, 1927*, Vol. 2, p. 173.

[38] *Ibid.*, p. 170. According to an instruction of April 8, 1927, all positions taken by the United States with respect to demands or sanctions had the approval of the president and the cabinet; see DS #893.00 Nanking/53.

[39] *Foreign Relations, 1927*, Vol. 2, pp. 167 (where MacMurray also opposed purely local reprisals), 170-76, 178, 181-86, 191, 194-95, 200-07, 212-16; Borg, *American Policy*, p. 143.

[40] In a speech at Manchester, England (date not given). See the abstract in "How China Loses Her Friends," *Far Eastern Review* 23:394, September 1927. Compare Chapman, *Chinese Revolution*, p. 140.

[41] The Russian interest in the incident is explicitly mentioned only twice in available documentation, both times as an argument for a "strong" policy; see the dispatches of MacMurray and Davis, March 29 and April 17, *Foreign Relations, 1927*, Vol. 2, pp. 166-68, 200. But American concern about Soviet influence had appeared earlier; see Pollard, *China's Foreign Relations*, pp. 278-79, n. 101. In the present case, it was doubtless implicit in considerations touching the Radicals and Communists within the Kuomintang. Although Congress had been curiously indifferent to the Russian connection during the debate on the Porter Resolution, the newspapers were quite alive to the issue; see Borg, *American Policy*, pp. 256, 263-65, 330-35.

[42] *Foreign Relations, 1927*, Vol. 2, pp. 164-66, 171-73, 180, 204-05; Borg, *American Policy*, pp. 203-04, 337. Some of the contradictory evidence on Chiang's attitudes is indicated in Isaacs, *Tragedy of Chinese Revolution*, pp. 150-54, 172, 175-82; Pollard, *China's Foreign Relations*, pp. 295-96; *Foreign Relations, 1927*, Vol. 2, pp. 147, 167, 213.

[43] *Ibid.*, pp. 219-35.

[44] *Ibid.*, pp. 232-34.

[45] *Foreign Relations, 1928*, Vol. 2, pp. 406, 323-30, 334-35. Pollard, *China's Foreign Relations*, p. 341, n. 32, indicates that Huang later lost his post partly because of his concessions to the United States.

[46] The notes appear in *Foreign Relations, 1928*, Vol. 2, pp. 331-33, 337. Similar settlements were made with Great Britain on August 9, France on October 1, Italy on October 8, 1928, and Japan on May 2, 1929; see *China Year Book, 1929-1930*, pp. 895-901.

[47] *Foreign Relations, 1928*, Vol. 2, pp. 352, 356-59, 366-69; *Foreign Relations, 1929*, Vol. 2, pp. 863-71, and n. 78; *Foreign Relations, 1932*, Vol. 4, pp. 621-22. The figures are approximate and have been reduced to American currency.

[48] *Foreign Relations, 1928*, Vol. 2, pp. 335, 338-40, 343-44, 348-56, 360-66, 369.

[49] The text of the treaty appears in *ibid.*, pp. 475-77. The British, French, Belgians, Italians, and Germans signed similar treaties in 1928; see Vinacke, *Far East*

in Modern Times, p. 458. On other aspects of American action see *Foreign Relations, 1928*, Vol. 2, pp. 192-96, 433-34, 467-68, 470, 472.

50 Vinacke, *Far East in Modern Times*, pp. 450-54; Isaacs, *Tragedy of Chinese Revolution*, pp. 295-99; Holcombe, *Chinese Revolution*, p. 347; H. G. W. Woodhead, *Extraterritoriality in China: The Case against Abolition*, pp. 14-28, 41-44 (Tientsin: Tientsin Press, 1929). This last is a polemical pamphlet.

51 Consul Davis reported that the 19th Division of the Sixth Army had not been disbanded, but absorbed into other units, and that only a handful of civilians at Nanking had been prosecuted; see *Foreign Relations, 1927*, Vol. 2, pp. 176, 199, 222, 226-27 (MacMurray). Hornbeck, newly appointed chief of the Far Eastern Division, feared that specific mention of "Communist" responsibility held troublesome potentialities, including embroilment with Russia; his memorandum on the subject, dated March 31, 1928, was too late to influence the final texts of the notes anyhow; see DS #893.00 Nanking/245.

52 H. G. W. Woodhead, editor, *The China Year Book, 1931*, pp. 2, 295; *The China Year Book, 1932*, pp. 2, 245; *The China Year Book, 1933*, pp. 2, 241 (Shanghai: North China Daily News and Herald, n.d.).

53 *Foreign Relations, 1928*, Vol. 2, pp. 323-24, 327-28.

54 Bryn-Jones, *Frank B. Kellogg*, pp. 215-21; Hornbeck, *China Today*, pp. 487-89. Strikingly, one finds Secretary of State Stimson, in July 1929, questioning a recommendation of MacMurray as "substituting for the independent policy followed hitherto, a policy of international cooperation," and as "a reversal of policy," which could lose the popular "support which the Coolidge administration had for its independent China policy" (*Foreign Relations, 1929*, Vol. 2, pp. 581-82). MacMurray's dire prophecy of a new Anglo-Japanese entente, of course, also went unfulfilled.

55 *Foreign Relations, 1927*, Vol. 2, pp. 217-18; Borg, *American Policy*, p. 305, n. 48; Bryn-Jones, *Frank B. Kellogg*, pp. 219-21.

CHAPTER VII

A Consul
and a Convict, 1933

In the early nineteen-thirties there were thirty million crossings of the Canadian-American border yearly. It would be surprising if the personal rights of their nationals did not sometimes become an issue between two countries which showed such a vast mutual interchange of population. One such episode, in 1933, illustrates the use of protest in dealing with a recurrent task of diplomacy: the protection of citizens who have run afoul of the law in a foreign country. It illustrates, too, the use of protest to assure the free functioning of official representatives abroad—in this case a consul—in the exercise of their duty to extend protection.

In one respect the particular incident was unusual. The common run of such cases concerns citizens arrested without reason or tried and condemned without justice. Here the United States did not challenge the conviction and sentence of the central figure. Its contention was rather that, once in prison, his treatment was inhumane and unfair. But in the important respects, the incident did follow the common run. The contention itself was a usual one: that minimal standards of justice were violated. The consul's approach to winning relief was a normal one, and the effort to assure the consul's status was based on an ordinary conception of what his functions implied.

On the Canadian side, two circumstances were significant elements in the setting of the case. The first of these was general and pertained to the country's external affairs: Canada's recognition that the United States must be a major reference point in foreign policy. At the period under discussion, this was less a matter of high politics than of elementary economics. Population structure and nature's endowment had oriented Canada toward an export economy, and this was heavily dependent on purchases by the United States. In 1929 the United States took about 45 per cent of its neighbor's $1,115,000,000 exports. The impact of the depression which began in that year was devastating and was compounded by the Hawley-Smoot Tariff's emphasis on agricultural protection. By 1932 Canadian exports had fallen to $535,000,000, of which the United States took only 32.5 per cent. The Conservative government of R. B. Bennett had itself resorted to high tariffs, in an effort to "blast its way into foreign markets," and had inspired the Ottawa Agreements of 1932, establishing Commonwealth preference. But the depression continued, and good relations with the United States were perhaps more clearly seen as necessary for Canada's national well-being.[1]

The second circumstance was more specific and was linked with the play of domestic politics. The governmental system of Canada was parliamentary, on the British model. Since confederation in 1867 the Liberals and the Conservatives had more or less alternated in governing the country, usually with narrow legislative majorities. Political rivalry remained keen. Here as elsewhere, a standard tactic of the opposition was to dramatize evidences of governmental mismanagement in order to undermine the majority's public support, and in 1933 an issue of this kind was available to the Liberal party. In the spring of that year and for many months thereafter, the conservative government was under heavy public criticism for alleged maladministration of the prisons.[2]

The political target of this attack was the minister of justice, who was legally responsible for the operation of Canada's national penal system. The active director of the system was really the superintendent of penitentiaries, who headed the Penitentiaries Branch of the Department of Justice. In 1933 there were seven national penitentiaries, having about 4,000 prisoners in their custody. Subject to the superintendent's regulations, the warden of each institution was its responsible executive officer.[3]

The incumbent superintendent had taken his post in August 1932. In October two prison riots occurred within the space of a few days at Kingston (or Portsmouth) Penitentiary, near Kingston, Ontario; a few weeks later there was a serious disturbance at an institution near Montreal; fourteen more outbreaks of greater or lesser gravity were to plague the Penitentiaries Branch during the next five years. After investigating the Kingston incident, the superintendent published his findings in January 1933.[4] Through the following spring and summer, twenty-seven alleged participants were brought to public trial. As might be expected, however, inmates on the witness stand testified to an impressive list of abuses in the administration of Kingston. Newspapers, civic societies, religious organizations, and prison reform groups were aroused and began to call for independent investigation and correction. A physician who had, it appears unjustly, served time in the Kingston institution published an account of his experiences.[5] Prominent lawyers who had donated their services as counsel for the accused prisoners strove to keep the issue before the public. Trade union groups and left-wing elements joined the agitation, especially over the assertedly spiteful handling of a Communist who had been jailed for subversive activities. It is even possible that some of Ontario's Conservative politicians, disgruntled over intraparty matters, welcomed the chance to embarrass their own party leadership.[6]

The case which was to become an issue between the United States and Canada sprang directly from the troubles in the penitentiary system and became enmeshed in their political potentialities. It was further complicated by two unfortunate failings of the superintendent, cited critically in the 1938 report of the Royal Commission which finally did investigate the penitentiaries. The commission charged, among other things, that he had been reckless in dismissing personnel (one suspects scapegoating) and that he had centralized at Ottawa control of the minutest details of prison management.[7]

On the American side the all-absorbing preoccupation of the recently inaugurated Roosevelt administration was domestic economic recovery. The government was aware that improved conditions of foreign trade would greatly contribute to this and that the Hawley-Smoot Tariff, along with Canadian retaliatory measures, was a serious obstacle to it. During this period Canada was second only to the United Kingdom as a purchaser of American goods. But whereas in 1929 the United States had exported $848,000,000 worth of goods to Canada, in 1932 the figure had dropped to $232,000,000; and whereas the 1929 figure had constituted 16 per cent of total American exports, the 1932 figure was only 14 per cent. On sheerly economic grounds, then, and apart from political considerations, the new administration was interested in maintaining and intensifying friendly relations with the Dominion. Accordingly, when Prime Minister Bennett visited Washington in April 1933 for multilateral talks preliminary to the London Economic Conference, Roosevelt invited him to the White House for conversations on Canadian-American affairs. Specific action looking toward the later reciprocal trade agreements was not taken, however, until early 1934, after which negotiations were carried on for a year and a half before the governments reached satisfactory terms.[8]

Curiously, another element in the American background had its base in Canada. It was the recognition by the legation at Ottawa of an odd facet of Canadian public psychology. It is true that between the United States and its northern neighbor lay the longest unfortified frontier in the world, that there had been no war between the two countries for 115 years, and that the two peoples shared important ethical, cultural, political, economic, and social ideals. But it is also true that there had been numerous angry controversies between them, especially over boundaries, border waters, and fisheries. In the Dominion the bitterness generated by these had been seasoned vaguely with the heritage of the earlier United Empire Loyalists and perhaps with the sensitivity of any small nation toward a powerful neighbor. As a result, latent public animosity toward the United States was easily aroused by the least friction, and the possibility of such a reaction had to be considered in any problem of Canadian-American relations.[9]

In the middle of May 1933 the American consul at Kingston, Ontario, was apprised of the situation of John O'Brien, a United States citizen imprisoned in the Kingston Penitentiary. The superintendent's report on the riots there had claimed that, during their course, several prisoners had attempted to release this man (designated in the document only as "Prisoner E") from a special cell block to which he was assigned. O'Brien himself, appearing as a defense witness at the public trials, testified that he had been in solitary confinement since August 1931. The consul was privately informed that the prisoner's physical and mental health was in jeopardy. According to a Toronto newspaper, O'Brien had requested an interview with his consul, but the request had been refused upon reference to the Department of Justice in Ottawa. The consul at Kingston immediately sought the warden's permission to visit the prisoner. He was told that his application had to be referred to the superintendent. The consul felt that his right to see O'Brien should not be questioned, and shortly thereafter he discussed this with State Department officials in Washington.[10]

Ottawa did grant permission for the interview. In conversation with O'Brien, then, and in conversation with the superintendent of penitentiaries, the consul pieced together the history of the case substantially along the following lines.[11] John O'Brien (the name was one of several aliases, but the present narrative will leave it at that) was a native American now in his early thirties. His citizenship was not disputed by Canadian authorities. He had a police record in the United States; this included three escapes or attempted escapes from prison or from custody; he had, however, never "drawn blood." He was serving twenty years at Kingston for robbery in Toronto. At the time of his trial, newspaper comment had unfortunately confused him with a certain dangerous desperado and had tagged him with the formidable but unmerited nickname, "Two-Gun." In August 1931, five months after his commitment, he had been accused—unjustly, he claimed—of conspiracy to escape. With several other inmates, he had been placed in a special cell block known as the Prison of Isolation. The others were restored to normal prison routine after from five to eleven months. O'Brien, however, had been continued in segregation throughout 1932 and was still there in June 1933.

The Prison of Isolation was not a dungeon and O'Brien was not confined to a "punishment cell." Light, air, food, and sanitation were as good as anywhere else in the institution. Under a special regimen prevailing there, however, the prisoner was not permitted to work in the prison shops, to take classes in the prison school, or to attend chapel. Originally he had been allowed no outdoor recreation and no exercise; he was currently permitted to walk in a segregated yard for forty minutes a day and to clean the corridor outside his cell for two hours a week. Cell assignments within the block were such that the only prisoners with whom he came in conversational contact at any time were a drug addict and a foreigner. It was the lack of work and conversation which preyed upon him most. He claimed that four of his neighbors had gone insane (officials asserted they were already insane when placed in the block) and feared a like fate for himself. Moreover, O'Brien's treatment had been meted out to him without a hearing or "prison trial," which had not, in fact, been stipulated by prison regulations until early 1933.

In the consul's judgment, the treatment accorded O'Brien was unjust and perhaps discriminatory, not in the sense that it was imposed because of nationality, but in the sense that it was differential as compared with that of the penitentiary's other inmates. Although he never said so in so many words, he obviously thought that it was also inhumane.[12]

In addition to requesting the conversation with the prisoner, the consul sought an interview with Kingston's warden. The warden deftly evaded this meeting and instead arranged an interview with the superintendent, who was visiting the penitentiary. Although the consul eschewed dealing directly with Ottawa authorities, he yielded to the circumstances. At this meeting in early June the superintendent admitted that O'Brien's segregation was of unprecedented length and that nothing had been proved against him. He said that action had necessarily been delayed by the business of dealing with the riots and the prosecutions. He pointed out, however, that the convict's isolation was really precautionary rather than punitive and that, in view of the record, the warden would not take responsibility for the security of the penitentiary if the man were released. Both the warden and he were willing, nevertheless, to attempt a gradual restoration to full prison privileges and to arrange for a prison trial as soon as the present court proceedings were over.

At this same interview, the superintendent explained that O'Brien's initial request to see his consul had been refused through a clerical error. He himself had not previously run into the problem of consular visits, but he now proposed to draft a regulation to the following effect. Consuls could apply to wardens for interviews with prisoners, stating their reasons; prisoners could request such interviews through their wardens. In routine matters the warden could permit the visit; in other instances he would refer the application to Ottawa. In every case the consul would be informed of the prisoner's request and of the reasons for any refusals. The superintendent foresaw no circumstance in which he would deny permission. He also yielded to the consul's argument that any guard who was present at an interview should be out of hearing. The American officer, however, was unwilling to comment formally on the proposed regulation until it had been reviewed at Washington.[13]

In mid-August the consul engaged in another series of conversations with the prisoner, the warden, and the superintendent. The public trials for riot were now over, yet O'Brien's status had in no way changed. The consul pressed the need of a prison trial as promised and of a determinate sentence if there was a finding of guilt. The warden renewed the promise. While the consul would not take the responsibility for making suggestions on prison administration, he seems now to have obliquely introduced a new idea, which the warden then put forward as his own: that a special shop be installed in the Prison of Isolation itself where segregated prisoners could work. To the American officer this looked like a good temporary solution, since it would give O'Brien some occupation, companionship, and a chance to prove his good will.[14]

September found the Canadian press and public giving considerable attention to the O'Brien case. One paper inferred from the United States minister's official silence that he and his government were satisfied. The consul now feared that the newspapers at home would take up the question and charge the State Department with negligence in the care of citizens abroad. Moreover, on a visit to the penitentiary, he found the prisoner deteriorating mentally and physically. There had been no alteration of his status; he had no work and no companionship. He looked pale and weak. He was bitter and inclined to be irrational.

True, the warden had the complete blueprints for the new work-shop; but he was now disclaiming the promise of a prison trial and asserting that the superintendent had meant not a judicial hearing but a testing of good will.

The consul therefore urged the State Department to consider a new move. In his judgment the workshop idea was a good temporary arrangement but no real solution. He sensed that public criticism had bent Dominion officials on justifying them-selves and that consequently even a prison trial would be futile; after it, the warden would probably return O'Brien to precau-tionary isolation. Interference with such an exercise of admin-istrative discretion would be delicate. Canadian authorities, however, were often willing to deport American prisoners when their terms were half up; they might be persuaded, as an easy way out for themselves, to advance this period for O'Brien.[15]

The State Department elicited from the United States De-partment of Justice the opinion that the prisoner's status, as described in the dispatches from Kingston, was equivalently solitary confinement. It learned from an American governor—who, so to speak, had a lien on O'Brien—that if deported, he would be returned to state prison to finish unserved time. On October 7 the State Department ordered the minister at Ottawa to make immediate representations against further solitary confinement without trial, insisting that O'Brien's discrimina-tory treatment was not justifiable and should be brought to an end at once.[16]

Prime Minister Bennett, who was also foreign minister, was at this time traveling in western Canada. Accordingly, it was the Dominion's undersecretary of state for External Affairs who was approached by the United States. The American minister talked with him on October 10 and 11; the first secretary of the legation conversed with him again on October 12 and left a covering memorandum. Meanwhile, several Canadian news-papers carried garbled versions of the State Department's instructions, generally to the effect that strong representations had been ordered.

In the discussions at Ottawa, the American officials urged definite steps to end the discriminatory treatment of O'Brien. He should not, they argued, be kept in exceptional punitive confinement without proof that his actions warranted this. The Canadian undersecretary replied that such a measure could be applied if authorities had reason to think it was necessary.

Apart from the issue itself, however, the undersecretary was worried over the effect of the case, and especially of current publicity, on the general relations between the two countries. According to him, the prime minister was personally acquainted with all the details of the case, defended strongly every aspect of the government's policy on the penitentiaries, and saw nothing wrong in the treatment of O'Brien. When the publicity was brought to his attention, he would doubtless be irritated and would feel that the United States was playing into the hands of his political opponents, who were using the Kingston riots to destroy his prestige in Ontario. The undersecretary especially feared that the prime minister's irritation would prejudice him in dealing with other matters of Canadian-American relations. When reminded by the Americans of the patient tack which they had fruitlessly taken to let the Conservatives settle the question with no appearance of pressure, the undersecretary had to acknowledge this gratefully.[17]

The memorandum which was left at the Department for External Affairs was not a formal protest. It was worded as an inquiry. It reviewed the legation's previous discussions with the Canadian Department of Justice, recalled the superintendent's promise of a prison trial, and noted that the trial had not taken place. It asked, therefore, for all the facts in the case and for action to establish O'Brien's guilt or innocence.[18]

About a week later, legation officials, joined now by the consul from Kingston, engaged in informal conversations with the legal adviser of the Department for External Affairs. The consul seems to have cleared up some of the Canadian authorities' own misapprehensions of the situation. On October 24 the legal adviser gave the legation a memorandum replying to the American note. It was understood that the prime minister had personally reviewed this reply.[19]

The memorandum followed the lines which the United States minister had anticipated. O'Brien's segregation was not punitive but preventive. It had been imposed by the authorities because his previous record and his performance at Kingston indicated a danger to prison security. The term "Prison of Isolation" was misleading; solitary confinement had been abolished in the penitentiary system. As of October 14 there were seventy-nine inmates in this cell block, and O'Brien could talk with those in the same range. The record of cell assignments on October 21 showed seven men within five cells of O'Brien. New facilities for work were almost complete. The prisoner had the chance to prove that he could be returned to the main body of inmates without imperiling security. Distribution of the convicts in cell blocks was an administrative matter. The United States would agree, it was assumed, that there was no occasion for reviewing the action of the penitentiary officials.[20]

This answer to the American objections appeared to be unyielding. Three days later, however, Kingston's warden himself returned from a trip to Ottawa and invited the consul to visit the penitentiary. The consul did so on October 31. O'Brien was now permitted outdoor athletics with several other prisoners. Whereas he still had no companionship as late as October 14, there were now three men within conversational distance of his cell. His treatment was in every respect on a par with that of others in the segregated group. The new workshop was under construction. The warden insisted, however, that he must use his own judgment on matters touching security, even if he lacked proof that would be irrefutable in a law court.[21]

In late November, construction of the new workshop was far behind schedule, but the consul saw no point in pressing for action. In late January the shop was completed. The warden now for the first time promised the American official a definite date for a review of the case with an eye to O'Brien's release from isolation. The consul recorded this conversation in a letter to the warden, in an effort to secure confirmation. The warden would not give this. He could not, he claimed, communicate directly with the consul on the matter, but could only recommend the promised action to the superintendent. The State Department felt that this raised a new issue which ought to be taken up with the Dominion government: the consuls' privilege of communicating directly with wardens in their districts concerning the welfare of American prisoners.[22]

By March 19 O'Brien had been working for over a month in the new shop, despite a siege of flu. Yet the warden would not consider his return to normal routine; he was not satisfied it was safe. The consul noted that in conversation the warden retreated from one position to another. The suspicion therefore grew that the warden would now take no further action while the United States showed an interest in the case. This observation suggested a new tactic to Washington. Under instructions from the State Department, the consul informed O'Brien in May that he would stop his regular visits and would come only if called for. Actually, even at this time, he had not been to the penitentiary for two-and-a-half months.[23]

Before another month passed, the situation was resolved. The warden (a new one, appointed June 15) got in touch with the consul and informed him that O'Brien had been well-behaved and that he had been moved from the Prison of Isolation. He had also been given a new job, which he liked and at which he had experience, as cook for the officers' mess. Another report from the warden in late July indicated that these new arrangements were working satisfactorily.[24]

While these lengthy negotiations over Convict O'Brien's personal status were proceeding, the United States also took up with the Canadian government the issues of consular privilege which arose from the discussions. The Department of State believed, with its consul at Kingston, that consuls should be permitted to visit Americans jailed in their districts without seeking authorization each time from officials at the seat of government. It also believed that the interviews should normally take place out of hearing of any guard. Accordingly, in July 1933 the acting secretary instructed the chargé d'affaires at Ottawa to discuss the first and more essential of these problems with the minister of justice. The granting of consular access to imprisoned nationals was asserted to be "the general practice of States."[25]

At first the minister of justice disputed the United States' view. He did not think a prisoner had any right to see his consul, although such a visit might be allowed as a courtesy to the consul. After discussion he expressed some willingness to formulate a rule permitting American consuls to interview their nationals upon application to the wardens. But he did not wish this rule to cover other nationalities, since he apparently feared visits so numerous as to disorganize discipline. As a possible pattern for his rule, he asked for a copy of the regulation in force in United States federal institutions. The State Department furnished the requested copy. In substance, this regulation authorized wardens to permit consular visits at reasonable hours, even though the inmate concerned was under special disciplinary control. The State Department also cited precedents and authorities to demonstrate that this was the practice of modern nations. A subsequent instruction to the legation reviewed the reports of American wardens on the practical application of the rule in their institutions.[26]

It will be remembered that, a month earlier, the Canadian superintendent had outlined for the consul at Kingston a proposed regulation. A copy of this regulation as promulgated was shown to the consul in September; it followed closely the scheme previously indicated by the superintendent. In November, under new instructions from the State Department, the American minister asked the Dominion government to eliminate the rule's requirement that requests be transmitted to Ottawa, in order to avoid delay and inconvenience for consuls and their imprisoned nationals. A circular of February 1934, after making specific reference to the existence of reciprocal arrangements with the United States, set forth a revision of the rule almost verbatim in the terms of the American regulation.[27]

Also in February 1934 the American minister followed Washington's instructions to take up the issue then raised at Kingston: the consular privilege of communicating directly with local wardens concerning the welfare of imprisoned nationals. The Canadian legal adviser orally informed the secretary of the legation that communications of this kind would be permitted, although wardens could refer them to higher authorities at their discretion.[28] One other detail had been brought up by the consul at Kingston after an interview with O'Brien in May 1934. On this occasion a guard appeared with orders to stay within hearing distance. When the consul objected that this had not been the practice during his previous visits, he was informed that a new rule had been instituted. The State Department apparently preferred not to press the consul's complaint. He was told to inform the new warden that, although the United States prison regulations did not deal specifically with the point, officials allowed interviews out of hearing unless this privilege was abused. The warden would not change his position, and Washington left the matter in abeyance pending the development of some case which might call for action.[29]

The Canadian Parliament debated the O'Brien case in the summer of 1934. The government was able to defend itself by asserting that the United States was completely satisfied.

In the consul's judgment, anticipation of this occasion had prompted the recent surrender to American demands. He understood that the exchange in Parliament would close the issue. He reported too that "many appreciate the friendly attitude taken by our government in its effort to avoid embarrassing the government at Ottawa."[30]

Such was the case of Convict O'Brien. The Canadian government had been perfectly truthful when, in October 1933, it publicly denied the newspaper reports that the United States had made formal representations. Neither the consul nor the minister ever spoke otherwise than informally. But diplomatic protest, as here understood, was made: Dominion authorities recognized that the American government was complaining, on legal and moral grounds, about a particular course of action and was asking redress of its grievance.

Relief for O'Brien was one American purpose. As the consul at Kingston—who appears not to have been a "bleeding heart" —later summarized it, this prisoner had been seventeen months without exercise, twenty-nine months without work, and twenty-seven months without having any normal fellow-convict within conversational distance of his cell. Whether or not this was "solitary confinement" depends on one's definition; the United States Department of Justice thought it was. There were times when, in the consul's opinion, this isolation was endangering the prisoner's physical health and mental balance. Moreover, the treatment had been meted out with no semblance of a hearing for the incident which precipitated the special confinement. Canada's defensive contention that the action was preventive, not punitive, was weakened by its reiterated promises of a hearing in due time.[31] The measures which the United States sought at various times in its efforts to correct the situation may be specified in these terms: (1) suitable companionship for the prisoner—an opportunity to converse and to engage in outdoor athletics with normal fellow-convicts; (2) some form of prison work to keep him occupied; (3) a prison trial, followed either by immediate restoration of full prison privileges or, if found guilty, by a determinate sentence which made allowance for punishment already suffered; (4) a gradual relaxation of the special discipline and a chance to prove good will with a view to resuming the normal routine; (5) as an alternative to settlement of the case within the Canadian penal system, early deportation to the United States (where he would be returned to a state prison to finish an uncompleted sentence).

The other prima facie American aims centered around the claimed consular right of access to nationals who were in jail. The United States sought assurance that consuls and prisoners had a free, mutual approach to each other. Two procedural details were included in this purpose: that the access be granted by local wardens without reference to central authorities and that interviews take place out of hearing of the guard. In addition, Washington wished to establish that consuls could communicate directly with local wardens concerning the treatment of their nationals in penitentiaries.[32] The United States had no ulterior purposes.

The United States' evaluation of the personal issue is best described as "low." O'Brien had a police record and had not fully paid his "debt to society." In the correspondence on his prospective deportation, American authorities did not appear anxious to have him back. And the consul was properly cautious about espousing a convicted criminal's cause. The State Department's fear of public criticism for apathetic handling of O'Brien's plight was remote; the American press, unlike the Canadian, gave little notice to the case. Nevertheless, the Americans, during most of the negotiations, showed little doubt that a satisfactory solution of this issue would be reached. The consul at Kingston did early sense administrative and political resistance among Canadian officials; hence, predictions were that progress would be slow.[33]

The United States' interest in consular privileges was rather high. In March and May 1934 the consul at Kingston feared that lack of firmness in this case might undermine all of the government's representations on behalf of its nationals. The large flow of American travelers, most of them in better standing than O'Brien, gave this great potential importance. The procedural details for exercise of the privilege were less meaningful. The United States' hopes of achieving what it sought on the issue were sanguine; the State Department's internal memoranda show no hesitancy about this.[34]

Canada, for its part, was not deeply concerned about consular privileges as long as their exercise could be restricted to American officials. The question of O'Brien's treatment, however, had more importance for Canada than its nature would have led one to expect. Problems of prison management are intrinsically difficult. The line between constructive firmness and mechanical rigor is thin. Relaxation of discipline may be called for in all justice; but if granted under fire, it will encourage restlessness and riot. On his record, it seems probable that O'Brien was not really feared as a desperate man; but he could be feared as a clever man and a risk to prison safety. Moreover, the warden had more than the convict and the consul on his mind; his superintendent already had a number of subordinates' scalps at his belt.[35]

Apart from penology, the case also had political overtones. The minister of justice was apprehensive of his personal political fate, and prison reform might have become an important subsidiary issue in the next general election, especially in Conservative Ontario. O'Brien's treatment was involved, then, in a hotly debated public question. Because of the politician's occupational phobia of admitting mistakes, confirmed by some misinformation in the Department of Justice on the intrinsic merits of its own position, the requested concessions represented a moderately high value to Dominion authorities.[36]

In estimating costs the United States counted mostly on the argument, rooted in the common juristic heritage of the two countries, that fairness and humanity demanded O'Brien's relief. The superintendent of penitentiaries once admitted that indefinite confinement without trial was "not right and contrary to British law." According to the Royal Commission which later investigated the prisons, the penal system "should be characterized by that firm dignity that is traditional in the British administration of justice." While noting with approval the procedural safeguards which existing regulations placed even on preventive segregation, the Commission complained that practice had violated the rules and had transformed an otherwise legitimate precaution into a punishment.[37]

Similarly, the United States contended that consular access to prisoners was a privilege established in international law: "the general practice of States." Because no treaty provision covered the point as between the two countries, the State Department argued from authority and precedent, deliberately avoiding instances which rested on treaty. It was not claimed that practice determined details like direct authorization by the warden, or attendance of a guard, or direct communication with the warden over the welfare of the prisoner; these points were placed on grounds of convenience. Implicit in the American position was a reciprocal grant of privileges to Canadians.[38]

Coldness as a sanction for the protest would have been accepted only with reluctance by the United States. This appraisal was manifest in the recommendations of both legation and consulate. The Canadian government was to be given every opportunity for remedying this situation on its own apparent initiative at periods when popular excitement was quiescent. Sharp remonstrance would meet resistance from the government, would do O'Brien no good, and might operate to unite the public against concession; the controversy would shift quickly from the treatment of the American prisoner to the comparison of law enforcement and prison conditions north and south of the border. The bare heading of one Canadian editorial testifies to the perceptiveness of the United States representatives: "What Shall We Do with Our Visiting Crooks?"[39] The United States was unwilling to impair friendly attitudes on more important problems, especially trade. Therefore, even when patience was wearing thin in the autumn of 1933, the consulate and the legation at all times used informal discussion rather than formal representations to achieve their ends. The American officers at Ottawa were especially upset, and complained to the State Department, over the press release which gave publicity to their October moves.[40] On the other hand, Canadian administrators who took a more detached view than their political superiors recognized and feared the mutuality of loss that a chilling of the United States' attitude toward Canada would bring.

The American government anticipated no countermeasures by Canada, wished no sanctions, and wanted to strike no bargains. However, compromises of sorts were at times envisioned, principally a gradualistic approach to O'Brien's reintegration into prison routine and his possible deportation to and resumption of his jail sentence in the United States.[41]

Two hazards peculiar to this case were recognized on the American side. The concrete suggestions which were sometimes solicited by Canadian authorities might have had an untoward effect in the administration of the penitentiaries, through, for example, a misplaced trust in O'Brien. The United States Department of Justice pointed this out to the State Department, but the consul had been conscious of the pitfall from the beginning. He consistently maintained with the appropriate prison officials that penology was their field of competence, not his. The consul was aware too that once his conception of his privileges was established, prisoners might trouble himself or his colleagues for interviews whenever they felt the need of distraction. This inevitable risk was accepted; only consuls' discretion in particular cases could meet it.[42]

The American protests achieved substantially what they sought in the access of consuls to their imprisoned nationals and in the approval of direct communication with wardens. Full relief for Convict O'Brien was also achieved, but only by dint of persistent interest and effort. The process took from May 1933, when the consul was first alerted, to June 1934. The prisoner received congenial companionship and facilities for athletic exercise only after five months, work after eight months, and desegregation after thirteen months. Although no formal prison trial was given O'Brien, under the circumstances this had become unnecessary.[43]

The protests did influence the outcome. Although the Canadian answer to the American memorandum took advantage of certain technicalities, in simple fact O'Brien's association with other prisoners only followed upon the United States' oral complaints and written note; on October 14 O'Brien was alone and on October 31 he was not. It can be conjectured that the appropriate Canadian ministers had themselves been misled by the information, technically correct but not quite complete, which came from their own governmental offices. The legation's remonstrance aroused their interest, the consul's report clarified their picture of the facts, and their legal adviser for External Affairs brought a more detached view than the prime minister or the minister of justice. Also behind the final release of the prisoner was apparently a wish to vacate, so to speak, the standing objection of the United States before it stirred up more trouble in Parliament.[44]

The actual cost was as expected. On consular access to wardens, reciprocity had already been implicitly granted in the existing federal prison regulations. While the consul at Kingston expended considerable energy in dealing with the issue, this was his duty. He successfully avoided responsibility for suggesting detailed methods of handling the prisoner, while at the same time he somehow conveyed the important notion of the special workshop. Moreover, as far as the case can be traced, such confidence as was placed in O'Brien was justified by his subsequent conduct in the Kingston Penitentiary. American officials accepted the anticipated gradual approach, the half-measures which, at different stages, were adequate temporary solutions. There was no call for the alternative compromise of deportation.[45]

The United States made no sacrifice of Canadian friendship. There were some tense moments, in October 1933, when the minister of justice almost issued an uncompromising statement to the press. But in the end the question was settled unobtrusively and the government was able to make a strong defense in Commons. "More important" substantive aspects of Canadian-American relations were not adversely affected. The failure of the Bennett regime to complete a trade agreement with the United States, and the success of the King regime—which won the elections of October 1935—in doing so, hinged on the two leaders' respective views of the trade agreement's merits rather than on outside considerations. The agreements of 1935 and 1938 were, of course, very helpful to the economies of both the United States and Canada. They also initiated an era of general conciliation in the relationships between the two countries which geography had linked so closely together.[46]

The episode illustrates how a simple demand can acquire unexpected magnitude in the eyes of the recipient because of the total situation in which it is presented. It also gives mild confirmation to the previously advanced hypothesis that questions of diplomatic and consular immunity between all nations, and questions of protection of nationals between stable "Western" countries, tend to be settled on their merits. At any rate, coercive power played no role in resolving the difficulties. A sensitive preference for moderation over vigor contributed to achievement. The case of the consul and the convict demonstrates a rational, successful, and substantially effective use of diplomatic protest.

NOTES

[1] George P. de T. Glazebrook, *A History of Canadian External Relations*, pp. 336-37, 398 (New York: Oxford University Press, 1950); Hugh L. Keenleyside and Gerard S. Brown, *Canada and the United States*, revised edition, pp. 280, 288, 291-94 (New York: Alfred A. Knopf, 1952); F. H. Soward, "Politics," in F. H. Soward and others, *Canada in World Affairs: The Pre-War Years*, p. 7 (New York: Oxford University Press, 1941). In the conduct of foreign affairs, Canada was independent of Great Britain. In 1927 the Canadians established a legation at Washington and received an American minister at Ottawa. Until 1946 the Dominion's prime minister customarily held the portfolio of External Affairs; see Glazebrook, *Canadian External Relations*, pp. 361-63, 384.

[2] Hugh McD. Clokie, "The Machinery of Government," in George W. Brown, editor, *Canada*, p. 309 (Berkeley: University of California Press, 1950); Frank H. Underhill, "Political Parties and Ideas," *ibid.*, pp. 332-36.

[3] Royal Commission to Investigate the Penal System of Canada, *Report of the Royal Commission to Investigate the Penal System of Canada* [henceforth cited as Royal Commission, *Report*], pp. 25-26 (Ottawa: J. O. Patenaude, 1938). See also *Canadian Annual Review of Public Affairs, 1934*, p. 177 (Toronto: Canadian Review Company, 1935); the figures cited discount a special institution for the Doukhobors.

[4] Department of Justice, *Report of the Superintendent of Penitentiaries re Kingston Penitentiary Disturbances, 1932.* Ottawa: F. A. Acland, 1933. (Henceforth cited as Superintendent, *Report.*)

[5] Oswald C. Withrow, *Shackling the Transgressor*, (Toronto: Thomas Nelson and Sons, 1933); see Frank H. Underhill's review of the book in *Canadian Forum* 14:30-31, October 1933.

[6] Royal Commission, *Report*, pp. 69-72, 86-88; "The Penitentiary Riots" and "Political Prisoners," *Canadian Forum* 13:84, December 1932; "Prisoners and Punishment," *ibid.*, 14:4, October 1933; DS #342.1121/32, consul at Kingston to Department, September 21, 1933.

[7] Royal Commission, *Report*, pp. 22-36, 43-44, 51; Superintendent, *Report, passim*, for his persistent references to the inefficiency and indiscretion of the Kingston Penitentiary's personnel.

[8] Cordell Hull, *The Memoirs of Cordell Hull*, Vol. 1, p. 246 (New York: The Macmillan Company, 1948); James M. Callahan, *American Foreign Policy in Canadian Relations*, pp. 557-58 (New York: The Macmillan Company, 1937); United States Department of Commerce, Bureau of Foreign and Domestic Commerce, *Foreign Commerce Yearbook, 1933*, pp. 345, 350 (Washington: Government Printing Office, 1934).

[9] DS #342.1121/65, minister at Ottawa to Department, November 2, 1933; Keenleyside and Brown, *Canada and the United States*, pp. 45-46, 79, 242-46, 268, 343-54.

10 *Foreign Relations, 1933*, Vol. 2, pp. 79-81; DS #342.1121/6, a Canadian's letter to the consul at Kingston; "Two-Gun O'Brien Asks Vainly for Interview with American Consul," *Toronto Star*, May 13, 1933; Royal Commission, *Report*, p. 75; Superintendent, *Report*, pp. 6-7, 10, 14.

11 DS #342.1121/8, consul at Kingston to Department, June 16, 1933.

12 *Foreign Relations, 1933*, Vol. 2, p. 80; DS #342.1121/43, consul at Kingston to Department, October 14, 1933.

13 DS # #342.1121/7 and 8, two dispatches from the consul at Kingston to Department, June 16, 1933.

14 DS # #342.1121/19 and 23, consul at Kingston to minister at Ottawa, August 23 and 16, 1933.

15 DS # #342.1121/26, 30, and 32, consul at Kingston to Department, September 15, 12, and 21, 1933; "Prisoner in Hole Two Years Refused Appeal to U.S. Minister, Ormond Dreading Public Inquiry," *Toronto Globe*, September 11, 1933; "Another Official Red Herring Exposed by W. M. Nickle, K. C.; Churchmen Demand Full Probe," *ibid.*, September 13, 1933. The erroneous inference was attributed to the *Kingston Whig-Standard*.

16 *Foreign Relations, 1933*, Vol. 2, p. 90; DS #342.1121/35, two instructions from Department to legation at Ottawa, October 7 and 11, 1933.

17 DS # #342.1121/48 and 47, minister at Ottawa to Department, October 16, 1933, and consul at Kingston to Department, October 13, 1933.

18 DS #342.1121/48, memorandum of legation for Canadian Department of External Affairs, October 12, 1933.

19 DS # #342.1121/61 and 65, minister at Ottawa to Department, October 24 and November 2, 1933; #342.1121/57, consul at Kingston to Department, October 23, 1933.

20 DS #342.1121/61, memorandum of Canadian Department of External Affairs for legation at Ottawa, October 24, 1933. #342.1121/65, a supplementary memorandum, October 27, corrected some errors of detail in the first.

21 DS # #342.1121/49 and 63, consul at Kingston to Department, October 16 and 31, 1933.

22 DS #342.1121/67, consul at Kingston to Department, November 24, 1933; #342.1121/73, consul at Kingston to Department, January 25, and Department to minister at Ottawa, February 2, 1934.

23 DS # #342.1121/79, 80, and 81, respectively consul at Kingston to minister at Ottawa, March 21, 1934; Department to consul at Kingston, May 15, 1934; and consul to Department, May 23, 1934. Compare #342.1121/67, consul to Department, November 24, 1933. The State Department decided on this maneuver in consultation with the United States Department of Justice; see #342.1121/80, Department of Justice to Department of State, May 7, 1934.

24 DS # #842.121/21, 342.1121/83 and 86, consul at Kingston to Department, June 18 (two) and July 16, 1934.

25 *Foreign Relations, 1933*, Vol. 2, pp. 81-82.

26 *Ibid.*, pp. 83-89.

27 *Ibid.*, pp. 90-91; *Foreign Relations, 1935*, Vol. 2, p. 60; DS #342.1121/42, consul at Kingston to Department, October 12, 1933.

28 DS #342.1121/76, first secretary at Ottawa to Department, February 14, 1934.

[29] DS # #342.1121/81, 82, and 85, respectively consul at Kingston to Department, May 23, 1934; Department to consul, June 19, 1934; and consul to minister at Ottawa, July 13, 1934, and (same file number) memorandum from Office of Coordination and Review to legal adviser, with longhand endorsement by the latter, August 3, 1934.

[30] DS #342.1121/87, consul at Kingston to Department, August 4, 1934; *Canadian Annual Review of Public Affairs, 1934*, pp. 119-20.

[31] *Foreign Relations, 1933*, Vol. 2, pp. 89-90; DS # #342.1121/8, 26, 43, and 87, consul at Kingston to Department, June 16, September 15, and October 14, 1933, and August 4, 1934; # #342.1121/35 and 55, minister at Ottawa to Department, October 7 and 24, 1933. Notice in Royal Commission, *Report*, pp. 44-46, the strictures on abuse of assertedly precautionary segregation.

[32] *Foreign Relations, 1933*, Vol. 2, pp. 82, 90-91; DS # #342.1121/76 and 82, first secretary at Ottawa to Department, February 14, and Department to consul at Kingston, June 19, 1934.

[33] DS # #342.1121/35 (two) and 48, Department to minister at Ottawa, October 11 and November 22, and memorandum of legal adviser, October 6, 1933; # #342.1121/10 and 48, chargé at Ottawa to Department, July 19, and minister at Ottawa to Department, October 16, 1933. It is perhaps indicative of the American government's general evaluation of the case that all the responsible work at Washington was done at the level of assistant secretary with the occasional intervention of the acting secretary. Protocol called for Hull's personal signature on a few communications to important officials within the United States.

[34] *Foreign Relations, 1933*, Vol. 2, pp. 82-89; DS #342.1121/9, exchange of memoranda between legal adviser and assistant legal adviser, June 30 and July 1, 1933; #342.1121/15 and 79, memorandum of assistant legal adviser for assistant secretary, August 11, 1933, and consul at Kingston to minister at Ottawa, March 21, 1934.

[35] DS # #342.1121/10, 76, 43, and 49, chargé at Ottawa to Department, July 19, 1933 and February 14, 1934; consul at Kingston to Department, October 14 and 16, 1933; Royal Commission, *Report*, pp. 26-36.

[36] DS # #342.1121/48, 50, and 65, minister at Ottawa to Department, October 16, 20, and November 2, 1933.

[37] DS #342.1121/8, consul at Kingston to Department, June 16, 1933; Royal Commission, *Report*, pp. 44-48, 65, 354.

[38] DS #342.1121/9, exchange of memoranda between the legal adviser and assistant legal adviser (particularly the latter's longhand notation), June 30 and July 1, 1933; # #342.1121/13 and 14, exchange of memoranda between Office of Coordination and Review and Office of Legal Adviser, August 7 and 8, 1933; # #342.1121/11 and 15, two memoranda of assistant legal adviser for assistant secretary, August 11, along with communication from Federal Bureau of Prisons to Department, July 28, 1933. The American position could be supported from the International Standard Minimum Rules—a draft code intended to be implemented by municipal action—which were then taking shape under the International Penal and Penitentiary Commission at Geneva and the League of Nations Assembly's Fifth Committee. According to Article 35, no

prisoner could be punished without opportunity to defend himself; Article 32
assured the alien prisoner's right to communicate with his consul (International
Prison Commission, *Improvements in Penal Administration: Standard Minimum
Rules for the Treatment of Prisoners*, Series of League of Nations Publications
IV, Social 1930 IV 10 [Geneva: League of Nations, 1930]).

39 *Ottawa Morning Journal*, October 16, 1933; the editorial argued that Canada
could not be moved by sentimentalism to tolerate the crime which was rampant
in the United States.

40 DS ##342.1121/48 and 65, minister at Ottawa to Department, October 16 and
November 2, 1933; #342.1121/47, consul at Kingston to Department, October
13, 1933. Actually, the American press seems to have paid little attention to
the entire episode. The *New York Times* did not specifically mention the
O'Brien case until it had been fully settled; see "American Prisoner Stirs Ottawa Debate," July 4, 1934. The troubles over prison reform were sometimes
noted.

41 DS ##342.1121/10, 48, and 65 (two), chargé at Ottawa to Department, July 19,
1933; minister at Ottawa to Department, October 16 and November 2, 1933;
Department to minister, November 21, 1933; ##342.1121/67 and 79, consul
at Kingston to Department, November 24, and to minister, March 21, 1933.

42 *Foreign Relations, 1933*, Vol. 2, p. 90; DS ##342.1121/19, 27, and 43, consul
at Kingston to minister at Ottawa, August 23, and to Department, September
15 and October 14, 1933.

43 *Foreign Relations, 1935*, Vol. 2, p. 60; DS ##342.1121/63, 83, and 79, consul
at Kingston to Department, October 31, 1933 and June 18, 1934, and to minister
at Ottawa, March 21, 1934; #342.1121/76, first secretary at Ottawa to Department, February 14, 1934.

44 DS #342.1121/61, memorandum of Department of External Affairs for legation
at Ottawa, October 24, 1933; ##342.1121/50 and 65, minister at Ottawa
to Department, October 20 and November 2, 1933—the former carries the
significant longhand notation that, according to a telephone call from the legation, an inmate had been placed in the cell next to O'Brien's; ##342.1121/57,
63, 67, and 87, consul at Kingston to Department, October 23, 31, November
24, 1933, and August 4, 1934.

45 *Foreign Relations, 1933*, Vol. 2, pp. 82-91; DS ##342.1121/19, 23, 26, and 86,
consul at Kingston to minister at Ottawa, August 23 and 16, 1933; and consul
to Department, September 15, 1933 and July 16, 1934.

46 DS ##342.1121/65 and 87, minister at Ottawa to Department, November 2,
1933, and consul at Kingston to Department, August 4, 1934; Keenleyside and
Brown, *Canada and the United States*, pp. 294-97; J. F. Parkinson, "Economics," in Soward, *Canada in World Affairs*, pp. 195-96, 198.

CHAPTER VIII

The Seventh Congress
of the Comintern, 1935

The United States' dealings with Soviet Russia have presented persistent perplexities for American statesmanship. A prime factor in the problem has been the peculiarity of the Soviet Union's revolutionary ideology; this factor touches the actions and reactions of both countries. An incident early in the formal relations between the two nations exemplifies the operation of diplomatic protest in the midst of these perplexities. The protest was prompted by the meeting of the Seventh All-World Congress of the Communist International, or Comintern, at Moscow in the summer of 1935.

The imperial monarchy of the Russian czars had fallen in March 1917. The Provisional Government which replaced it was itself overthrown in November through a coup effected by the Bolsheviks, the extreme Left of Russian politics. In the face of counterrevolutionary action from several quarters, sometimes aided financially and militarily by the Allied and Associated Powers, the Bolsheviks gradually consolidated their effective dominion over most of the former Russian Empire. Professing to follow the economic and social philosophy of Karl Marx, their government undertook to reorganize society on collectivist lines. It nationalized the land and the banks, placed control of the factories in the hands of the workers, and little by little suppressed private trade. It repudiated the debts of its predecessor governments. It was aggressively atheistic and materialistic. It employed terror unsparingly in winning and implementing its rule. It prophesied confidently that its own proletarian revolution would quickly be extended throughout the world.[1]

Whatever the nominal structure of the Soviet government, the country was actually a dictatorship, ruled first by Vladimir Lenin, then by Joseph Stalin, each with a small circle of intimate collaborators. A highly important instrument of domestic control was the Communist party, which was not a political party in the traditional sense but an activist elite, tightly knit, highly disciplined, deeply imbued with the Marxist revolutionary philosophy, and ruled as the nation was, autocratically. Under such centralized direction, the Bolsheviks, for all their rigid adherence to Marxist aims, could be flexible in the choice of means. Political and social reality in other countries and economic reality in Russia, for example, compelled Lenin to "postpone" the revolution in 1921 and to restore productivity through the modified capitalism of the New Economic Policy.[2]

However, postponement did not mean renunciation. This was the ideological peculiarity which troubled Soviet-American relations. For world revolution was not merely retained as an objective and an ideal; it was given an institutional tool in the Communist International, founded at Moscow in 1919. This was composed of radical extremists from an ever-widening roster of countries. It was organized into national sections which were identical with the various national Communist parties and which were patterned on the Communist party in the Soviet Union. Nominally the policies of the international body were laid down by periodic all-world congresses; actually control was dictatorial. The periods between congresses became longer and longer, and debate at the congresses became less and less real. Four years separated the Fifth Congress from the Sixth, and seven more years passed before the Seventh; and while the Fifth saw an open fight between Stalin and Leon Trotsky, the Seventh could be characterized as "well-rehearsed."

Nominally the Comintern was also truly international and had no connections with the Soviet regime. Actually it was completely dominated by Russians as an instrument of the Moscow government. The Russians could assert pre-eminence as experts, as the engineers of the only successful proletarian revolution. The Soviet state could claim the loyalty of Comintern members anywhere in the world and could enlist their advocacy of Russian interests, because Russia stood as the sole territorial base from which revolutions elsewhere could be supported. At this point the new ideology fused with the more traditional preoccupations of diplomacy. The avowed purpose of the Comintern was the achievement of the revolution in other countries; as in Russia, its general strategy was to foment restlessness and discontent among the masses and to capitalize on the consequent social disorder by seizing power and instituting the dictatorship of the proletariat.[3]

The Communist International was involved in the uprisings in Germany of 1920 and 1923, in Bulgaria of 1923, and in China of 1924-1927. All proved abortive. In the self-criticism and adaptation of methods which followed upon successive failures, the Comintern alternated two fundamental tactics. At times it insulated itself uncompromisingly from the very breath of gradualism or irenicism; calculated, remorseless, immediate terrorism and violence were the order of the day; there could be no collaboration even with leftist elements who thought otherwise. At other times it shunned premature violence and husbanded strength for future action by present cooperation with anyone whose short-term aims were similar, especially the Socialists. At the Sixth Comintern Congress in 1928 the pendulum had swung to self-insulation and revolutionary purity, and it was still there as late as December of 1933.[4]

The organization, purposes, and methods of the Comintern were the same in the United States as elsewhere. Overtly the Communist party participated in politics by nominating candidates for public office in national and local elections, and its press propagandized the movement's ideas. Covertly the Communists attempted to intensify the public agitation over heated public controversies and sought to infiltrate mass organizations and governmental posts. The degree of the party's success in its "Fifth Column" operations has become a matter of bitter debate and will indefinitely remain such. Its enrolled membership and its showing at the polls, however, were always insignificant. In the 1932 election it carried only 0.25 per cent of the popular vote for president.[5]

The Communist International was, as has been suggested, a unique component of the Russian setting. More commonplace factors touched upon national and international economics, domestic politics, and the political relations of the Soviet Union with the world at large. It should be noted, however, that the motivations of leadership in Russia must be more the object of conjecture than anywhere else. Reliable versions of significant public facts are hard to come by, and evidences of the central personalities' private sentiments are even more elusive than these.

In 1928 the New Economic Policy was supplanted by the New Socialist Offensive, as Stalin set in motion the First Five-Year Plan. This laid down schedules for a vast expansion of industrial plant and for the mechanization and collectivization of agriculture. The exhausting human effort required to meet the schedule was evoked through enthusiasm inspired by propaganda and through fear inspired by ruthless repression. Foreign trade necessarily occupied a crucial position in the Plan. Capital goods, of which the United States was an important source, had to be imported on a large scale. A large volume of exports was essential to pay for the imports, especially in view of the Soviet

Union's inability to get long-term credits abroad. This phase of the program met unexpected difficulties. The depression of 1929 narrowed the market and drove down the prices of Soviet commodities. Forced sales of some of these brought into play the restrictive measures of other governments against "dumping" and "slave labor." Imports accordingly had to be reduced; the year 1933 found them at low ebb and found the Russians in dire need of foreign advances. The Plan was pronounced a success, however, and was terminated earlier than originally intended. A Second Five-Year Plan was instituted in 1935, pitched at a somewhat more conservative level and favored by the world-wide improvement in market conditions.[6]

At home, under the First Five-Year Plan, the unrelieved strain of constant effort and the serious privations resulting from famine and from curtailed importation of consumers' goods appear to have caused widespread public unrest. More critical from the viewpoint of the Soviet powers-that-be, there appears to have been exceptional tension within the circle of leadership. In December 1934 the mysterious assassination of Stalin's close collaborator, Serge Kirov, precipitated a major purge which was marked by the public trials, early in the following year, of several old-time Bolsheviks. That Stalin himself apparently instigated the crime and then prosecuted his potential opponents for it bears dramatic witness to the perils which the times held for the Soviet hierarchy.[7]

On the international political scene, the rise of expansionist powers to the east and to the west worried Moscow. The Manchuria Incident in September 1931 and subsequent troubles over the Chinese Eastern Railway and the border of Outer Mongolia (a Soviet protectorate) all made the Kremlin fearful of a Japanese attack. The Soviet Union's response vacillated between conciliation and severity, and for several years the prospect fluctuated between stabilization and active hostility. In 1933 the situation was tense; in the fall of 1934 the Russians thought war possible the following spring; in mid-1935 the peril had not vanished but had receded. The rise of Hitler in Germany, in February 1933, aggravated the Soviet's anxieties by calling up the specter of a two-front war. Early attempts to deal directly with the Third Reich proved fruitless.[8]

Beyond its direct approach to Germany and Japan, Moscow sought strength in the support of other powers. As against Japan, it responded favorably to Nationalist China's proffer of renewed relations in December 1932. Fear of a Fascist coup in France impelled the Comintern to shift its line toward fostering a united front with the Socialists in June 1934. In counteracting the German military threat, the Soviet signed mutual assistance pacts with France and Czechoslovakia in May 1935. To meet the menace from both east and west, Russia improved its relations with Great Britain, joined the League of Nations in September 1934, and, above all, intensified its efforts toward an entente with the United States.[9]

On the American side, the general mood and policy of isolationism continued. From 1919 far into the thirties the United States was simply unwilling to assume any serious responsibility for cooperative action on international issues in Europe and Asia.

With respect to the Soviet Union, the attitude adopted in 1917 persisted as official policy. By 1924 all other major powers had recognized the new government; the United States had not. Behind this position lay a widespread popular revulsion from the Kremlin's persecution of religion and its terroristic reign over its own people. At the official level, the specific considerations which were at different times asserted to bar recognition were the Bolshevik repudiation of predecessor governments' debts, the refusal to compensate American nationals for damages inflicted by Bolshevik policies, and the promotion of revolutionary ideas and activities in the United States itself. To the rebuff of nonrecognition, the American government joined other unfriendly measures: the State Department's disapproval of long-term credits for the Soviet Union; the Treasury's refusal to accept Soviet gold; and embargoes or discriminatory customs treatment—based on charges of "dumping" and "slave labor"—for matches, pulpwood, lumber, and asbestos of Soviet origin. All these handicapped Russian commercial operations and the dealings of American entrepreneurs with Russia.[10]

Despite these obstacles, American firms in the nineteen-twenties developed a small (relative to total United States exports) but active trade with the Soviet Union. The Russian side of this business was conducted by Amtorg, a company incorporated in New York. From 1926 through 1929 American exports to Russia were exceeded only by those of Germany; in 1924-1925 and again in 1930, they headed the list. During the decade there was steady support in some circles for diplomatic recognition. The depression of 1929 gave new impetus to this movement. Especially in view of Soviet requirements under the First Five-Year Plan, businessmen and newspaper editors came to regard renewed formal relations as the open-sesame to a stupendous market, estimated by one commentator as likely to take $5,000,000,000 of American goods in three-and-a-half years. Russian commercial bulletins published in the United States seconded this idea.

The Hoover administration remained deaf to the plea, but its successor responded. Curiously, while the new government was deeply interested in economics, its main concern here seems to have been politics. It realized that the popular conception of a huge potential market was exaggerated. It could nevertheless capitalize on this conception to achieve another end. In the president's opinion, the policy of nonrecognition had failed and had become anomalous. He and his close advisers were clearly anxious about Japan's intentions and possibly about Germany's. Without being very specific as to how their gesture would become fully operative, they envisioned a more friendly attitude toward the Soviet Union as a restraining influence both in the Pacific and in Europe.[11]

Accordingly, President Roosevelt extended recognition to the Soviet government. Before coming to a decision, the president had canvassed the situation through his personal advisers and through the State Department. The experience of other countries made it luminously clear that recognition first and settlement of differences afterwards was a futile formula. In view especially of the heavy economic and political pressure under which the Soviet Union was then laboring, opinion was unanimous that all outstanding disagreements between the two countries could and should be resolved before the Soviet government was recognized. The principal points which were singled out were Russia's repudiated debts and the Comintern's subversive activities in the United States. The president arranged for Maxim Litvinov, people's commissar for foreign affairs, to discuss these matters in Washington. Out of these conversations came an exchange of letters and memoranda, dated November 15 and 16, 1933, in which the renewal of relations was formalized and a number of undertakings—some unilateral, some reciprocal—were set forth.[12]

The documents included an agreement "in principle" on the settlement of the Russian debts. This issue had proved to be the most refractory of those discussed, and the agreement was reached in a private conversation between the president and the commissar. Unfortunately the joint memorandum was hastily and carelessly drafted and thus contained the seeds of further misunderstanding.[13]

The documents also included a pledge by Litvinov forswearing Soviet participation in the propagandizing of proletarian revolution in the United States. Since the remonstrance which the American government made two years later was based only on the fourth paragraph of this assurance, this section alone need be summarized here. It was, wrote the commissar, the fixed policy of his government not to permit the formation or residence on its territory of any organization—and to prevent the activity on its territory of any organization or of its representatives—which aimed at preparing or effecting an alteration, by force, of the political or social order of the United States. Roosevelt engaged the Executive of the United States to reciprocate within the limits of its legal powers.

The commissar's undertaking had been carefully drawn by State Department experts as an iron-clad legal guarantee against Comintern activities in the United States, although they were not overly confident that a legal guarantee was a practical assurance. Specific mention of the Communist International was studiously avoided, in order to preclude such a simple subterfuge as changing its name; instead the organization was designated by an "operational definition." The pledge was also designed to obviate the evasive claim that the Communist International and the Soviet government were distinct and unrelated institutions; Russia was to prevent the proscribed activities by anyone on its territory. Foolproof though the engagement might be, before he even left the country Litvinov twice indicated to newspapermen that it did not affect the Comintern and that one must not read into it any more than it said.[14]

The immediate impact which United States' recognition of Russia had on Germany is not clear, but Japanese leaders were sobered. The Soviet government demonstratively transferred to its Washington embassy the man who then headed its mission in Tokyo, Alexander Troyanovsky. However, disillusion quickly followed as the reality of American isolationism dawned upon the Soviet leaders and appeared more clearly than before to the Japanese.[15]

Negotiations to implement the agreement "in principle" on the debt dragged into early 1935 and terminated in complete failure. Even the Soviet need of loans did not bring the Kremlin to terms. The ambiguities of the original document made it possible for each side, with plausibility, to accuse the other of bad faith. Soviet-American relations notably cooled.[16]

Only in the field of trade was there any accomplishment. Immediately after the renewal of relations, each country withdrew some of its discriminatory measures against the commerce of the other, the Soviet Union reducing port charges and the United States ending both its special tonnage dues on Russian vessels and its special customs rulings on matches, pulpwood, lumber, and asbestos. In 1933 exports to Russia continued their downward trend, instead of expanding as prophesied, and the next year they recovered but slightly. A modified reciprocal trade agreement of 1935, however, raised them to $30,000,000. In return for a guarantee of purchases to this amount, the United States granted Russia most-favored-nation tariff rates. The agreement was renewed and improved several times until 1940.[17]

Even while the reciprocal trade agreement with the Soviet Union was in preparation, however, events were tending toward the incident which is of interest here. A few weeks later it actually happened.

In mid-1934 the American ambassador in Moscow, William C. Bullitt, acting on the State Department's instructions, informally took up with Litvinov a series of occurrences which were regarded as violations of the latter's antipropaganda pledge. The State Department wished to warn the commissar for foreign affairs that any further breach of that engagement at the Seventh Congress of the Communist International, scheduled for that summer, would be a serious obstacle to friendly relations. In the fall the ambassador reported a postponement of the Congress. He proposed two interpretations of this step: one, that it was to placate the other powers, especially France, with whom negotiations were afoot for an alliance; the other, that it was to give time for swinging the Socialists toward the united front which would emerge as the Congress' "line."[18]

By early July 1935 it was clear that the Congress was definitely planned for the near future. The American ambassador, having inquired as to Washington's attitude, on July 8 informally broached the subject with the Soviet foreign commissar. He indicated that, if the Congress should concern itself in any way with the United States, relations would be so gravely prejudiced that he could not predict the consequences. Litvinov, in a half-jesting manner, brushed the matter aside as something which neither he nor Stalin knew anything about. Less than a week later the ambassador repeated his advices to the Soviet official; but he also counseled the State Department to consider what action it intended to take if his representations were again ignored.[19]

From July 25 to August 20 the Seventh Congress of the Communist International met at Moscow. Although the full text of the proceedings and resolutions was not published until some time later, the American embassy followed the Congress' activities as best it could, mostly through the newspapers. As the sessions went on, the following pertinent facts appeared. At least ten members of the Soviet governmental apparatus, including Stalin, had either taken part in the meetings or were elected to office in the Comintern. At least nine Americans, including Earl Browder and William Z. Foster, had participated in the sessions. One of the nine had presided over the Congress on several occasions, two were elected to the Presidium and three to the Central Executive Committee of the organization, five were members of various working committees, and seven made speeches. Among other things the speeches by Americans reported "paving the way for Bolshevist mass-work" through active recruitment of party members, leadership in the organization of the unemployed, establishment of Communist cells in the factories, a dominant role in the violent strike of West Coast longshoremen—among whom influence was regarded as important because of their role in the transportation of armament—a judgment that the strike in the coming year might well be worse, and a conviction that Democrats and Republicans alike were really Fascists. Others beside Americans made comments which attracted the embassy's attention. Thus Georgi Dimitrov, general secretary of the Comintern, asserted that in the United States the effort to revive capitalism had collapsed, that the bourgeois parties were alienating the masses, and that it was time to bring together the downtrodden worker and the discontented farmer in a mass Farm-Labor party. Finally, in its resolutions for the guidance of the Executive Committee, the Congress reaffirmed as the general objective of the Communist International the assurance of the conditions for victory in the proletarian revolution. None of the Congress resolutions, however, dealt specifically with the United States.[20]

In a sense, the extraction of the more offensive phrases from the proceedings of the Seventh Congress is unfair. For the entire context was the new party line, the united front (chiefly with the moderate Left) against Fascism; and the concern was principally with Europe, not the United States. The extracts make it clear, however, that the Comintern meeting in Moscow did discuss and prescribe measures for the American situation. The extracts also make it clear that the Comintern's measures had been and would continue to be tainted with conspiracy and Bolshevik-style violence, and that its stated aim everywhere was still the revolution. The anti-Fascist orientation of the struggle was scarcely a mitigating factor when the established order in the United States was characterized as Fascist.[21]

The American ambassador judged, and the State Department agreed, that the activities of the Seventh Comintern Congress violated the Soviet Union's undertaking not to sanction revolutionary propaganda in the United States. On August 23 the embassy was informed that the president and the secretary of state had decided to lodge a formal protest. Curiously, Bullitt had not recommended this, and there is no record of any conversation with anyone concerning the decision. However, the president did approve the draft of the document. After a revision that incorporated two verbal changes which were suggested by the ambassador and which considerably sharpened its tone, the note was delivered on August 25. In the absence of Litvinov, it was handed to Nicolai Krestinski, acting commissar for foreign affairs. The latter told Bullitt that, if the note touched the Comintern, it would assuredly be rejected; he would, nevertheless, read it.[22]

The American communication called the Soviet government's attention to "the activities, involving interference in the internal affairs of the United States," which had taken place on Russian territory in connection with the Congress of the International. It entered a most emphatic protest against this flagrant violation of Litvinov's pledge, especially of its fourth paragraph. The American government assumed that the Soviet regime must know the aims and activities of such an institution as the Congress. Therefore, it need not detail evidence of those aims and activities as they pertained to the political and social order of the United States or to the formulation of policies for the Communist organization in the United States. Nor need it list the American Communists who were active at the Congress. In discussing earlier violations of the Soviet promise, the ambassador had told the foreign commissar that the American people resented most strongly interference in their affairs, "regardless of . . . [its] nature or probable result." He had said too that strict observance of the guarantee was essential for continued normal and friendly relations. Especially in the current international situation, the United States government would regret the impairment of such relations. Nevertheless, it anticipated the most serious consequences if the Soviet government were unable or unwilling "to take appropriate measures to prevent further acts in disregard" of its solemn pledge to the United States.[23]

Two days later the acting commissar gave Bullitt the Soviet reply. This note reaffirmed the government's respect for all its obligations, including those assumed in its antipropaganda pledge, but the American complaint had cited no facts which constituted a breach of that undertaking. It was not new to the United States government that the Soviet Union could not take upon itself any responsibility for the Communist International. Since no obligation was touched, the American note had to be rejected. The Soviet government agreed that mutual noninterference in internal affairs was essential to friendly relations, and it aimed at improved collaboration in order to advance the interests of both peoples and to contribute to the establishment of universal peace.[24]

Oral protests by the British, Italian, and Latvian diplomatic representatives in Moscow were likewise rejected. In a brief press statement, the Russian ambassador in Washington took occasion to cite the vast amount of propaganda in the United States against the Soviet Union. *Pravda* carried a short, unilluminating account of the exchange of notes between Russia and the United States.[25]

The president and the secretary of state considered measures for dealing with the rejection of their protest. Again there is no record of any conversations. They barred the American ambassador's original recommendation, which would have involved Roosevelt's taking the opportunity of some speech to unmask the united front, to castigate the Soviet government's bad faith, and to announce certain diplomatic sanctions. Instead, on August 31 Secretary Hull gave a statement to the press. According to the secretary, the language of the antipropaganda promise irrefutably covered the activities of the Third International which had its headquarters in Moscow. Since the Soviet reply did not deny either the fact or the orientation of the Comintern's activities, but simply disavowed any responsibility for them, that reply was tantamount to a repudiation of Litvinov's pledge.

In view of the government's absolute power, it certainly could not plead inability to control the organization. Whether the Soviet government was going to persist in its attitude, and permit further offensive activities, remained to be seen. If so, then the friendly and official relations between the two countries would be seriously impaired, and cooperative opportunities for great good would be lost.[26]

The secretary did not invoke the diplomatic sanctions suggested by the ambassador in Moscow; the president preferred to hold these in reserve. The Soviet press made brief note of Hull's statement but gave no details. Information reached Bullitt that critical comments were unlikely because the Russians did not wish to envenom relations any further. Neither the United States nor the Soviet Union took any subsequent public or official action.[27]

Two later informal conversations touched the problem, but did not advance its solution. In the first of them, in October 1935, Ambassador Troyanovsky pressed upon the assistant chief of the State Department's Division of Eastern European Affairs the mitigating factors in the Congress' activities, especially the swing to the united front. The American official rebutted each point, particularly insisting that the new line altered tactics but not objectives. A month later, in Moscow, Ambassador Bullitt and the chief of Eastern European Affairs gathered from Litvinov that the Soviet government would not change its attitude on the Comintern and that, in view of the United States' aloofness from active interest in international affairs, friendly relations with that country were not important for the Soviet Union. The ambassador here challenged the commissar's claim that, in conversation with Roosevelt, he had effectively exempted the Third International from the operation of his pledge.[28]

In view of the impasse, however, it seems noteworthy that when the Sixth Congress of the Communist International of

Youth met at Moscow from September 25 to October 11, Soviet newspapers gave it almost no attention and appear consciously to have minimized or ignored the role played by Americans in its deliberations. Three Americans were elected to the Presidium, at least one to the Executive Committee, and one to the Secretariat. One speech by an American about conditions in the United States received a very abbreviated notice.[29] It is a fact, whatever the explanation of the fact, that no Congress of the Comintern itself was ever again held; Stalin announced the dissolution of the organization in 1943. But this does not mean it ceased to function.[30]

Russian-American relations did not substantially improve for several years. In fact they deteriorated, as the Soviet Union divided Poland with Germany, warred on Finland, and seized the Baltic States. On the positive side, it can be said that through 1940 the trade agreements were renewed and commerce expanded; but Soviet purchases never exceeded 4.3 per cent (in 1931) of total American exports. Only in 1941, when Hitler's attack linked Russia's fortunes with those of Great Britain and France, did American policy toward the Soviet Union change.[31]

Analysis of the United States' objectives in its protest must distinguish between action before and action after the Comintern met. In his informal representations prior to the meeting, the American ambassador was warning Soviet officials against any treatment of United States affairs in its deliberations. Initially he was very optimistic, because he interpreted previous postponements as concessions to foreign pressure, and he understood that Litvinov especially resented the Comintern as a handicap to his policies of conciliation and alliance. By early July of 1935 Bullitt's optimism was tempered with misgiving. Litvinov's professed ignorance of the Congress and his rather heated claim that the International was excluded from his original promise foreshadowed reliance on the fiction that the Soviet government knew nothing of the institution. At this very time, on the other hand, there was evidence of intensified efforts in some Kremlin circles to call off the meeting, and on this basis Ambassador Bullitt recommended that the reciprocal trade agreement, then ready for signing, be not delayed. At different periods in the pre-Congress phase he appears to have expected the simple cancellation of the sessions, or the omission of American affairs from its proceedings, or a vague "restraining hand" on its activities in this regard, or the complete concealment of its deliberations, or no concession whatsoever. The State Department's prima facie aim was clearly the one stated by its representative; it can only be assumed that its actual expectations were identical with his.[32]

Once the Comintern Congress had met, the Department of State sought to assure through its protest that the Soviet government would "take appropriate measures to prevent further acts in disregard of the solemn pledge given by it" to the United States. The acts particularly in question were those covered by the fourth paragraph of the Soviet undertaking: activity on Russian territory by any group aiming at a change through force in the American political and social order. If specified, this should have meant the dissolution of all real ties between the Communist International (and similar institutions) and the Communist organization in the United States, and silence on American affairs in the future deliberations of that body. The American complaint was not intended to affect any other issue outstanding with Russia. It was not a bargaining counter in the debt settlement, for example, or a justification for a previously determined sanction (as Foreign Commissar Litvinov once implied).[33]

The protest perhaps had a deeper purpose touching either the wider meaning of the Comintern or merely domestic politics. On this the documentary history of the note is not helpful. The draft first appeared as an adjunct of several memoranda in which the Eastern European Division analyzed the Congress. The secretary and the assistant secretary agreed that it should be sent, obtained the president's approval, and cabled it to Moscow. There is no indication of who first suggested a protest or of any conversations on its pros and cons.[34]

In the State Department's view, the Comintern was deadly serious about its aims. It had fomented uprisings elsewhere, although it is true they were futile. Shortly before the Congress the ambassador in Moscow recorded his conviction that proletarian upheaval was still the Soviet objective; and somewhat after the Congress the assistant chief of the Eastern European Division seconded this judgment. Moscow's policy control and financial help of the American Communist party seemed indisputable. Futhermore, at the Seventh Congress one American delegate had boasted of the Communists' leading role in the violent San Francisco strike and had promised more; other American delegates had reported progressive infiltration of various mass movements. Yet the United States could neither have regarded the Comintern's activity as an imminent threat to American security, nor have viewed a reiterated juridical promise as an effective remedy for whatever threat there was. For the State Department recognized that the American Communist apparatus was too weak to initiate a coup and was aware that eight of the thirteen countries which held Soviet anti-Comintern pledges had already complained of their violation. Bullitt, moreover, had specifically recommended against protest as being futile. In a sense, nevertheless, the United States had to protest; Russia had broken a promise and the American government as a matter of record could not let this pass. Substantively, the State Department could at best hope to harass the Communists' system of communication by driving them completely underground. The State Department's evaluation of its end would be "low," or perhaps "moderately high." One could say that the issue was less one of domestic security than of domestic tranquillity. As the note put it, the American people resent foreign interference in their internal affairs "regardless of the . . . probable result of such interference."[35]

On the other hand, the protest may have been concerned only with the appearances of Communist enterprise. Whatever the real danger, a clamorous public had to be satisfied. The pledge itself, it has been suggested,[36] was in large measure intended to make recognition palatable for some sectors of the population. When the Seventh Congress met in 1935, there were public pressures on the government to act. The secretary of state feared the Hearst press's using the occasion to mobilize opinion against Russia. One Washington newspaper attributed the protest to some dicta of Dimitrov which seemed to urge Communist support for Roosevelt. If the protest's purpose was to quiet public criticism and disavow an unwelcome political endorsement, the administration's hopes could have been high. A sufficient response would have been nonpublicity for the Comintern's treatment of American affairs, without any real break in the ties between the Third International and the American Communist movement.[37]

The Soviet government placed a high value on the concessions implied in complete fulfillment of American demands. However the Communist International had failed as a revolutionary catalyst, and however it had embarrassed the Commissariat of Foreign Affairs, the institution held potentially great advantages for Russia. It enabled the Soviet Union to operate directly on social conditions, public opinion, and governmental officials abroad, in support of its own diplomacy. The Seventh Congress itself was mobilizing international sentiment and action against Russia's most likely adversary. Moreover, the social myth of the proletarian revolution had been the heart and soul of the Soviet government's seizure and expansion of power. The universalization of this struggle very probably remained a real objective of its foreign policy. Even if it did not, the myth had imprisoned its makers. Lip service, at least, had to continue. In 1935 its abandonment would have complicated an already tense political situation. One long-time Bolshevik told Bullitt that world revolution was their religion and that they would, to a man, oppose even Stalin if he should renounce this cause.[38]

The United States did not expect the force or eloquence of its legal argument to move the Kremlin. It would, of course, stand by its own reciprocal pledge, within the limits of presidential power. Its chief reliance was on the cooling of Soviet-American relations; and this it was ready to accept. Bullitt had warned the Russian authorities that relations would be gravely prejudiced; the protest admonished that friendly relations would be precluded; the secretary publicly stated that friendship would be impaired. The United States was unwilling to employ any of the other sanctions which Bullitt suggested. As the ambassador himself argued in a reversal of position at the height of the crisis, breach of relations would have cost the United States a post in Russia, whereas it would not have cost Russia its Amtorg or other "private" agencies. The cancelling of consular exequaturs, rigorous control of Soviet visas, or demonstrative reduction of the American embassy's staff in Moscow all might have brought Soviet retaliation. Besides, similar and stronger sanctions had not yet settled the debt.[39]

The direct response to the United States' protest was completely unsatisfactory. The convocation of the Congress and the open participation in it of Americans constituted a rejection of Ambassador Bullitt's informal representations and a disappointment of even his most modest hopes. The Soviet Union's reply to the embassy's formal note conceded absolutely nothing. The Third International was to go its way unhindered, with its channels of communication intact. The curious reserve, a short time later, about things American in press reports on the Sixth Congress of the Communist International of Youth was perhaps an unacknowledged reaction to Washington's remonstrance. But this did not alter the actuality of Americans' participation in these deliberations. The Comintern's failure ever again to assemble in an All-World Congress was not a consequence of the United States' diplomatic action. The increasing complications of international affairs and the persistence of internal tensions kept the Kremlin thoroughly occupied for several years. The dissolution of the Communist International in 1943 did stem very tenuously from various nations' earlier complaints; these assured the Soviet Union that its gesture would be welcome. It was, but it deceived no one in official circles. Not even then, and certainly not before, was there any abatement of Communist activity in the United States.[40]

As anticipated, the cost to the United States of its note to Russia was chiefly the continuance and maybe the aggravation of bitterness between the two countries. Relations remained correct but cold. Failure to settle the pre-Soviet debt, various minor irritations, and possibly disappointment with the volume of trade had so disillusioned the administration that this eventuality was not an overwhelming loss.[41] Some commentators suggest that the long-run price was high, that closer ties might have saved the United States from Japan, and Europe from Germany.[42] The suggestion rests on doubtful assumptions about both nations' intentions. In the United States, isolationism still ruled; as late as 1937 a presidential bid to act was vetoed by the people. As for Russia, the observation of the American ambassador in July 1935 may have been correct: The Soviet Union was not against war, but against war which involved itself, especially when it was unprepared. A war, in its own time, of France and Britain against Germany and of the United States against Japan would simply be a welcome opportunity for the revolution.[43]

The United States did not meet Russia's negative reply with any serious consequence, as had been threatened. Herein lay an apparently unanticipated sacrifice. Whether the threat had been conscious bluff or unconscious miscalculation, the failure to follow through on it diminished prestige. The pragmatic importance of this may have been great or small, but its tendency was probably to encourage disregard of later American complaints. The country had been placed in the unhappy position of first shaking its fist, then wagging its finger.[44]

Some of the influences which contributed to the unsatisfying denouement were such as might be expected in any international dispute. American officials were careless in formulating their abstract aims and their concrete expectations, in evaluating their objectives, and in appraising suitable means and likely costs. Particularly surprising, in view of Bullitt's more perceptive dispatches, was the inflated estimate of the value which the Soviet Union placed on American friendship. The Russians had not sought the renewal of relations for its own sake. Two years after recognition they had received no loan from the United States and no rails for doubletracking the Trans-Siberian Railway; and they had now concluded, as Commissar Litvinov told the American ambassador, that the United States would take no interest or action in international affairs. Meanwhile, the world market for the Russians' exports had greatly improved; they were in the League of Nations, more friendly with Great Britain, allied with France and Czechoslovakia, and on less hostile terms with Japan. Perhaps the Soviet government shrewdly judged too that a nation which had been ready to sign a reciprocal trade agreement in July would not be ready to break diplomatic relations in August.

Other influences behind the diplomatic failure were rooted in the ideological peculiarities of the Bolshevik tradition. The episode originated in an institutional embodiment of Soviet social philosophy. The establishment within one country of propaganda agencies and even of filibusterers' organizations against another country is not new, but the official associations of such groups have seldom been as obvious or as permanent as those of the international communist movement in Moscow. To be faced with such an institution was an unfamiliar experience. Whether governmental patronage of the proletarian revolution was real and spontaneous, or fictitious but politically necessary, was irrelevant. For whatever the answer, the unyielding devotion of Soviet leadership to the preparation of this cataclysm was unfathomable for outsiders.

The United States' protest over the Seventh All-World Congress of the Communist International failed to accomplish any international purpose. Of that there is no doubt. But one wonders whether any other genuinely feasible instrument would have succeeded in these circumstances.

NOTES

[1] Merle Fainsod, *How Russia Is Ruled*, pp. 82-86, 90-97, 357-60 (Cambridge: Harvard University Press, 1953); Samuel N. Harper, *The Government of the Soviet Union*, pp. 30-32 (New York: D. Van Nostrand Company, 1938); John A. White, *The Siberian Intervention*, pp. 15-19, 259-60, 331, and *passim* (Princeton: Princeton University Press, 1950); *Papers Relating to the Foreign Relations of the United States, 1918. Russia*, Vol. 3, pp. 32-33 (Washington: Government Printing Office, 1932); Nicholas S. Timasheff, *Religion in Soviet Russia*, pp. 10-14, 21-37 (New York: Sheed and Ward, 1942).

[2] Fainsod, *How Russia Is Ruled*, pp. 137-38, 149-50; Harper, *Government of Soviet Union*, pp. 53, 65-68, 90-92.

[3] Franz Borkenau, *The Communist International*, pp. 26, 164-65, 197-98, 270, 339, 358-59, 385 (London: Faber and Faber, 1938); Michael T. Florinsky, *Toward an Understanding of the U.S.S.R.*, p. 219 (New York: The Macmillan Company, 1939); Barrington Moore, Jr., *Soviet Politics: The Dilemma of Power*, pp. 198-200 (Cambridge: Harvard University Press, 1950).

[4] Borkenau, *Communist International*, pp. 153-60, 221, 241-42, 252; Max Beloff, *The Foreign Policy of Soviet Russia, 1929-1941*, Vol. 1, pp. 46, 186 (London: Oxford University Press, 1947).

[5] Borkenau, *Communist International*, pp. 206-07, 368; Beloff, *Foreign Policy of Russia*, Vol. 1, p. 118.

[6] Harper, *Government of Soviet Union*, pp. 35-40; Alexander Baykov, *Soviet Foreign Trade*, pp. 18, 47-50 (Princeton: Princeton University Press, 1946); Robert T. Browder, *The Origins of Soviet-American Diplomacy*, pp. 46-47 (Princeton: Princeton University Press, 1953).

[7] Fainsod, *How Russia Is Ruled*, pp. 103, 148, 366-67. The Kirov assassination is attributed to Stalin by Alexander Orlov, *The Secret History of Stalin's Crimes*, pp. 10-24 (New York: Random House, 1953). Orlov's version was perhaps confirmed by Khrushchev in his Special Report to the 20th Congress of the

Communist Party of the Soviet Union; see Nikita S. Khrushchev, *The Crimes of the Stalin Era*, pp. S22-S23 (New York: The New Leader, 1956).

[8] Beloff, *Foreign Policy of Russia*, Vol. 1, pp. 61-68, 77-82, 97-103, 167-68, 171-75; DS #861.5017 Living Conditions/769, ambassador at Moscow to Department, October 2, 1934.

[9] Beloff, *Foreign Policy of Russia*, Vol. 1, pp. 112-15, 135-37, 151-52, 155-56, 188-89; Moore, *Soviet Politics*, pp. 354-56; Browder, *Soviet-American Diplomacy*, pp. 55-59, 65-66, 72-73, 94-95, 128.

[10] *Ibid.*, pp. 12-13, 16-18, 22, 33-34; Mikhail V. Condoide, *Russian-American Trade*, pp. 78-81, 84 (Columbus: Ohio State University Bureau of Business Research, 1946).

[11] Browder, *Soviet-American Diplomacy*, pp. 21-32, 36-48, 68-69, 81-82, 103-04, 108-12, 219; William A. Williams, *American-Russian Relations, 1781-1947*, pp. 210-18 (New York: Rinehart and Company, 1952); Meno Lovenstein, *American Opinion of Soviet Russia*, pp. 107-09, 137-40 (Washington: American Council on Public Affairs, 1941).

[12] Browder, *Soviet-American Diplomacy*, pp. 99-101, 104-07, 113-14, 116-18, 128, 131-34; Cordell Hull, *The Memoirs of Cordell Hull*, Vol. 1, pp. 294-301 (New York: The Macmillan Company, 1948); *Papers Relating to the Foreign Relations of the United States. The Soviet Union, 1933-1939* [henceforth cited as *Soviet Union*], pp. 6-18, 28-37 (Washington: Government Printing Office, 1952); Henry Morgenthau, Jr., "The Morgenthau Diaries, III," *Collier's* 120:20-21, October 11, 1947.

[13] Browder, *Soviet-American Diplomacy*, pp. 135-41; *Soviet Union*, pp. 26-27.

[14] Browder, *Soviet-American Diplomacy*, pp. 131-32, 143-44, 150, 174; Hull, *Memoirs*, Vol. 1, pp. 299-301; *Soviet Union*, pp. 28-29.

[15] Browder, *Soviet-American Diplomacy*, pp. 193-94, 197-202.

[16] *Ibid.*, pp. 179-91; Hull, *Memoirs*, Vol. 1, p. 303; *Soviet Union*, p. 158.

[17] Browder, *Soviet-American Diplomacy*, pp. 176-78, 194-95, 225; Condoide, *Russian-American Trade*, pp. 85-88.

[18] *Soviet Union*, pp. 132-34, 156-57; DS # #861.00 Congress, Communist International, VII/2 and 6, dispatches of September 26 and October 2, 1934; #861.5017 Living Conditions/769, dispatch of October 2, 1934, pp. 11, 14-15.

[19] *Soviet Union*, pp. 219-23.

[20] *Ibid.*, pp. 228-44, 257; DS # #861.00 Congress, Communist International, VII/25, 28, 34, 37, 38, 41, 47, 64, 65, and 66, dispatches of July 29 to August 22, 1935; # #861.00 Congress, Communist International, VII/99 and 114, memoranda from Eastern European Division to secretary, August 2 and 20, 1935. Some of the data also appears in *VII Congress of the Communist International: Abridged Stenographic Record of the Proceedings*, pp. 6, 83-88 (Moscow: Foreign Languages Publishing House, 1939).

[21] Williams, *American-Russian Relations*, pp. 239-41 (which is, however, notably inaccurate); DS #861.00 Congress, Communist International, VII/124, chargé at Riga to Department, December 24, 1936, pp. 339-40; this document is an analytic review of the proceedings of the Congress.

[22] *Soviet Union*, pp. 244-49; DS # #861.00 Congress, Communist International, VII/70, 71, 73, 79, 99, and 114. These are, respectively, assistant secretary to

president and reply, August 22, 1935; ambassador at Moscow to Department and reply, August 24, 1935; two memoranda, Eastern European Division to secretary, August 2 and 20, 1935.

[23] *Soviet Union*, pp. 250-51.

[24] *Ibid.*, pp. 251-53.

[25] *Ibid.*, pp. 242, 253-56.

[26] *Ibid.*, pp. 246-48, 253-54, 257-59.

[27] *Ibid.*, p. 259.

[28] *Ibid.*, pp. 260-62, 264-65.

[29] *Ibid.*, pp. 260, 262-64, 266-68; DS # #800.00B Congress, Communist International of Youth/20 and 23, dispatches, September 27 and October 26, 1935.

[30] Hull, *Memoirs*, Vol. 2, pp. 1251-52; Franz Borkenau, *European Communism*, pp. 282-83 (New York: Harper and Brothers, 1953).

[31] Hull, *Memoirs*, Vol. 1, pp. 657-58, 685, 701-02, 704-10; Vol. 2, p. 967; Condoide, *Russian-American Trade*, pp. 91, 95-96.

[32] *Soviet Union*, pp. 156-58, 222-24; DS # #861.5017 Living Conditions/769, 861.00 Congress, Communist International, VII/2 and 6, dispatches of October 2, September 26, and October 2, 1934. Regarding the attribution of postponement to fear of foreign repercussions, however, the last cited document carries a longhand notation: "Time will tell!" A similar note appears on a memorandum reporting this information to the undersecretary, #861.00 Congress, Communist International, VII/8, November 1, 1934. Both comments appear to have been made by the assistant chief of the Eastern European Affairs Division.

[33] *Soviet Union*, pp. 158, 250-51. Although the Eastern European Affairs Division felt that other clauses of the pledge were violated, these were not pressed; see DS #861.00 Congress, Communist International, VII/114, memorandum for secretary, August 20, 1935 (Memorandum "C").

[34] DS # #861.00 Congress, Communist International, VII/114, 70, and 71, memorandum from Eastern European Affairs Division to secretary, August 20; assistant secretary to president and reply, August 22, 1935; *Soviet Union*, p. 249.

[35] *Ibid.*, pp. 224-27, 245-46, 251, 260-62; DS #811.00B/1608, special memorandum (one of a series) by Eastern European Affairs Division on problems of recognition, October 20, 1933, pp. 40-44, 47-49, 56, 73-74, 97-98; #861.00 Congress, Communist International, VII/114, memorandum from Eastern European Affairs Division to secretary, August 20, 1933 (Memorandum "A"); Hull, *Memoirs*, Vol. 1, pp. 300, 305-06; Vol. 2, pp. 1288-89.

[36] Browder, *Soviet-American Diplomacy*, pp. 143-44; compare pp. 103-04.

[37] *Soviet Union*, pp. 241-42, 261; Browder, *Soviet-American Diplomacy*, p. 209, n. 34; "Moscow Activities Protested by Woll," *New York Times*, August 4, 1935; "Roosevelt Held Choice of Reds," (Washington) *Evening Star*, August 26, 1935.

[38] *Soviet Union*, p. 225; Beloff, *Foreign Policy of Russia*, Vol. 1, p. 93; Borkenau, *Communist International*, pp. 332-33, 388-89, 425-26; Browder, *Soviet-American Diplomacy*, p. 157; Harper, *Government of Soviet Union*, pp. 177-78, 193.

[39] *Soviet Union*, pp. 133, 156-58, 170-71, 222, 244-51, 259; Browder, *Soviet-American Diplomacy*, pp. 188, 221.

[40] *Soviet Union*, pp. 252-53, 262-68; DS # #800.00B Communist International of Youth/20 and 23, dispatches of September 27 and October 26, 1935; William C. Bullitt, *The Great Globe Itself*, p. 70 (New York: Charles Scribner's Sons, 1946); Hull, *Memoirs*, Vol. 2, p. 1252; Borkenau, *European Communism*, pp. 279-80, 282-83.

[41] *Soviet Union*, pp. 294-96; Browder, *Soviet-American Diplomacy*, pp. 212-13.

[42] Williams, *American-Russian Relations*, pp. 240-41; Louis Fischer, *Men and Politics*, pp. 307-08 (New York: Duell, Sloan and Pearce, 1941).

[43] *Soviet Union*, pp. 225-27.

[44] Fischer, *Men and Politics*, pp. 306-07; "A Diplomatic Deadlock," editorial, *New York Times*, August 29, 1935; Samuel N. Harper, *The Russia I Believe in*, p. 219 (Chicago: The University of Chicago Press, 1945).

CHAPTER IX

The Pattern
and Its Meaning

The focal question of the present study is whether and in what circumstances diplomatic protest is an effective instrument of foreign policy. The search for the answer has been carried on through a twofold examination of American experience: a superficial survey of many cases and an intensive scrutiny of a few. The double task is finished. It is necessary only to trace out clearly the lines of whatever pattern may have emerged and to seek its meaning.

The conclusions of the general survey need only the briefest restatement. With respect to simple effectiveness, about 55 per cent of the United States' diplomatic protests appear to have achieved their stated purpose, while 25 per cent assuredly did not. In 20 per cent of the instances studied, the results were either impossible to uncover in the published documents (uncertain), or impossible to assess decisively (doubtful). Whenever the absolute numbers were at all large, the proportion has been roughly the same for all subject-matter categories, at most times, and with most recipient nations. The United States, incidentally, has approached the Great Powers as readily and as successfully as it has the small powers.

Circumstances adversely influencing the record of effectiveness were principally revolution and war. Nations torn by rebellion have tended to respond unsatisfactorily to representations aimed at protection of nationals or at maintaining reasonable conditions of commerce. Nations involved in warfare with third parties have tended to reject remonstrances touching conditions of commerce or the complainant's national security (but in these instances threats under the latter heading were never really serious). If the impact of these circumstances is analyzed, strong support emerges for the generalization that nations do weigh profit and loss; governments show resistance when the cost of yielding to a protest is high relative to the gain which yielding will bring. Modest support emerges for the generalization that nations respond readily to the requirements of established international usage which carry assurance of reciprocal treatment, as in cases concerned with diplomatic and consular immunities.

Although the mere presentation of the case histories has afforded insight into the operation of protest, comparison of them should be much more helpful in the derivation of useful general observations.

Some pervasive elements of the pattern concern the mechanics of policy making. In facing incidents which might call for diplomatic action, the American government has usually given ample consideration to its problem, but it has shown an unfortunate inclination toward afterthought rather than forethought. In the episodes with Rumania, China, and Canada, the essential complaint was made first and only later was attention given to measures for meeting resistance. The same thing was true with two of the three major complaints to Great Britain. The prior consideration of an approach to the Soviet Union was hasty. The programing of action has consistently been far removed from the logical "model" set forth in Chapter 2. In itself this is not a defect, but there has been little fresh analysis, at least at the outset, of any situation in terms of ends and means. Instead, action has followed a stimulus-response scheme, based either on a standing policy—requiring, for example, quick protest to defend petroleum interests abroad—or on a deeply ingrained reverence for the law. Behavior of this kind is understandable in a case like John O'Brien's where the United States' contention was unquestionable and the issue was not overwhelmingly important. But there should have been more circumspection when the ramifications were as far-reaching as those of neutral rights in a major war.

Other elements of the emerging pattern touch substantive policy objectives. The United States has rarely attempted through diplomatic protest to achieve any purpose not intrinsically related to its prima facie demand. In no case was the complaint intended, for example, to neutralize the other nation's remonstrances to the American government or to enhance the United States' strategic situation. The notes to Great Britain in 1914-1915 perhaps had as partial objectives a nebulous bargain to assist American businessmen and the establishment of President Wilson's acceptability as mediator. But dominantly here, and exclusively in other instances, the positive ulterior purpose was merely an extension of the prima facie aim: the protection of all nationals or the general maintenance of conditions for trade. Even within the framework of prima facie ends, forethought was neglected. The American government made virtually no effort to specify in advance what partial concessions might be regarded as an adequate response. Wilson made a vague gesture in this direction after the British reply to the protest of December 1914. Calculations on this aspect of policy were likewise delayed, for more or less lengthy periods, in dealing with the Rumanian Mining Act, the Nanking incident, and the mistreatment of John O'Brien. The prospect of outright failure was seldom faced squarely in the initial phase of the different international episodes.

This study has deliberately prescinded from the domestic political aims of diplomatic protest. From the casual indications of the cases investigated, however, it appears that these are sometimes highly relevant, sometimes nonexistent. No such objectives motivated the note to China; they were mildly operative in the approach to Rumania and Canada; they were very important, and maybe primary, in the notes to Great Britain and Russia.

In the estimate of probable costs, lack of forethought again characterized American action. The closest approximation to a full advance consideration of likely sacrifices appeared in Ambassador Bullitt's prior advices to the State Department on the Comintern incident. President Wilson did a little of this kind of thinking in early 1915. When the United States did get around to estimating the price of backing up its complaints, it anticipated little more than the intrinsic costs. Curiously, even in this regard American policy makers paid little attention to the implications which their legal arguments held for the country's own future conduct. Only in the O'Brien case was this facet canvassed at an early date, and incompletely at that. It was comparatively late in World War I when Secretary Lansing foresaw strategic handicaps in the American contentions vis-à-vis Great Britain; and the Nanking incident was virtually settled by the time the State Department's Far Eastern Division noted possible embarrassments on protection of nationals, arising from American federalism.

The United States did not principally rely on the abstract persuasive force of its arguments. The implicit threat of strained relations was felt to carry the weight, but always as linked with the recipient's circumstances. In other words, the total situation brought to bear on other governments additional pressure which Washington did not create but on which it could capitalize through mere coolness. In this respect, there were miscalculations as to the degree but not as to the fact. Great Britain's dire necessity was not fully appreciated. Russia's anxieties were overestimated. The United States discerned with substantial accuracy, however, that Rumania, China, and Canada needed its support more than it needed theirs.

The United States shied away from every resort to active sanctions. These were regarded sometimes as unfeasible, sometimes as inefficacious, almost always as too expensive. Vis-à-vis the Chinese Nationalists, the diplomatic sanction of nonrecognition was used; vis-à-vis the Soviet government, that of a strong statement to the press. Only with Rumania did action approach coercion, when the temporary recall of the American minister was followed by the obstruction of loans and investments. Incidentally, in dealing with China and Russia the United States indulged in overstatement which verged on bluff.

In anticipating costs, much more than in formulating aims, ulterior considerations were influential. Persistently, sacrifices which the American government was unwilling to make inhibited its action. The fear of economic depression and of war itself in 1914 and the quest for Chinese stability in 1927, especially as against Communism, moderated the pressure on Great Britain and Nationalist China. A vague belief in the desirability of international cooperation operated similarly, but much less strongly, in dealing with Canada and the Soviet Union. By contrast, where other American political and economic interests were least vulnerable, in the Rumanian case, the United States used the most stringent of the sanctions recorded.

In the instances cited, American officials showed no naiveté about the power aspect of international relations. They did make some erroneous judgments of detail, but the significant weakness, if there was one, was in the will, not in the intellect. As things actually turned out, the United States did not clearly sacrifice any large value for its protests. The possible failure to win from England all that might have been won and the alienation of Russia at a crucial period in history appear as losses too speculative to be significant. The considerable concessions made to China after 1928 were carefully dissociated from the settlement of the Nanking incident. Loss of prestige and the swallowing of pride had to be faced in dealing with the British, the Chinese, and the Soviets, most impressively with the last-named. But this did no serious harm to American spiritual or material interests.

The concessions which the United States actually won came slowly in every case: a year with China and Canada, and five years with Rumania. Patience is obviously necessary in the use of diplomatic protest. Substantively, Washington achieved virtually complete success with Rumania, China, and Canada. It failed substantially but not totally with Great Britain. It accomplished nothing with the Soviet Union. In the successful cases, United States' expectations had been firm; the valuation of objectives, on its part, had run from low to moderately high; the valuation of concession, on the part of the recipients, from moderately high to high. The United States' anticipations on the main issues of neutral rights, apart from the legal purpose, were not sanguine. The English placed an extremely high value on any surrender; but here the minor gains, to which moderate importance was assigned by both parties, roughly corresponded with the protesting nation's hopes. American pessimism regarding Russia was not an expectation of total failure. In Soviet eyes, partial concessions ought not to have had the same high value that a complete sundering of the Comintern's ties with the American Communist party assuredly had. Yet somehow this is the way things worked.

From the case studies, then, as from the general survey, success seems a more likely outcome of protest than failure. The studies additionally indicate that the achievements may be substantial and quite highly valued by the recipient nation. Moreover, technical rationality may mark the use of the instrument even in substantial failure. The case studies do not confirm the judgment that the Great Powers will bow to diplomatic protest as readily as small ones; but it must be remembered that with Britain, at least, a concession of exceptionally high value was at stake.

In no instance, not even in so simple a matter as that of
John O'Brien, was the American protest wholly efficacious
by itself. With respect to the circumstances that contribute to
success, this is noteworthy. In the O'Brien case, even a common
juristic heritage and a strong argument from traditional international practice had to be supplemented by Canada's own
recognition of the wider implications which the United States'
friendship and hostility held. Purely diplomatic sanctions seem
almost always to get their strength from the concrete situation
of the recipient. Confirmation may be found in Nationalist
China's eager quest of American recognition and in Great
Britain's self-confessed "timidity," for all the lack of concession, about tightening the blockade. Above all, it may be found
in the history of the Rumanian Mining Act, wherein the United
States accomplished its purpose only by clinging tenaciously
to its position until the financially embarrassed Bratianu government fell from power. The operative relationship of the
legal to the political function of diplomatic protest appeared
with sufficient clarity to deserve special mention. Formal American objection founded postwar claims against Great Britain,
kept open some questions on the Rumanian Mining Act until
a friendly government succeeded the Liberals, and helped move
China toward agreement on satisfactory terms.

The case studies demonstrate nothing conclusive about the
type of approach which is most likely to win concessions. In two
successful instances the American representations were severe,
but with Canada they were mild and sympathetic. On the other
hand, neither the stern attitude toward the Soviet Union nor the
indulgent attitude toward Great Britain accomplished much;
in the latter case, it was possibly quite harmful.

The suggestion, derived from theoretical analysis, that
the protesting nation's capacity for action influences results
was neither confirmed nor discredited. In dealing with China
and Canada, the United States' own values strongly inhibited

the action of which the country was abstractly capable; yet its protests were eminently successful. This capacity—or, more properly, the lack of it—had more importance in the difficulties with England and Russia, since here the concrete situation of the United States virtually nullified abstract persuasive capabilities. A lack of leverage for the United States also contributed to failure. Resources were not wanting, but a point of application was. High cost and uncertain efficacy made the American government unwilling to use particular measures; Great Britain and the Soviet Union were not vulnerable to the sort of action that was left.

A correlation of sorts appeared between disparity of basic resources, enormously favorable to the United States, and successful diplomatic action. Curiously, the influence of this factor was passive rather than active; greater resources gave the protesting country superior staying power vis-à-vis Rumania and China. Great Britain, on the other hand, employed its more nearly equal reserves to counteract American pressure.

In all five cases, resistance to American demands was partly but strongly motivated by the domestic politics of the recipient. The mere presence of such considerations is not decisive, for in only two cases, in both of which the central issue had considerable weight of its own, was resistance equivalent to failure. But the tendency of these considerations is to increase, in the eyes of the government to which representations are directed, the aggregate value of the concession asked. Inattention to this fact, when the international aspect of the matter did not seem critical, occasioned some surprises for American policy makers. The phenomenon appears most clearly in Canada, where acquiescence in an intrinsically trivial request was temporarily blocked by an unblushing anxiety for its possible effect on the voters. This feature of the studies confirms the earlier judgment that the size of the request, as viewed by the recipient country in the given situation, is highly significant.

The cases do not necessarily support the supposition that more effective domestic control in the recipient country makes for more satisfactory response to protest. Nationalist China's government had only tenuous authority within its jurisdiction, yet it did what it could to comply with American demands. Soviet Russia's government had virtually absolute power, yet it did nothing.

Beyond its meaning for practical effectiveness, the pattern also has significance for the theory of international relations. On the American side, although considerations involving power were present in three instances, they were marginal and late in making their appearance. President Wilson recognized early that the World War would inevitably affect his country's position in the world, but only after eight months did the idea that the Allies' fight was America's become a factor in his decisions. Awareness of the opportunity to check Russian influence in China became operative only some time after the protest over Nanking. The power factor consistently exercised its influence less as the object of active search than as a restraint on the quest for other values. This is not to say that moral ideals anywhere exercised an overriding influence. They were at work, however, and were most strikingly operative in restraining American action vis-à-vis China and in defining United States objectives vis-à-vis Canada. The American unwillingness to use any severe sanctions is a recurring feature of the cases. If in this regard the case studies do confirm in depth the results of the general survey, the record speaks well for the accomplishments of non-coercive instruments in suitable circumstances.

The power factor did play a dominant role in Great Britain's response to American pressure, and the gravity of the crisis blurred juridical perceptions. But within the British community, power seems to have remained subordinate to other values. In the other cases the motivating force for the recipient nations was notably less and sometimes completely negligible.

On the basis of American experience, therefore, diplomatic protest seems likely to succeed more often than not, although absolutely vital concessions are not to be expected. The key to its effectiveness lies not so much in the force of its argumentation as in the implicit threat of diplomatic chill. This means that much depends on the value which the recipient, in the concrete circumstances, places on United States friendship. A careful look at these circumstances is always essential in gauging the likely response and in preparing early for needed compromises or sanctions. The success of protest is, moreover, the success of an essentially noncoercive instrument. While power relations are part of the background in almost every instance, their influence is usually indirect and passive, operating through the total situation to inhibit action or furnish immunity. Legal ideals, ethical attitudes, economic ends, and personal ambitions meantime play significant roles. A complete theory of international politics, then, demands a thorough inquiry reaching beyond power to the numerous facets of social value—the things, the concepts, the sentiments and attitudes prized by communities—which do limit resort to violence. Fully understood, these may or may not make force the permanent servant of man in international society.

---

1. Manuscripts

Edward M. House Collection. Yale University Library.
United States Department of State Files. United States National Archives.

2. Published Diplomatic Papers

United States Department of State. *Papers Relating to the Foreign Relations of the United States with the Annual Message of the President.* Washington: Government Printing Office, 1861- (Annual. Imprint varies.)

———— *Papers Relating to the Foreign Relations of the United States. The Lansing Papers*, Vol. 1. Washington: Government Printing Office, 1939.

———— *Papers Relating to the Foreign Relations of the United States, 1918. Russia*, Vol. 3. Washington: Government Printing Office, 1932.

———— *Papers Relating to the Foreign Relations of the United States. The Soviet Union, 1933-1939.* Washington: Government Printing Office, 1952.

3. Books and Periodicals

Almond, Gabriel A. *The American People and Foreign Policy.* New York: Harcourt, Brace and Company, 1950.

American Petroleum Institute Bulletin 5:1, March 7, 1924.

Baker, Ray S. *Woodrow Wilson: Life and Letters*, Vols. 5 and 6. Garden City: Doubleday, Doran and Company, 1935-1937.

———— and William E. Dodd, *The Public Papers of Woodrow Wilson: The New Democracy*, 2 vols. New York: Harper and Brothers, 1926.

Basch, Antonin. *The Danube Basin and the German Economic Sphere.* New York: Columbia University Press, 1943.

Baykov, Alexander. *Soviet Foreign Trade*. Princeton: Princeton University Press, 1946.

Beloff, Max. *The Foreign Policy of Soviet Russia, 1929-1941*, Vol. 1. London: Oxford University Press, 1947.

Bemis, Samuel F. *A Diplomatic History of the United States*, fourth edition. New York: Henry Holt and Company, 1955.

Borchard, Edwin M. "The Neutrality Claims against Great Britain." *American Journal of International Law* 21:764-68, October 1927.

Borg, Dorothy. *American Policy and the Chinese Revolution, 1925-1928*. New York: American Institute of Pacific Relations, 1947.

Borkenau, Franz. *The Communist International*. London: Faber and Faber, 1938.

———— *European Communism*. New York: Harper and Brothers, 1953.

Brokaw, Albert D. "Oil." *Foreign Affairs* 6:89-105, October 1927.

Browder, Robert P. *The Origins of Soviet-American Diplomacy*. Princeton: Princeton University Press, 1953.

Brown, George W., editor. *Canada*. Berkeley: University of California Press, 1950.

Bruel, Erik. "La Protestation au droit international." *Revue de droit international* 10:364-70, 1932.

Bryan, William J. and Mary B. Bryan. *The Memoirs of William Jennings Bryan*. Philadelphia: John C. Winston Company, 1925.

Bryn-Jones, David. *Frank B. Kellogg*. New York: G. P. Putnam's Sons, 1937.

Bullitt, William C. *The Great Globe Itself*. New York: Charles Scribner's Sons, 1946.

Callahan, James M. *American Foreign Policy in Canadian Relations*. New York: The Macmillan Company, 1937.

Calvo, Carlos. *Dictionnaire de droit international public et privé*, Vol. 2. Berlin: Puttkammer and Mühlbrecht, 1885.

Canada, Department of Justice. *Report of the Superintendent of Penitentiaries re Kingston Penitentiary Disturbances, 1932*. Ottawa: F. A. Acland, 1933.

Canada, Royal Commission to Investigate the Penal System of Canada. *Report of the Royal Commission to Investigate the Penal System of Canada*. Ottawa: J. O. Patenaude, 1938.

Canadian Annual Review of Public Affairs, 1934. Toronto: Canadian Review Company, 1935.

Carr, Edward H. *The Twenty Years' Crisis, 1919-1939,* second edition. London: The Macmillan Company, 1949.

Chang, H. H. *Chiang Kai-shek.* Garden City: Doubleday, Doran and Company, 1944.

Chapman, H. Owen. *The Chinese Revolution, 1926-1927.* London: Constable and Company, 1928.

Clark, Charles U. *United Roumania.* New York: Dodd, Mead and Company, 1932.

Clark, Evans, editor. *Boycotts and Peace.* New York: Harper and Brothers, 1932.

Clark, Grover. *Economic Rivalries in China.* New Haven: Yale University Press, 1932.

Clokie, Hugh McD. "The Machinery of Government." In George W. Brown, editor, *Canada,* pp. 297-313. Berkeley: University of California Press, 1950.

Clyde, Paul H., editor. *United States Policy toward China: Diplomatic and Public Documents, 1839-1939.* Durham: The Duke University Press, 1940.

Condoide, Mikhail V. *Russian-American Trade.* Columbus: Ohio State University Bureau of Business Research, 1946.

Cussy, Ferdinand de. *Dictionnaire ou manuel lexique du diplomate et du consul.* Leipzig: F. A. Brockhaus, 1846.

Dahl, Robert A. *Congress and Foreign Policy.* New York: Harcourt, Brace and Company, 1950.

———— and Charles E. Lindblom. *Politics, Economics and Welfare.* New York: Harper and Brothers, 1953.

Denny, Ludwell. *We Fight for Oil.* New York: Alfred A. Knopf, 1928.

Dulles, John Foster. "Practicable Sanctions." In Evans Clark, editor, *Boycotts and Peace,* pp. 17-22. New York: Harper and Brothers, 1932.

L'Economiste roumain nos. 2-6, pp. 1-51, 1924.

Fainsod, Merle. *How Russia Is Ruled.* Cambridge: Harvard University Press, 1953.

Feis, Herbert. *Petroleum and American Foreign Policy.* Stanford: Food Research Institute, 1944.

Fischer, Louis. *Men and Politics*. New York: Duell, Sloan and Pearce, 1941.

———— *The Soviets in World Affairs*, second edition, Vol. 2. Princeton: Princeton University Press, 1951.

Florinsky, Michael T. *Toward an Understanding of the U.S.S.R.* New York: The Macmillan Company, 1939.

Foulke, Roland R. *Treatise on International Law*, Vol. 1. Philadelphia: John C. Winston Company, 1920.

Garner, James W. "Violations of Maritime Law by the Allied Powers during the World War." *American Journal of International Law* 25:26-49, January 1931.

Glazebrook, George P. de T. *A History of Canadian External Relations*. New York: Oxford University Press, 1950.

Grey, Edward. *Twenty-Five Years, 1892-1916*, Vol. 2. New York: Frederick A. Stokes Company, 1925.

Guichard, Louis. *The Naval Blockade, 1914-18*. London: Philip Allan and Company, 1930.

Gwynn, Stephen, editor. *The Letters and Friendships of Sir Cecil Spring-Rice*, Vol. 2. Boston: Houghton Mifflin Company, 1929.

Hanna, Margaret M. and Alice M. Ball. *Style Manual of the Department of State*. Washington: Government Printing Office, 1937.

Harper, Samuel N. *The Government of the Soviet Union*. New York: D. Van Nostrand Company, 1938.

———— *The Russia I Believe in*. Chicago: The University of Chicago Press, 1945.

Heilborn, Paul. *System des Völkerrechts*. Berlin: Julius Springer, 1896.

Hendrick, Burton J. *The Life and Letters of Walter H. Page*. 3 vols. Garden City: Doubleday, Page and Company, 1925-1926.

Hilsman, Roger, Jr. "Intelligence and Policy-Making in Foreign Affairs." *World Politics* 5:1-45, October 1952.

Hindmarsh, Albert E. *Force in Peace*. Cambridge: Harvard University Press, 1933.

Hobart, Alice T. *Within the Walls of Nanking*. London: Jonathan Cape, 1928.

Hoffman, Karl. *Oelpolitik*. Berlin: Ring-Verlag, 1927.

Holcombe, Arthur N. *The Chinese Revolution*. Cambridge: Harvard University Press, 1930.

Hornbeck, Stanley K. *China Today: Political. World Peace Foundation Pamphlets*, Vol. 10, pp. 413-566. Boston: World Peace Foundation, 1927.

Houston, David F. *Eight Years with Wilson's Cabinet*, Vol. 1. Garden City: Doubleday, Page and Company, 1926.

"How China Loses Her Friends." *Far Eastern Review* 23:394, September 1927.

Hull, Cordell. *The Memoirs of Cordell Hull*. 2 vols. New York: The Macmillan Company, 1948.

International Prison Commission. *Improvements in Penal Administration: Standard Minimum Rules for the Treatment of Prisoners.* Series of League of Nations Publications IV, Social 1930 IV 10. Geneva: League of Nations, 1930.

Isaacs, Harold R. *The Tragedy of the Chinese Revolution*, revised edition. Stanford: Stanford University Press, 1951.

Kaplan, Morton A. "An Introduction to the Strategy of Statecraft." *World Politics* 4:548-76, July 1952.

Keenleyside, Hugh L. and Gerard S. Brown. *Canada and the United States*, revised edition. New York: Alfred A. Knopf, 1952.

Khrushchev, Nikita S. *The Crimes of the Stalin Era* (Special Report to the 20th Congress of the Communist Party of the Soviet Union). New York: The New Leader, 1956.

Kunz, Josef L. "Protest im Völkerrecht." In Karl Strupp, editor, *Wörterbuch des Völkerrechts und der Diplomatie*, Vol. 2, pp. 329-30. Berlin: Walter de Gruyter, 1925.

Langer, Robert. *Seizure of Territory*. Princeton: Princeton University Press, 1947.

Lansing, Robert. *The War Memoirs of Robert Lansing*. Indianapolis: Bobbs-Merrill Company, 1935.

Lasswell, Harold D. and Abraham Kaplan. *Power and Society*. New Haven: Yale University Press, 1950.

Lerner, Daniel and Harold D. Lasswell, editors. *The Policy Sciences*. Stanford: Stanford University Press, 1951.

Link, Arthur A. *Wilson: The Struggle for Neutrality, 1914-1915*. Princeton: Princeton University Press, 1960.

Liszt, Franz von. *Völkerrecht*, twelfth edition revised by Max Fleischmann. Berlin: Julius Springer, 1925.

Lloyd George, David. *War Memoirs of David Lloyd George*, Vol. 2. Boston: Little, Brown and Company, 1933.

Logio, George C. *Rumania*. Manchester: Sheratt and Hughes, 1932.

Lovenstein, Meno. *American Opinion of Soviet Russia*. Washington: American Council on Public Affairs, 1941.

McCamy, James L. *The Administration of American Foreign Affairs*. New York: Alfred A. Knopf, 1950.

McGuire, Carl. "Point Four and the National Power of the United States." *American Journal of Economics and Sociology* 11:343-56, April 1952.

McLaughlin, C. H. "Neutral Rights under International Law in the European War, 1939-1941." *Minnesota Law Review* 26:1-49 and 177-212, December 1941 and January 1942.

Madgearu, Virgil. *Rumania's New Economic Policy*. London: P. S. King and Son, 1930.

Manoliou, Florin E. *La Réconstruction économique et financière de la Roumanie et les partis politiques*. Paris: Librarie Universitaire J. Gambier, 1931.

Marshall, Charles B. "The Nature of Foreign Policy." *United States Department of State Bulletin* 26:415-20, March 17, 1952.

Martens, Charles de. *Le Guide diplomatique*, fourth edition, Vol. 2. Paris: Gavelot Jeune, 1851.

May, Ernest R. *The World War and American Isolation, 1914-1917*. Cambridge: Harvard University Press, 1959.

Meisel, H. *Cours de style diplomatique*, Vol. 1. Dresden: Chr. Arnold, 1823.

The Mining Law [of 1929]. Bucharest: Cultura Nationala, 1929.

Moore, Barrington, Jr. *Soviet Politics: The Dilemma of Power*. Cambridge: Harvard University Press, 1950.

Moreuil, L. J. A. *Dictionnaire des chancelleries*, Vol. 2. Paris: Jules Renouard, 1855.

Morgenthau, Hans J. *Politics among Nations*, third edition. New York: Alfred A. Knopf, 1960.

——— *Scientific Man vs. Power Politics*. Chicago: The University of Chicago Press, 1946.

Morgenthau, Henry, Jr. "The Morgenthau Diaries, III." *Collier's* 120:20-21 and 72-79, October 11, 1947.

Morris, Henry C. "Development of the Foreign Oil Policy of the United States." *Annals of the American Academy of Political and Social Science* 116:262-63, November 1924.

Morrissey, Alice M. *The American Defense of Neutral Rights, 1914-1917.* Cambridge: Harvard University Press, 1939.

Nicolson, Harold. *Diplomacy,* second edition. London: Oxford University Press, 1950.

Notter, Harley. *The Origins of the Foreign Policy of Woodrow Wilson.* Baltimore: The Johns Hopkins Press, 1937.

Noyes, Alexander D. *Financial Chapters of the War.* New York: Charles Scribner's Sons, 1916.

Oppenheim, Lassa. *International Law,* seventh edition edited by Hersch Lauterpacht, Vol. 1. New York: Longmans, Green and Company, 1952.

Orlov, Alexander. *The Secret History of Stalin's Crimes.* New York: Random House, 1953.

Parkinson, J. F. "Economics." In F. H. Soward and others, *Canada in World Affairs: The Pre-War Years,* pp. 175-224. New York: Oxford University Press, 1941.

Pasvolsky, Leo. *The Economic Nationalism of the Danubian States.* London: George Allen and Unwin, 1928.

"Penitentiary Riots." *Canadian Forum* 13:84, December 1932.

Pfluger, Franz. *Die einseitigen Rechtsgeschäfte im Völkerrechts.* Zürich: Schulthess, 1936.

Pilpel, Georges. *Le Pétrole en Roumanie.* Strasbourg: Editions Universitaires de Strasbourg, 1925.

Pizanty, Mihail. *Petroleum in Roumania.* Bucharest: Cultura Nationala, 1930.

"Political Prisoners." *Canadian Forum* 13:82, December 1932.

Pollard, Robert T. *China's Foreign Relations.* New York: The Macmillan Company, 1933.

"Prisoners and Punishment." *Canadian Forum* 14:4, October 1933.

Pusey, Merlo J. *Charles Evans Hughes,* Vol. 2. New York: The Macmillan Company, 1951.

Report of the Standard Oil Company (Incorporated in New Jersey) for the Year Ended December 31, 1928.

Rivier, Alphonse. *Principes du droit des gens*, Vol. 2. Paris: Arthur Rousseau, 1896.

Roberts, Henry L. *Rumania*. New Haven: Yale University Press, 1951.

Roucek, Joseph S. *Contemporary Roumania and Her Problems*. Stanford: Stanford University Press, 1932.

Schmitt, Bernadotte E. *The Coming of the War, 1914*, Vol. 1. New York: Charles Scribner's Sons, 1930.

Scott, James Brown, editor. *The Declaration of London, February 26, 1909*. New York: Oxford University Press, 1919.

VII Congress of the Communist International: Abridged Stenographic Record of the Proceedings. Moscow: Foreign Languages Publishing House, 1939.

Seymour, Charles, editor. *The Intimate Papers of Colonel House*, Vols. 1 and 2. Boston: Houghton Mifflin Company, 1926.

Siney, Marion C. *The Allied Blockade of Germany, 1914-1916*. Ann Arbor: The University of Michigan Press, 1957.

Soward, F. H. "Politics." In F. H. Soward and others, *Canada in World Affairs: The Pre-War Years*, pp. 3-171. New York: Oxford University Press, 1941.

―――― and others. *Canada in World Affairs: The Pre-War Years*. New York: Oxford University Press, 1941.

Spykman, Nicholas J. *America's Strategy in World Politics*. New York: Harcourt, Brace and Company, 1942.

Stowell, Ellery C. *International Law*. New York: Henry Holt and Company, 1931.

Strausz-Hupé, Robert and Stefan T. Possony. *International Relations*, second edition. New York: McGraw-Hill Book Company, 1954.

Strupp, Karl, editor. *Wörterbuch des Völkerrechts und der Diplomatie*, Vol. 2. Berlin: Walter de Gruyter, 1925.

Syrett, Harold C. "The Business Press and American Neutrality, 1914-1917." *Mississippi Valley Historical Review* 32:215-30, September 1945.

Tansill, Charles C. *America Goes to War*. Boston: Little, Brown and Company, 1938.

Timasheff, Nicholas S. *Religion in Soviet Russia*. New York: Sheed and Ward, 1942.

Tumulty, Joseph P. *Woodrow Wilson as I Know Him.* Garden City: Doubleday, Page and Company, 1921.

Turlington, Edgar. *Neutrality, Its History, Economics, and Law: The World War Period.* New York: Columbia University Press, 1936.

Underhill, Frank H. "Political Parties and Ideas." In George W. Brown, editor, *Canada*, pp. 331-52. Berkeley: University of California Press, 1950.

———— Review of Withrow's *Shackling the Transgressor. Canadian Forum* 14:30-31, October 1933.

United States Congress. *Congressional Record.* 69th Cong., 2nd Sess. Vol. 68. Washington: Government Printing Office, 1927.

United States Department of Commerce. Bureau of Foreign and Domestic Commerce. *Foreign Commerce Yearbook, 1933.* Washington: Government Printing Office, 1934.

United States Department of State. *Our Foreign Policy, 1952.* State Department Publication 4466. Washington: Government Printing Office, 1952.

United States World War Foreign Debt Commission. *Combined Annual Reports of the World War Foreign Debt Commission.* Washington: Government Printing Office, 1927.

Vinacke, Harold M. *A History of the Far East in Modern Times*, sixth edition. New York: Appleton-Century-Crofts, 1959.

Walters, Francis P. *A History of the League of Nations*, Vol. 2. New York: Oxford University Press, 1952.

White, John A. *The Siberian Intervention.* Princeton: Princeton University Press, 1950.

Wieger, Leon. *Chine moderne*, Vol. 7. Siensien: Hien-Hien, 1926-1927.

Williams, William A. *American-Russian Relations, 1781-1947.* New York: Rinehart and Company, 1952.

Withrow, Oswald C. *Shackling the Transgressor.* Toronto: Thomas Nelson and Sons, 1933.

Woodhead, H. G. W., editor. *The China Year Book.* The 1929-1930 volume was published in Tientsin by the Tientsin Press; the 1931, 1932, and 1933 volumes were published in Shanghai by the North China Daily News and Herald.

———— *Extraterritoriality in China: The Case Against Abolition.* Tientsin: Tientsin Press, 1929.

Wright, Quincy. *The Control of American Foreign Relations.* New York: The Macmillan Company, 1922.

———— "The Denunciation of Treaty Violators." *American Journal of International Law* 32:526-35, July 1938.

215

About this book

Diplomatic Protest in Foreign Policy was designed by William Nicoll of Edit, Inc. It was set in the composing room of Tamwill Corporation. The text is 12 on 14 Bodoni Book; the reduced matter, 10 on 12; and the notes 8 on 10. The display type is Bodoni Book (Mono 875).

It was printed by Photopress, Inc. on Warren's 1854 60# paper and bound by A. C. Engdahl and Company, Inc. in Bancroft cloth.